CAMPER'S DIGEST

2nd Edition

Edited by Erwin and Peggy Bauer

DIGEST BOOKS, INC., NORTHFIELD, ILL.

CAMPER'S DIGEST STAFF

Erwin A. Bauer
Peggy Bauer
Editors
Mary MacDonald
Art Director
Sheldon L. Factor
Associate Publisher
Cover Photo by Bill Browning

ISBN 0-695-80452-9   Library of Congress Catalog Card #73-102640

FOREWORD

Peggy and Erwin Bauer

THERE ARE FEW activities engaged and indulged in by more people in America today than camping. Camping is—well, a group of college students, shirtless, with 40-pound backpacks and shoulder length hair heading into a wilderness area. It's my son, Paul, canoeing with the YMCA Explorers along Canadian waterways and the retired couple from Michigan in their sleek mobile home headed for an Arizona winter. It's the two of us driving, tenting and fishing the length of Baja California.

Camping can be done as cheaply as staying at home or even cheaper. It can be as luxurious as a bungalow-sized motor home complete with a bathtub, TV, and a bar hove-to at Las Vegas. It can be bicycling in Alaska, boating in Florida, fishing on the Texas Gulf Coast or touring the Pacific shores.

The duration of a camping trip is as flexible as any other aspect. The young family can go to a nearby area for the Friday-at-five-to-Sunday-night weekend; some spend ten days or two weeks on a Montana pack-trip; and many have foresaken the homestead entirely for the convenience, low-cost and freedom of a motor home.

Great numbers of people use camping as a means of pursuing a hobby. Consider the fisherman, the hunter, and the shell collector; the botanist at the edge of spring's retreating ice collecting marsh marigolds; and that army of citizens who are amateur photographers. I have a friend from New Jersey who last summer earned college credits for an ecology course by camping Idaho's White Cloud area with her study group. Another family "collects" lighthouses. They visit every one they can; learn its history, photograph it and write it up in their journal.

How far from home will the camper venture? My fourth grader received a tiny tent for his February birthday and spent the night in the backyard in it warmed by a thin sleeping bag and a large friendly dog. That was camping. There is an organization out of Boston which sponsors flights to Europe where a camping vehicle awaits the traveler. From the airport the tourist roams the continent pretty much as he chooses—and that's camping, too.

There is, of course, one important factor which limits the horizons of some campers and that is the new high price of gasoline and the scarcity of petroleum products. Campers who own the very large bring-it-all-with-you vehicles must make greater changes in their habits than some others. The long, high-speed excursions will cease and in their place will arise single-destination camping trips to places closer to home.

In all other respects camping promises to become more important to more people than ever before. The equipment used, the areas visited, the duration of the stay and the quality and texture of the experience will continue to proliferate. Meet new people or leave the human race behind; go high or low; wet or dry; for a weekend or the season—there is some mode of camping for everyone. We hope that this book will enlarge your thoughts on camping possibilities and prod your imagination. From the almost infinite ways to go we hope you will choose what suits you best, pleases you most and brings you the fullest measure of enjoyment.

Peggy Bauer

CONTENTS

5 QUESTIONS BEGINNING FAMILY CAMPERS ASK MOST

by CLAY PRESCOTT

Fishing and camping are synonymous.

FOR SURE, Americans are enthusiastic campers. And why not? America's foundation was built on camping. Thumb back through the history books and you'll find it was campers like Daniel Boone, Lewis and Clark, and Teddy Roosevelt (and maybe even John Wayne) who wove our country into a nation. Boone spent few nights in frontier inns; more often he slept on the forest floor. Lewis and Clark found no Howard Johnsons in their search for the Northwest Passage; and Roosevelt's North Dakota didn't exactly blossom with neon-lit places of food and lodging. For them, camping was a necessity; for us it is recreation.

In an unprecedented camping revival, we stream forth from our confines of asphalt, concrete, glass, and steel to commune with the sights, sounds, smells, and feel of Nature. This migration has reached astronomical proportions and we have fallen into a paradox: never before have so many people wanted to go camping, and never before have our campgrounds been so crowded. And never before have we had camping made so easy for us. A fantastic variety of recreational vehicles and other sophisticated camping paraphernalia has been made available to us. Considering the overall camping picture, the issue becomes a complex one for the beginning camper. Here are five of the most important questions he should ask himself before he makes his first camping move.

1. What Camping Equipment Do I Buy?

Don't buy! At least not until you've become familiar with the type of camping you plan to do. Rent. You can rent everything from simple backpacks to plush motorhomes. The latter duplicates, and sometimes exceeds the comforts of living at home. Most are totally self-contained and, when fully stocked with food and water, you can actually make a complete camping trip without ever getting out of it. Other recreational vehicles include the mini-motorhome, pick-up truck campers, camping trailers and van conversions. You can get every comfort in these too, or settle for Spartan-like vehicles that provide little more than storage and beds. The canvas-sided camp trailer comes closest to camping depicted in the outdoor magazines that have been stored away for 20 years, and still has extreme mobility. It folds into a compact wheeled box for travel. Most demanding of all, is the tent, which, of course, requires time to set up.

Backpacking is the most rugged branch of camping. Here you must depend upon your own two legs for locomotion. If you have small children, don't count on taking them along until they are older. As family campers, we own a van conversion, using it for camping trips as long as a month, but still we take off on "spur hikes" with backpacks from our van conversion base.

In choosing a recreational vehicle and other camping equipment, invite your family to go shopping with you and ask them to express their opinions. Tons of information on camping equipment and recreational is available just for the writing. Subscribe to RV and camping magazines; buy current issues and familiarize yourself with what is available today and how to get the most from it.

2. What Kind of Clothing Will We Need for Camping?

This depends upon where you'll be camping. A National Park Service foreman I worked for once told me to always bring along a jacket. Good advice. Especially if you plan to camp in the mountain West. Temperatures can drop sharply here even in mid-summer. In the Kaibab Forest on the North Rim of Grand Canyon I've seen shirtsleeve weather one day and snow on the ground the next. Too, thunderstorms can blow up quickly and unexpectedly dur-

Canoeing and camping go together; both are keys to solitude.

No matter what kind of camping it is, campers seem to get the most out of life.

At Lees Ferry, near the entrance of Glen Canyon, Arizona, these tenters find solitude. This national recreational area campground is often empty.

ing summer and early fall, so take along rainwear. If you're traveling with a recreational vehicle, usually you'll have plenty of space to take along clothing to meet all situations. We even take dress clothing in our van in case we suddenly decide to dine in a fashionable restaurant.

If you're backpacking, you must be more specific, paring your clothing to the barest necessities, and make sure it's practical clothing. On trails I've seen backpackers without hats, wearing shorts and shortsleeve shirts. Their arms and legs suffered the full brunt of thorns and brush, and insects they had encountered. Long pants and long sleeves not only protect you from these hazards but from overexposure to the sun as well. Although I've seen backpackers poorly clothed, rare is the one with inadequate boots or shoes. Footwear is extremely important to campers even if they do nothing more than step out of their luxury RV and walk across a field to take a picture.

3. What Kinds of Foods Are Best for Camping?

Unless you intend to backpack, the same kinds of foods you eat at home are best for your camping trip. We make every effort to duplicate home meals. Do the same and you'll end your trip feeling better than when you left. Just because you're camping doesn't mean you have to go on a steady diet of marshmallows and hot dogs. Consider these as treats and use them sparingly. With proper refrigeration (most recreational vehicles have either a refrigerator or an ice box) you can have fresh meats, milk, fruits and vegetables, and other perishables for the duration of your camp trip.

In the outdoors you'll be waking up earlier and perhaps going to bed shortly after dark. Like wildlife, you'll be making the most of the daylight hours. With your three regular meals spread over a wider span of hours, you and your family will probably burn up more energy. Some

Insects can be a nuisance at certain times of the year, so campers should take along bug repellant as part of their standard gear. Also, it is wise to have rain gear such as the young lady is wearing.

Group camping can be fun too. This party is on a sand bar in the bottom of Grand Canyon on a nine-day, river-running campout. They must take proper clothing and food for a comfortable trip.

backpackers prepare a mixture caled "gorp" for these breaks. Gorp consists of a mixture of small candies like M & M's, raisins, peanuts, cereals, and what-have-you. You can make up your own favorites. Kids love gorp, but save it for the "energy breaks."

We've never been keen on dehydrated and freeze-dried foods, but they have been tremendously improved in the past few years. I've heard conditioned backpackers say they taste as good or better than fresh food. Because of weight restrictions, dehydrated and freeze-dried foods are vital to the backpacker. We feel they're also important to RV campers. On extended trips where we've run short of ice and couldn't get more, like on the Sonora, Mexico, coast, dehydrated and freeze-dried foods literally save the day, or days. Falling in roughly the same category, "convenience" foods, prepackaged items such as "skillet dinners" are fine also. Whether you travel with a backpack or deluxe RV, eat properly. Don't spoil a great campout because you got far out with food.

4. Where Do I Camp?

As mentioned earlier, our campgrounds are overflowing, primarily those in our national parks and monuments during the summer vacation months. Grand Canyon, for example, suffers under such extreme camping pressure that during June, July, and August, thousands of recreationists must be turned away. Commercial campgrounds springing up all over the nation have helped to alleviate pressure in our public campgrounds by giving this overflow a place to overnight. These private campgrounds generally offer more convenience and facilities. One of the primary factors bunching up the Nation's camping population is the general reluctance to leave the paved road. Once in Idaho we passed campground after campground literally jammed with people. Near dark, having previously selected a camp-

Nothing beats breakfast outdoors. Here, on a camp trip down the Salmon River in Idaho, the camp cook grills fresh-caught trout and french toast. ➤

Any camper who can take time mid-week in the spring or fall will find normally congested areas unpeopled. These camper-picknickers had this spot all to themselves.

Some of the best camping to be found isn't in campgrounds.

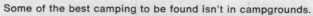

Some people find tent campers the way to go. They require only a few minutes to set up.

ground from a directory, we turned off the paved road and drove five miles over back country roads to reach it. Only two camping rigs occupied the 20-plus available sites. The same sparse camping conditions can often be found near parks like Grand Canyon. I have never seen Ten X Campground, a Kaibab National Forest site, full. Yet it lies just 10 miles south of Grand Canyon National Park, and one mile off the paved road. Frequently I meet campers who are unaware that they may camp just about anywhere they want in National Forests. Some of our finest campsites have been in a small opening in an aspen and fir forest, perhaps 10 miles from our nearest neighbor.

Once summer crowds subside, the National Park Service may close off portions of campgrounds because of such drastic thinning of camper ranks.

Though most of us lust for the camping solitude and scenery of distant places, our camping is largely done near home. If you're an average camper who gets an annual two-week vacation, no doubt you'll splurge on a long-range camping trip. After that you can camp the weekends or not at all. How far can you get on a weekend? Not too far, or you'll lose your valuable camping time to getting there and getting back. Woodall's *Trailering Parks and Campgrounds Directory,* and Sunset's *Western Campsite Directory* (if you live in or plan to camp in the West) pinpoint thousands of campsites. Using these books, we have located excellent campsites, many nearly vacant. State and federal agencies such as game and fish departments, travel bureaus, and parks departments have free publications of campsites and campgrounds.

In all, with a little experience you'll learn where the crowds are and where they aren't, and you can make your camping plans accordingly.

In certain areas, campers will find local wildlife quite tame. Big game animals should be avoided, and no animals at all handled.

Your RV can serve as a base from which to make backpack trips.

5. How Long Does it Take to Become a "Real" Camper?

A beginning camper can be accepted as a "real" camper on his first time out. He will be judged primarily for his camping manners, and secondly on his ability to meet the outdoors. I've been in campgrounds where semi-intoxicated singers have yodeled well into the late hours. A little campfire singing is fine, but don't show your ignorance by lack of consideration for other campers. Some of them turn in with the chickens, so keep it low. Aesthetics are an important part of the camping experience, not only in the enjoyment of scenery but in solitude. Camping should give you recreation, literally, re-creation. Without it you merely duplicate routine in a new locale.

Campers by nature are a friendly lot. If you're having difficulty parking your RV or driving your tent pegs, you probably won't have to ask for help because more often than not, they'll volunteer. Don't be embarassed to take a little help, because we've all had to learn. Your day will come soon when you can pass on camping knowledge.

When you depart the campground be sure you've left a clean campsite, maybe even a little cleaner than you found it. Pick up all your litter and dispose of it in campground trash cans. If you're camping in the forest by yourself, don't bury your trash because the first coyote, fox, or dog that comes along will dig it up and scatter it all over the landscape. Take it with you and find a proper place to put it.

The answer to each of these five questions could be expanded into several chapters. They should be considered a basis from which to expand your camping knowledge. You will become polished by experience. And you will find that camping is not escape from reality, but a chance to deal with a "new" reality. One that will teach you to be self-reliant, and perhaps a new set of values as well.

Backpackers can get a "legitimate" leg up on the journey by setting out from a camper driven to a trail head.

Good camp-keeping leaves the campsite as natural and clean as you found it; or maybe even better than you found it.

Conservation and Camp-Keeping

by G. O. STEINDLER

Using a Coleman propane stove instead of a wood fire leaves no scar on the landscape and eliminates the need to burn up a national resource, timber.

CAMPERS ARE on the move—both on wheels and afoot! In 1970, 450,000 new RVs hit the high road to camping adventure joining the 2¼ million RVs already in use. By 1972 the RV sales figure had jumped to 740,000 new units, and now we have over 6½ million RV families "getting away from it all." At the other end of the camping spectrum, backpacking is undergoing a similar boom.

This fantastic increase in all phases of camping is exerting tremendous pressures on our wilderness areas. State and national campgrounds are enlarging facilities, but cannot keep up with the demand for more camp sites. Privately owned chains of camp resorts are springing up all over the country. They have—to some extent—helped fill the demand for camping facilities and provide campground luxuries unheard of even a few years ago.

Many camping families will continue to seek the more sophisticated pleasures of these modern luxury resorts, but there is an equally important trend in the opposite direction. As campers gain confidence in their equipment and in their outdoor skills they tend to seek more isolated camp sites in wilderness areas. With all the amenities of

modern living in an RV, "roughing it" in the far-off places may mean doing without a cable TV hook-up and an Olympic swimming pool. Even the hardiest breed of campers—the backpackers—are finding it easier to get into remote areas, thanks to their streamlined and sophisticated lightweight gear.

With the vast areas of wilderness still ours to enjoy, the actions of one camping group might appear to have little effect on the environment, either for good or bad. But multiply that impact by the ever-increasing millions of campers, and you have a powerful force at work in the environment.

Much of our present-day knowledge of woodcraft and wilderness camping techniques has been handed down from our pioneer outdoor writers like Nessmuk, Seneca and Kephart, and propagated as gospel by a few of our modern writers. Some of this woods lore is still of practical value to modern campers—but only in terms of survival situations. If these old-time camping practices are followed by today's campers, it won't take very long to wreak ecological havoc upon our remaining wilderness.

In 1889 Nessmuk wrote: "I have made a successful and entirely satisfactory expedition with a tin cup and a pocket knife. Meat can be broiled on a stick. Flour can be transferred into a dough in the hollow of a clean piece of bark and baked on a flat stone, a chip or a piece of bark . . ."

Few campers would ever consider venturing forth with such spartan gear, let alone relying on available wood for all their cooking. Most campers are aware that cutting green wood sticks for broiling (or any other purpose) can no longer be considered ecologically responsible behavior, but they don't realize that dead wood should not be cut or broken off trees or standing snags. These trees are an integral part of the wilderness scene. They should be left not only for aesthetic reasons, but also to provide homes for small mammals and birds and to finally disintegrate and return to the soil in the natural cycle of things.

Even the formerly ubiquitous down wood is fast becoming a precious commodity in some remote areas and should be left for survival situations. Although backpackers carry along highly efficient lightweight stoves, there seems to be a tendency to unpack the stove only when available wood is too wet to ignite readily, or when hikers are in a tearing hurry to eat and be on their way. Although cooking over a wood fire or a glowing bed of coals is traditional in camping, it is becoming a luxury we can now ill afford.

When firewood is available and open fires are permitted, keep your campfire small and leave some wood for other campers. If there is no established fire site, choose the location with care. It must be on mineral soil that you can rake clear of all leaves, twigs and combustibles for an area at least six feet in diameter. Rake the ground litter well away from the fire site and then spread it over the ground when you leave so as to conceal any sign of your presence. Be certain that there are no overhanging branches that might be dried by the heat of the fire and then set ablaze by a popping spark. Sparks could also cause trouble if the fire is too close to your tent or vehicle —keep it at least ten feet downwind.

Fires should never be built in places that will show the scars even though such locations may be safe as far as fire hazards are concerned. Plants on mountainside meadows are delicate and slow-growing, and it takes years to eliminate the marks of a campfire. A bare rock outcropping will remain blackened for a lifetime, and the fire may also alter the crystalline rock structure, causing crumbling and flaking.

Before a match is ever set to tinder have at least one bucket of water close at hand in case a sudden gust of wind starts trouble. Never leave a fire untended for a second and make sure the fire is dead out before you walk away. Only when the entire fire site is cool to the touch and there are no signs of still-steaming wood can you leave the area with a clear conscience. If you have used dry rocks to define your fire spot and to act as supports for your wire grid, return them to their original locations and partially bury them, blackened side down.

Despite all the discussion in the various media about water pollution, most of us take for granted an inexhaustible supply of safe water at the turn of a faucet—at least until we start camping. Then, whether backpacking or travelling in a self-contained camping rig, every precious drop of water takes on new importance. Even a 50-gallon pressurized water system in a motor home can be woefully inadequate if water is used foolishly. It is possible to operate efficiently and hygienically with a minimum of water —and it would not hurt to carry over the same techniques of water conservation at home.

Proper dishwashing is absolutely essential for health

Whether backpacking, tenting or camping in a luxurious rig like this, lack of consideration for the environment and those campers to follow is inexcusable. As more of us enjoy the out-of-doors it becomes more important for each of us to be alert to what we leave behind.

There's no trash collection in this area, so these hunters will use the cardboard carton for their refuse and dispose of it properly at the next opportunity.

reasons, but does not require copious amounts of water to do it thoroughly. Wipe cooking pots, utensils and plates thoroughly with paper towels before food particles have a chance to harden. Then only a minimum of scalding soapy water will do a thorough cleaning job, followed by a rinse in hot water.

Unfortunately, we can no longer assume the purity of any water dipped from a lake or even a swiftly moving mountain stream, no matter how clear and sparkling it may appear. When you camp outside established camp-

grounds, carry water purifying tablets with you, and use them to treat water used for all purposes, except for the toilet in a camping rig. Water can, of course, be purified by boiling it vigorously for at least 10-15 minutes. However, this is an unnecessary use of fuel and your camping time!

All waste water—from dishes, laundry, and bathing—should be disposed of properly in the wilderness to prevent further pollution of the water supply—unless you have a camping rig with a holding tank. Dig a pit well away from the lake or stream near camp and downhill from the water supply, piling the soil from the excavation to one side. Each time you dispose of waste water in the pit, add a good amount of soil to cover it thus preventing any odor or greasy film from attracting insects to the site. When you are ready to move on, fill in the pit completely, mounding the soil slightly so that rains settling the soil will not leave a depression. Cover the bare earth with leaves and ground litter.

No matter how carefully you dispose of waste water, it can still pollute our water supply if cleaning products containing phosphates are used. There seems to be some confusion about products that are environmentally safe to use for dishes, laundry and bathing. Many manufacturers use the word "biodegradable" to imply that a product will not harm the environment. However, biodegradable means only that the product breaks down quickly into its chemical components.

By law, all detergents as well as soaps are now biodegradable, but all we have eliminated by this action is the great masses of detergent suds that used to foam down streams and bubble along the shores of lakes. If a cleaning product contains phosphates, they will seep through the soil and eventually return—unchanged—to the water supply. This will happen no matter where you dump waste water, for even sewage treatment plants do not as yet eliminate phosphates.

Phosphates are fertilizers, and once they reach the water supply, they encourage the growth of aquatic plants. Such over-fertilization, or eutrophication, of a body of water decreases the oxygen supply in the water, causing fish to die, and ultimately creating a "dead" lake. This process of eutrophication does occur naturally, but at a much slower rate. Since we have begun to use phosphate detergents in quantity, the process has been accelerated. For example, it has taken man only 50 years to turn Lake Erie into a dead lake, when it would have taken nature 50,000 years to accomplish the job.

Finding out if your favorite cleaning products contain phosphates may not be a simple matter. Some of them list the components in terminology only a chemist can understand—an "anionic surfactant," for instance, is a phosphate compound found in some dishwashing liquids. Soaps contain no phosphates, but not all products in cake or bar form are soaps—deodorant bars that "leave you cleaner than soap" and the various "campers' soaps" that lather well and rinse off easily in cold or salt water undoubtedly contain phosphate compounds. Most laundry detergents contain phosphates, but there are a number of them now available that are phosphate-free.

Cleaning products with phosphates are highly efficient in removing grease and soil, particularly in hard water. However, it's just as easy to do the job with products that are environmentally safe. A few drops of household ammonia added to soap suds in the dishpan will remove a greasy film on dishes as thoroughly as any dishwashing liquid. Ammonia on a damp sponge will remove grease spatters from a camp stove in a flash, just wipe off the residue with a paper towel. Grease and baked-on food particles on wire grilles are easily removed after soaking in hot suds to which ammonia has been added.

Many of the scouring powders contain phosphates, and the sandy residue is difficult to remove from pots and pans in hard water. Soap-filled scouring pads work well, but food particles collect in the steel wool and can attract insects. Sponges with green nylon mesh on one side work well without any additional scouring powder needed. Food particles rinse out easily, and the sponges may be sterilized by boiling.

When you launder in hard water, soap and phosphate-free detergents may combine with minerals in the water to form a soap scum that clings to the clothes. However, if you add washing soda, this combines with the scum and precipitates it as a fine grit which falls away from the clothes, allowing the soap to do a thorough job.

Despite nationwide anti-litter campaigns, we still have plenty of thoughtless campers who leave a trail of trash across the country. Keep your own camp site clear of all litter—a junior-size rake is handy for the job—and carry a litter bag with you on hikes, not only for your own gum and candy wrappers, flash cubes, etc., but for the debris you may find cluttering the woodland trails and the streams. If you see any snarls of monofilament line, add them to your collection lest they entrap some woodland creature. Sure, it's not your litter, but pick it up anyway. Trash scattered over millions of acres of wilderness is extremely expensive to collect, and we must all share ultimately in the cost of keeping our wild places from being turned into massive trash heaps. A few years ago, it cost $90,000 to clear out the trash dumped in one season in the Boundary Waters Canoe Area in Minnesota—there were 180 tons of the stuff to be hauled away, at a cost of $500 a ton!

In some wilderness areas, you must pack out what you pack in; in others, you are forbidden by law to bring in cans or bottles. But whenever you camp outside an established campground with proper disposal facilities, you must consider it an unwritten law to be responsible for your own trash. If you can carry in cans of food, you can surely tote out the empties. Rinse the cans thoroughly to remove food particles and odor, remove both ends and flatten; then collect them in a plastic garbage sack, along with all aluminum foil, plastic, beverage cans (with the pop-tops inside), film wrappers, 35mm film cassettes, old flashlight batteries, etc. Glass containers have no place in camp since they're too easily broken. But if you do take such risks, be sure to tote the empty glass back to the nearest garbage can or recycling center.

Disposal of solid organic waste—coffee grounds, corn cobs, bones and the like—poses a problem in remote areas where there are no garbage cans. You can't bury it—in some areas, this is forbidden, and in any case, animals with their keen sense of smell will only dig it up and scatter it over the landscape. You can't burn it—even when fires are permitted, you will be polluting the air with burning garbage. If you are vehicle-camping, you can collect a fair amount of such waste in a three-pound coffee can with plastic lid, and dispose of it outside the wilderness. But probably the best solution for wheel campers is to emulate the backpackers and use dehydrated and freeze-dry foods on wilderness jaunts. This way there is very little organic waste, if any, to dispose of.

Luring animals to your campsite, either deliberately by scattering tidbits about, or by leaving crumbs and scraps of food through careless camp-keeping, is completely irresponsible. Animals are perfectly capable of surviving without your free lunch, but once accustomed to handouts, even the cute chipmunks and squirrels become a nuisance. Then too, you may attract more than you bargained for—a porcupine may consider your ax handle or canoe paddle an irresistible midnight snack, to say nothing of the bacon you planned for tomorrow's breakfast. Canny old raccoons who've become experienced campground scroungers have been known to open latches on ice chests.

Of course, the most publicized camp nuisances are bears. In remote areas where bears are unaccustomed to man, they are usually shy and will vanish at the first whiff of human scent. Unfortunately, they have been turned into

Feeding wild animals, no matter how tempting, is bad practice. Would anyone want this fellow in the tent during the night?

bums and renegades in our parks through lack of understanding of bear behavior and disregard for the rules against feeding them. Damaged camp gear, bashed-in car windows, and occasionally severely mauled campers, can be the result of thoughtless actions of campers. When trouble does occur, park officials are then forced to remove the bears and perhaps even destroy them, thus depriving us of one more aspect of a true wilderness experience.

The natural instinct for a bear is to consider all food within his territory as his own. Once he has acquired a taste for our food instead of his normal diet and has overcome his natural fear of man through continued close contact, the bear will stop at nothing to take what he instinctively feels belongs to him. To thwart a bear's keen sense of smell, keep all food in air-tight, smell-proof containers, in coolers or refrigerators. Thorough cleanup after every meal and prompt garbage disposal is a must. Some authorities on bears even recommend the use of an odorless room deodorant spray, such as Lysol, to kill cooking odors in camp.

If you're a tent camper, never keep food or candy in your tent. Mr. Bruin may decide to help himself by walking in one side of the tent and out the other without unzipping the flaps. The smell of blood, carrion and the entrails of fish or game will attract carnivores for miles around. Savvy outdoorsmen clean fish and game well away from camp and promptly bury the entrails deeply.

Although the chances are slim if you've tended to your camp-keeping, should a bear wander into camp while you're eating, let him take over as you withdraw slowly and quietly. It's worth the price of a meal and few battered pots just to watch from a safe vantage point. Notify the authorities and move camp if they suggest it, since bears will very often return to the same spot, having staked their claim on the territory.

Keeping a tidy camp is no problem when everyone pitches in on the chores, and you'll seldom be bothered by insect or animal invaders. If you leave a camp site in a little better shape than you found it, and make it a matter of pride never to leave any signs of your presence in the wilderness, then there will still be beautiful wild places for camping five or ten years from now.

As one ecologist put it: "Remember, if you're not part of the solution in the preservation of our only Earth, you're part of the problem!"

Venture Out at Cudjoe Key—palm branches sway lazily as gentle Gulf Stream breezes soothe the sun bleached coral. Join in the endless round of activities or just relax and savor the quiet contentment of your own tropical recreational vehicle village.

THERE'VE BEEN SOME CHANGES

by JIM RUTHERFOORD

AS THE ALARM CLOCK raucously greeted the new day I went below to stir up a hearty breakfast of fried ham and eggs, hot biscuits and honey. The coffee water was already perking merrily thanks to my foresight of setting the electric timer the night before.

While the ham sizzled in the pan, its aroma wafted to one and all by the electric vent fan, I went outside to check my little fishing boat bobbing safe and secure, tackle aboard and ready for a morning of fishing in Florida's Indian River. Back inside, I turned off the stereo music and switched on the small color TV set in time to receive a weather report which forecast a fine day for any outdoors sport.

The doorbell rang. I greeted my good friend and fishing buddy, Bobby Lord, who had driven out from his home in Jensen Beach to join me for breakfast and for a go at the spotted weakfish which were practically polluting the river.

"Well, Old Buddy, how's camping?", asked Bobby.

For the moment I had forgot that I was "camping" but that is what it was. Our 27-foot ElDorado chassis mount camper was parked in one of the nearly 1600 plush, beautifully landscaped sites hard by one of the many canals which lead into the Indian River on the Intra-Coastal Waterway. Each site is serviced with connections for pure water, heavy duty electricity, sewer and cable TV. Even telephone connections are built into the sites and are available at regular rates.

The place was Nettles Island Outdoor Resort, one of five locations of Outdoor Resorts of America, Inc. in Florida and at Gatlinburg, Tenn., all of which are country club-like operations that foretell a new era in vehicular camping, or recreational vehicle travel as it is more properly called. Bobby Lord is one of the principals in the Nashville, Tennessee based ORA corporation which has established this new breed of RV park in the belief that a large segment of the American population is willing to pay just a little bit more for a true resort atmosphere though they travel and live on wheels. They believe too, that many people who haven't the resourcefulness or liking for the "smoky-fire burned-bacon wet-tent" school of camping will buy and use recreational vehicles when they are assured of comfort, nighttime security, organized family recreation activities, interesting things to do and sights to see nearby. The popularity of the Outdoor Resorts of America, Inc. operations and other similar developments have proved their point quite well. So well in fact that ORA is planning additional locations in at least two western states and one in southern Michigan; the latter to be a year 'round operation with late season emphasis on winter sports.

Gulf Oil Company now operates five of their Venture Out Resorts in Florida, Tennessee and Arizona and is looking at other locations for similar development.

Both Outdoor Resorts and Venture Out are based on the condominium concept. The company sells completely equipped lots, usually about 30 x 60 feet in size, to an individual who may then use the lot for his own recreational vehicle vacations or rent it through the local management to other RVacationers, thereby realizing a return on his investment. Such rentals are usually on a 50/50 basis. In addition the lot owner pays a moderate ($17-$20 per month) condominium fee for upkeep of roads and grounds, operation of pools and other services. Lot prices may run from as low as $5000 to $20,000 or more depending upon the resort's location and the desirability of the particular lot and the appreciation of the overall development.

But the good thing to know is that you don't have to be a lot owner at one of these condominium resorts to enjoy the full resort life.

The Bryn Mawr Group, a Ft. Lauderdale based corporation, is developing a chain of oceanside CampResorts strictly for transients along Florida's east coast and is looking at properties elsewhere on the Atlantic Seaboard. On a smaller scale they are almost equally as luxurious as the larger resorts of Venture Out and Outdoor Resorts of America. Let's look at some of these resorts individually.

NETTLES ISLAND (ORA)

Situated on Hutchinson Island on U. S. A1A, this resort is reached via U.S. 1 south from Ft. Pierce via Jensen Beach. The resort derives its name from the manmade island dredged up from the mud and sand of the Indian River. Covering more than 450 acres bordering on both the Atlantic Ocean and the Indian River, this is the newest and most complete of the ORA resorts.

In addition to full service, hard surfaced vehicle pads and patios and hard surfaced streets, the resort features a large, two-story recreation building with sauna baths, showers, and indoor games. The second floor of the building houses a large meeting room overlooking the Olympic size outdoor pool, three tennis courts and a miniature golf course. The building is the center for language classes, handicraft courses, dances and other group recreation.

On the causeway separating the mainland RV complex from that on the island are located a full service marina, a complete shopping center with drug store, beauty salons, barber shop, clothing store and supermarket. A full service marina offers fuel and maintenance for the boats of guests as well as boaters using the Intra-Coastal Waterway of the Indian River.

Across U. S. A1A, but on the ORA property, is a large Sheraton Motor Inn with restaurant, cocktail lounges, meeting rooms. Here also is a beach club, an outdoor bar and more than 1200 feet of beachfront. All facilities are available to site tenants and the motel is a popular spot for guests of tenants or for campers who may wish to dine out occasionally.

Check-in procedure is similar to that of a motel or hotel. The traveler chooses a site from a large map in the resort office and, once assigned, the renter may go and come at will without fear that his site will be occupied on his return. He signs a chit for site rental and other charges, such as restaurant, marina, boat and equipment rental. Payment is made upon departure. Bobby Lord told me during my stay there last winter, they had had only three "skip payments" during the two years the resort has been in operation and two of those paid when billed by mail.

Pets and trail bikes are allowed in the resort although both bike riders and pet owners must abide by the posted rules.

Resort rules are strictly, though diplomatically, enforced and night security guards check all incoming cars and other vehicles.

VENTURE OUT, Ft. Pierce, Fla.

This is one of the Gulf Oil Company owned properties. Located just a mile south of the ORA complex, this RV resort features a beach club, waterside sites on the Indian

The beautifully land-scaped entrance to Outdoor Resorts of America at Nettles Island is an introduction to the tropical "fun in the sun" that lies in this 130 acre recreational vehicle resort. There are 1585 sites with complete convenience facilities, plus indoor and outdoor recreation areas.

River, organized recreational activities, a marina and shopping center. A nice touch, when I visited the RV complex a few years ago, is attendant parking of the renters' travel trailers by use of a small tractor which takes the vehicle from the check-in area to the site assigned where attendants assist in levelling the RV and making the service connections. Sites and streets are paved and service connections conveniently located.

BRYN MAWR CAMPRESORT, Ft. Pierce, Fla.

This is the newest and largest of the Bryn Mawr Group's RV resort parks.

Located on A1A about 8 miles north of Ft. Pierce and north of Ft. Pierce Inlet, this park, like all Bryn Mawr CampResorts, is operated strictly for transients, not as a condominium operation as are the ORA and Venture Out properties.

This resort features hard surfaced pad and patios and concrete patio tables. There is a large heated pool and a kiddy playground and an attractively designed recreation building is at poolside as are the shuffleboard courts. Several tennis courts are located in the park and tiled bath houses and laundry facilities are conveniently spotted throughout the 400-site park. All sites feature full service hookups including cable TV connections.

This property also runs from the ocean to the Indian River. Launching ramps and a boat basin are located on the river side of the complex.

A fine feature of the Bryn Mawr CampResort at Ft. Pierce is its landscaping. It was developed with the least possible disturbance to natural growth. Native palm trees were left in place wherever possible and the area abounds with them as well as with smaller shrubs and plants, yet it is sufficiently open to the faintest breeze.

Fresh water is furnished by the resort's own desalination plant while a sewage disposal plant provides tertiary treatment that returns pure water to the river.

VENTURE OUT, Panama City Beach, Fla.

This Gulf Oil Company resort is worthy of special mention as it is the only such deluxe camping resort on the

Gulf Coast of Florida.

Situated on Thomas Drive adjacent to St. Andrews State Park, this resort is close to all beach activities. In fact the pool and beach club are situated amid sea oats-covered dunes in the sugar-white sands of Florida's "Miracle Strip" beach. This area is rapidly becoming a year 'round resort where northerners, even Canadians, who appreciate the mild winter climate, vacation.

The physical layout of the resort is superb. Every site has water and heavy-duty electric service while sewer connections may be made at either of two convenient points depending upon vehicle size and configuration.

A unique "late arrival area", also equipped with 3-way hookups, holds transients overnight so that they do not disturb other guests by driving through the resort or spotting their vehicles on site in the dark. This is a popular feature with lot owners as well as transients. Security guards make sure the rule is enforced and provide assistance in parking.

Venture Out's $2-million Treasure Island Marina, located on Grand Lagoon of St. Andrews Bay is a part of the multi-million dollar complex. It provides barn storage for boats up to 26 feet in length. Big fork lifts pick your boat out of the water, move it into the storage building and "file it away" in one of scores of three-tiered cradles. Covered slip storage is provided for larger boats.

Treasure Island Marina also offers a complete line of boats, motors, marine accessories and fishing tackle and will make arrangements for charter boats for those who don't trail their own. As in all the RV resorts mentioned here, there are organized recreation programs, swimming instruction, movies, dances and other social activities. Since this resort is close to area shopping centers, no store is provided. Excellent convenience stores, liquor stores, restaurants and night clubs are to be found within a mile or so of the resort.

* * *

The Bryn Mawr, Outdoor Resorts and Venture Out resorts are truly bargains in camping fun, convenience and comfort. All are multi-million dollar developments. The Nettles Island ORA resort was built at a cost of more

This is Camping? Property owners and guest enjoy backyard boating fun at Venture Out at St. Lucie. When they tire of the salt, surf and sand, a refreshing olympic-sized swimming pool awaits. Recreation is stressed and a well-rounded program of activities in addition to modern recreational facilities is available to all.

than $13-million. Yet site rental fees, which are all-inclusive, are often less than one would pay for inferior accomodations. Fees range from $4 per night for the winter rates at Venture Out's Panama City Beach resort to $9 at Nettles Island. There is no extra persons duty, no extra charge for sewer service or for use of air conditioners or heaters. Nettles Island Resort even provides free bus or golf cart "taxi" service to points within the 450-acre complex. Use of pools, sauna baths, tennis courts and most social activities are included in the site rental cost. Some of the resorts even provide cable TV connections with only a refundable deposit for the connecting cable.

Unique in the recreational vehicle travel field is Outdoor Resorts of America's Outpost at Jennings, Florida. Located at the first interchange in Florida of I-75 south, the Outpost offers a large, full service RV travel park with recreational vehicle service center capable of performing any repair or maintenance service on any make of RV or its appliances. A service station dispenses motor fuels and oils and lubrication service while several especially designed RV wash bays remove road grime before the RVacationer travels further into the "Sunshine State".

The Outdoor Resorts Outpost is the world's first service plaza designed especially for recreational vehicles and,

with nearly 5-million RV's on America's highways today, there is clearly a need for more.

If you are a backpacker, a tent camper on one who loves the rugged life in the boondocks, such resort RV parks may not be your cup of tea, but Bryn Mawr, Outdoor Resorts and Venture Out are filling a need long awaited by thousands of RVacationers who enjoy the comforts of home—away from home.

Bryn Mawr CampResort locations: Key Largo, Ft. Pierce, and St. Augustine, Florida. Information Address: Bryn Mawr CampResorts, 2755 East Oakland Park Blvd., Ft. Lauderdale, FA 33306.

Outdoor Resorts of America locations: Long Key, Nettles Island, Orlando, Jennings, Florida; Gatlinburg, Tennessee. Information Address: Outdoor Resorts of America Inc., Suite 100, 311 Plus Park Blvd., Nashville, TN 37217.

Venture Out locations: Cudjo Key, Ft. Pierce, Panama City Beach, Florida; Gatlinburg, Tennessee; Mesa, Arizona. Information address: Venture Out In America, Inc., 3445 Peachtree Rd., NE, Atlanta, GA 30326.

Campgear Care and Repair

Photos by author

A ground cloth is worth its cost—the minimum effort required to use it and its fine ability to protect the floor of the tent make it a fine investment.

by MARV LINDBERG

FALL OF THE year is a time for falling leaves, frost on the pumpkin, ice on the pond and, regrettably, an end to camping for most families with kids in school. Fall is also the time to prepare for the first camping trip next spring— the time to clean what's soiled, fix what's broken, sharpen what's dull, tighten what's loose and paint what needs it.

Preparing your camp gear for winter storage is like putting money in the bank—you'll get interest on your investment when you withdraw the principal in the spring.

The chore is much easier if you have kept abreast of the wear and tear during the camping season and you have exercised reasonable care of your gear in use.

A ground cloth for your tent is well worth its price in protecting the tent floor from dirt and sharp stones. Use a

ground cloth or heavy plastic that is about two feet longer and wider than the floor size of your tent. Fold or roll the extra material back under itself to a size a few inches smaller than the size of the tent floor to avoid trapping rain water that runs off the tent. The fold forms a rounded edge that keeps surface water from running under the tent between the tent floor and the ground cloth.

A sheet of 4- or 6-mil, lightweight plastic, such as a painter's drop cloth, used *inside* the tent serves to catch the dirt and sand normally tracked into the tent—especially at the beach. Use a sheet of plastic the same size as the floor of the tent. Sew a strip of cotton bias tape along the outer edges of the plastic, using a long stitch so as not to perforate the plastic too closely. Sew small loops of round elastic to

A tent fly protects the tent from weather, tree sap and bird droppings—and a large one will also cover the table.

the bias tape at each corner and one or more loops along each edge. Sew buttons to the inside corners of the tent and along the seam where the tent wall joins the floor, spaced to match the elastic loops on the plastic.

You can now fasten the elastic loops to the buttons to hold the plastic in place. Instead of sweeping out the tent, just unbutton the plastic and take it outside and shake out the dirt. Remove the sheet of plastic when you store the tent.

To help keep dirt out of your tent altogether, obtain a couple of rubber floor mats to place outside the tent door. When traveling between campgrounds, place the mats on the floor of the car. A piece of carpet just inside the tent door also helps.

A tent fly will protect your tent from tree sap, bird droppings, exposure to the weather and keep your tent cooler on hot days. With two poles and extra guy lines, the fly can be set to form a peaked roof over the tent. With four corner poles, it can be set at an angle with one edge higher than the other, but this setup is more apt to suffer from wind.

If you get one large enough, it can serve as a shelter for your dining area as well, but you'll need extra poles. By varying the height of the poles, and using extra grommets, extra guy lines can be used to draw down the edge of the overhead fly between the poles to form gutters at selected places along the edge of the fly.

A canvas repair kit should be part of your camp gear. The manufacturer can furnish scraps of canvas and advise you as to what type of cement can be used on their tent fabrics.

Most cotton canvas tents can be patched with a cement obtained from any tent and awning dealer. Other all-purpose cements are usually effective on fabrics—check the directions first. Most such cements require a first coat on both the patch and the area to be covered. Let the first coat dry, then apply a second coat and press the patch in place. Be sure to round off all corners on the patch for better results.

When you have access to an electric iron, dry finish tents can be patched with iron-on patches sold in fabric stores in various weights of fabric, such as jean patches. You may even find some the same color as your tent.

Pinhole leaks can be stopped with wax. With a set of heavy duty straight and curved needles and waxed thread, emergency patches can be sewn in place. When it comes time to store your tent, replace any emergency patch with a permanent one.

Before storing the tent, set it up in your back yard and vacuum it inside and out. Use a brush along all seams to get rid of dirt and insects. Wash it down with a spray from your garden hose. Use a soft bristle brush on stubborn stains. A mild soap may be helpful but don't use a detergent. Then, be certain the tent is absolutely dry before storage in a dry area. A fabric bag offers additional protection.

If you have experienced a problem with leaks through the fabric, check with the manufacturer, if possible, to determine what repellent treatment to use. If this is not possible, there are both spray and brush-on solutions that may solve the problem.

If you need to clean or treat the bottom of your tent, turn it upside down, and, using telescoping poles or short 2 x 2's with a nail in one end to fit into the grommets, and guy lines to anchor them, raise the tent floor to waist height for easy accessibility and a smooth, taut surface on which to work.

Tent poles should be separated and upended to be sure no water is trapped inside. Any corrosion can be removed with a fine grade of steel wool.

The usual reason grommets pull out is because the tent was set with the guy lines too taut. When it rains, the canvas will shrink and pull out the grommets. Leave a little slack in the guy lines or loosen them when it rains.

If grommets have pulled loose, they can be replaced by a tent and awning shop, or you can buy a grommet kit at most hardware stores. The same applies to seams that need repair, or you can buy a hand sewing awl to do it yourself.

Lanterns and stoves also need attention. On those using gasoline, check the gaskets on tank filler caps and replace if necessary. An occasional drop or two of oil on the leather in the pump will keep it soft. For storage, drain any remaining gasoline from the tank.

If your lantern or stove has not been operating properly, the fault may be in the generator. Check the needle in the gas tip first to see if it is broken or corroded with gum or carbon which can be removed with steel wool. The generator itself may require cleaning or replacement. When cleaning, be careful not to bend the needle tip or enlarge the orifice in the gas tip on the stove generator.

To check for proper shut-off on a stove valve and generator assembly, pump plenty of air pressure in the tank and dip the gas tip end in a glass of water. Open the valve stem and bubbles will appear in the water. Close the valve firmly, and if no more bubbles appear, the valve is operating properly. If bubbles persist, remove the valve stem and check for obstructions in the seat, such as a broken thread or packing.

If either lamp or stove appear to be starved for fuel, the fault may be an accumulation of gum on the lower end of the needle in the fuel tube inside the tank. Remove the entire valve assembly from the tank and clean off the end of the needle protruding from the fuel tube. To assure a tight seal on the threads of the valve assembly to the tank, rub a wet bar of soap over the threads before reassembly.

To check for a leak at the pump, have air pressure in the tank and, with the pump in closed position, dip the pump end of the tank in water and check for bubbles. Replace parts or the pump as needed.

Remove the burners on the stove, being careful to note the arrangement of burner rings if such are used. Remove accumulated carbon, oil lightly and reassemble.

If an accumulation of carbon is especially difficult to remove, soak it for a few days in fresh gasoline. Any tall bottle does well for soaking a stove generator. Use a wire brush or steel wool to remove rust on all other areas subjected to heat and apply a coat of light oil. Plug the venturi opening (the tube the generator fits into on a stove) with a piece of cloth to keep insects out.

To preserve the enamel finish, use a good paste wax. A spare generator for lantern and stove should be a part of your emergency gear. A spare mantle can be taped to the bottom of a lantern. A funnel with a fine wire mesh or felt filter should be used at all times.

Propane appliances need little attention except for rusted areas. Usually, the orifice can be removed and reversed in its position and cleaned out with pressure from the propane tank. If not, use a fine needle, being careful not to enlarge the orifice.

You will probably do a better job and do it more easily if the working area is at a comfortable height and in good light. Here the tent bottom gets a needed cleaning.

Repairing either tent seams or grommets can be done at home with supplies from the hardware store.

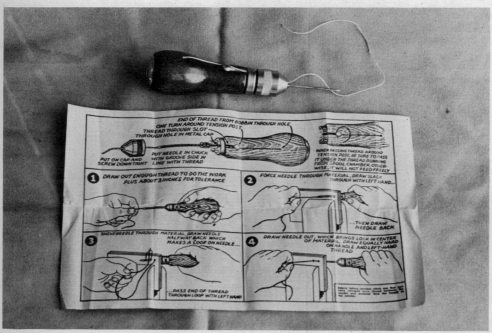

If, when in use, you notice a "garlic" smell, check all fittings for leaks. Never use a match! Use soap suds, shaving cream or a child's bubble soap, daubed on each fitting. Remove disposable cylinders from the appliance when not in use. Valves on bulk tanks should be closed whether full or empty. This is a good time to add an ounce or two of alcohol to an empty bulk tank to absorb any water that may be in the tank.

A broken mantle on any type of lantern should be replaced immediately. It not only deposits soot on the globe, but can break it. Use an old toothbrush to clean the screen in the mantle housing.

While camping, sleeping bags should be aired daily to remove body moisture. To keep them clean, use a liner. You can make a liner from 81-inch sheeting available at a fabric store. Be sure to pre-shrink it before cutting to size.

Tabs to hold it in place can be made from short strips of twill tape and metal snaps, or make the tabs long enough to tie together. Sew tabs to the liner and to the sleeping bag in matching pairs.

If the bag needs cleaning, take it to a reliable dry cleaner who uses the proper solution for the purpose. "Do-it-yourself" dry cleaning may not have the proper solution. Be sure to air the bag well before use.

Zippers will work better if given a coat of wax. For storage, if possible, hang the bag. If not, fold it loosely and store it in a plastic bag or flat carton. If storage space is a problem, consider the space under beds.

Before storing air mattresses, hold them up by one end and shake them. Then, shake them from the other end. This distributes the powder inside the mattress. Air mattresses should be rolled for storage. Constant folding in the same

Assuring the shut-off valve for the stove and generator works properly is essential for safe operation once the "season" opens.

Soap suds—never use a match—indicate a leak in the propane system which can and must be repaired.

place may cause a crack in the rubber. Store them in a cool, dry area away from heat or sunlight.

A dull ax or knife is a dangerous tool. Keep them sharp at all times. Both should have a sheath to avoid personal injury when not in use. Treat the sheath with neatsfoot oil to keep the leather soft. If the ax head is loose, tighten it with a metal wedge. If the handle is nicked, smooth it with sandpaper and rub it down with linseed oil. Never paint an ax handle. The paint makes the handle slippery and a rough surface will result from chipped paint.

Remove any dirt from a spade, touch up the edges with a file and apply a coat of oil. If your saw doesn't have a blade protector, one can be made from a piece of garden hose split open lengthwise and held in place by rubber bands cut from an old innertube.

Now is the time to write the bulb and battery numbers for battery lanterns on a piece of adhesive tape and attach it someplace inside the battery housing for future reference. If there's room, put in a spare bulb. Remove the battery to avoid corrosion inside the case. Batteries can be stored in a refrigerator to lengthen their life.

Coolers and water jugs should be washed, then rinsed with water containing baking soda. Store them with lids or covers open or ajar. Check your backpacks, camp chairs and cots for tears in the fabric, loose rivets or cracks in the metal frames.

There will no doubt be camp gear not mentioned here. You know what you demand of it in use. Check it to be sure it is capable of the job for another season. If not, the fall of the year is also a good time to pick up a bargain on new equipment. Dealers may be anxious to reduce their inventory at lowered prices.

If you tackle these chores in the fall of the year, you can rest assured your first trip the next spring will be enjoyable. And that first sunny weekend has a way of sneaking up on you. If you don't—consider the consequences of putting up with a family who wanted to go camping, but had to stay home while you caught up on your camp gear repair instead.

The small motor home is easier to drive than its bigger brothers but provides sufficient interior space for at least three persons.

The Motorhome "Minis"--

by BYRON W. DALRYMPLE

DURING A RECENT camping vacation my wife and I covered some four thousand miles, using as our mobile camp a compact RV of a type that has become known over the past several years as a "mini-motorhome." Day after day as I drove I was continually astonished at the ease with which the rig handled, at the places I was able to take it, and at its total comfort.

Shortly after finishing that tour I became involved in producing a film for national TV distribution in which another "mini" was, so to speak, one of our stars. By the time I had completed that experience I was fully convinced that mini-motorhomes are the brightest RV invention to date and the best thing that has ever happened to the recreational vehicle industry and its customers.

Certainly right now this is the *biggest* news in the industry. Since the first one was exhibited several years ago at the massive annual Louisville RV show, the idea has caught on until the highways are now teeming with minis and practically every manufacturer in the field is turning out models. Basically the true mini-motorhome is a kind of unique cross or compromise between a full-fledged motorhome and a frame-mounted pickup camper. It is a motorhome body of modest size built on a van chassis, with the van cab retained and an overcab bunk thrusting above it.

When the first ones appeared they were passed off by both pickup camper enthusiasts and owners of full-fledged motorhomes as some sort of gimmick. But within the first year production zoomed over 500 percent. It has kept right on. Today many factories are chronically behind on orders. There are provocative reasons for this popularity. One of them is the fundamental agility and handling ease of these well-balanced, compact units. Let me illustrate from a reverse experience.

During the year a couple of years ago I used two different models of standard motorhomes of a well-known make. One was a 22-footer, the other a 24. Both were mounted on heavy truck chassis, and outfitted with dual rear wheels. They were, admittedly, excellent units, roomy and comfortable. But in each case, after making extended family tours, I was actually relieved to get home and park the ponderous, unwieldy monsters.

On an interstate, to be sure, they rolled along easily. But any side road or quasi-back-in trail was a creep-along ordeal. Turning around and street parking were major operations. Gas mileage was particularly frightening—5 and 6 miles. When we were parked somewhere we certainly enjoyed the interior comfort and all the gadgets. But after a few days or so I dreaded moving. I kept having the feeling that there must be some compromise possible that would offer all the basic comforts, plus a reasonable amount of living room, and still allow one to travel almost as with a small pickup camper or a passenger car.

Part of this feeling, I'm sure, stems from our long experience with what are nowadays termed "RVs", and with a rather diligent constant search for a unit that would com-bine the best points of several types and eliminate as many disadvantages as possible. Long before pickup campers and motorhomes had even been dreamed of—back in the 1940s —I was hauling trailers of various lengths hither and yon. We tried very small ones and found them too cramped for long tours. We tried big, heavy ones and I despised every mile of towing. We experimented with light-weight aluminum units in medium length and, for trailers, considered these the best compromise. The one undeniable advantage of a trailer in today's RV world where many types are available, is that it can be detached from the car at the campsite.

When the pickup coach came along in the middle and late 1950s the idea seemed to me to be perfect. We tried small ones, even with low headroom, standard eight-footers, then larger "tail draggers", and finally big ones of the frame-mounted type up to 12 feet and more on stretch-frame pickups. These certainly balanced better than the slide-in models, but they handled like—well—trucks. We even dropped back for a time to retry tent campers. They are great—so far as a light tow package is concerned. But I figured my tent days were pretty well over, except for true tenting trips back into wilderness areas on horseback or 4WD jaunts.

Just why it took so long for the RV industry to discover the workhorse delivery van is a curious matter. But finally a few designers were hit over the head with a flash of insight. Why not use a husky one-ton van chassis, maybe stretch the frame a bit until such time as the automotive manufacturers caught on to demand and built a special one. With large 10-ply tires, and a cab with bucket seats, this basic chassis was just waiting to have a small motorhome— or should we say a frame-mount-type pickup camper?— married to it. It was simply a matter of retaining the cab, padding its rear archway handsomely. The overcab bunk would reach out above the cab.

In a standard pickup all that room up front was lost to the hood and motor compartment. With the van used, the driver would sit over the front wheels, just as in a regular full-sized motorhome. A unit of 18 to 20 feet overall—19 is a general average—would become a "mini" motorhome, far easier to handle and park than the big jobs, and lighter, too. It had the immense advantage and convenience of two cab doors in addition to the body door, a substantial safety feature. It could go a lot of places that standard motorhomes could not, or at least not without difficulty. And it would have almost as much room and certainly just as much comfort as the larger models. Further, gas mileage was almost certain to be higher.

The one I am presently using and extremely pleased with is a Diamond, built by Coons Manufacturing, Oswego, Kansas. This firm is owned by Bud Coons, one of the charter people in the RV business, with vast knowledge and experience. It is on a Ford van chassis, has single rear wheels with super-rugged tires. At 60 miles an hour I average 10 miles to the gallon, twice what I got on one of the big motor-

My Favorite Modern RVs

On our Texas ranch the roads are rough and steep, but the mini takes it easily.

homes. Because of its compactness I can turn it around or park it in a very small space, and on the highway it handles literally like any passenger car. It is far better balanced than most pickup campers I've used.

Now have a look inside. This particular model is in my estimation the best interior design of any RV we've ever used. The dinette at rear right makes into an excellent bed, and across from it a gaucho pulls out to become a second rear bed, both running lengthwise of the interior. An extremely convenient design trick here is that with both beds made up there is still a narrow aisle between them, leading forward. The bathroom, of very ample size with shower, lavatory and toilet, is on the left. Anyone wanting to use the bathroom after the rear beds are made up doesn't have to crawl over anybody else, as in many units. You just walk down the aisle.

There is a neatly designed divider between the dinette and the galley, which is up front and right. Across from it is an electric-gas refrigerator. At the far rear large storage compartments are at the head of the beds. There is also unusually large locked trunk space, outside, rear. But one of my greatest joys in the design of this mini unit is the overcab bed. I often sleep here, and for years I have cussed overcabs, or refused to sleep in them because I banged my head or got claustrophobia. Bud Coons has designed this mini with a kind of "waterfall roof" from front to rear. In other words, the roof slants up higher above the overcab. A person of average height can actually sit up in this bunk. It offers immense sleeping comfort, and has small steps leading up to it.

All told, this mini has inside it everything that large motorhomes have. Body air conditiong (there is automotive air conditioning in the cab) and generator are options as on all motorhomes. The only thing lacking in the compact unit as opposed to the full-fledged standards is a couple of feet of living room. I say "a couple of feet" because even in the ponderous 24 to 30 footers interior designs are too commonly so inept that much room is wasted so far as usefulness and general comfort are concerned. On the minis, with less space to work with, designers have to show ingenuity. The small loss of space is well compensated for in handling ease and versatility.

But price, to many buyers, has even greater appeal. The first motorhome we ever used, a borrowed unit, had a retail price tag of $16,500. Many cost much more today. Over the past several years the motorhome builders have been trying desperately to cut corners and shorten models and raise production enough so that they could market a motorhome at $10,000 or less. A few have succeeded, with most models selling just barely under that figure.

Conversely, the mini-motorhome concept was, to begin with, a more economical idea chiefly because the cab portion of the vehicle was already there on the chassis. Thus the minis were launched, depending on interior equipment, a good bit cheaper in price than the standard motorhomes. The average retail price today of a 19 footer fully equipped with everything one needs runs somewhere around $8,500. They can be had for a lot less, with equipment pared down. Even with air conditioning and generator the very best ones stay under $10,000. Thus, in my opinion at least, they offer everything the larger units do, plus much more agility and driving ease, at lower cost.

A telling point is that when you put, say, $9,500 into a mini you are buying a plush unit with all the extras. When you put that much into a standard motorhome you are buying a somewhat stripped down model, often no larger than

Smallest of the motorhome family is the van conversion, a kind of "mini-mini."

The van conversion may be the way to go for those who prefer lower price, higher milage and easier driving. Pop-up top allows comfortable stand-up space inside and the wide-open doors make access and egress easy.

a mini. To give a succinct idea of how firm and valid the mini trend is, consider the fact that the very largest builders of full-size motorhomes have been forced to begin marketing their own mini versions!

In Texas where we live we have a hill-country ranch some miles from our home. It is exceedingly rugged and scenic, the access is difficult, and our ranch roads are little more than trails. In trying out various RVs I have for some years given them the "last test" by having a go at the ranch. The hills are steep, the winding trails rough. I have often taken pickup campers in, but have had occasional problems with big ones. Not long ago a friend was here with a motorhome and bragging quite heavily as to how far "back in" he could take it. I drove him down to the ranch in my Jeep Wagoneer and showed him around. I suggested that he take the motorhome down for an overnight campout.

"You have to be kidding!" he said. "In the first place my

wheelbase is too long, and in the second I might get down a couple of those rough hills but never back up. This isn't motorhome country."

I couldn't resist. "We bring the mini down here," I told him. "You park yours at our house and we'll use mine."

I'm sure he went for it hoping I'd get hung up. But having had it there previously I knew there were no problems. On any of the fairly high RVs—pickup campers, minis, standard motorhomes—there are obviously overhead problems. You have to watch for low limbs, etc. But aside from that I can go anywhere with this unit I have gone with a good sized camper.

This reminds me of one caution to prospective mini owners. When driving a pickup camper you will note that the overcab thrusts forward over the truck hood, but not clear to the front. The van cab has no appreciable hood. Thus the overcab thrusts past the front of the vehicle. When you park, let's say, at a drive-in grocery or any other building that has an outthrust roof or awning, you must use care. In the camper you could park with front wheels against the curb. In the mini you can't, without striking the overcab.

There has been some confusion among prospective buyers regarding the term "mini-motorhome," for that term has here and there been applied also to another unique use of the workhorse delivery van, the *conversion*. These van conversions might suitably be called: mini-mini motorhomes." They are the most compact form of the motorhome so far concocted, and when properly executed the conversion is indeed a most useful and super-agile RV. I put one over the jumps for several months last year and was totally sold on the idea for specific uses.

Basically the van conversion is simply a van that has had the roof, or a portion of it, removed and replaced by a raised section to allow full stand-up headroom inside. Then the interior is furnished exactly like a motorhome in miniature. Of all RVs these come closest to a compromise with the family car. Quite a few owners even drive them back and forth to work, and quite a few wives drive them shopping and to cart kids around.

The van conversion is no wider than a passenger car, and no longer. It is somewhat higher — if you have one with a raised roof that stays up permanently. Some versions have a roof section either of fiberglass with canvas sides or all of fiberglass that raises for camping and lowers for the road. In these, of course, overhead clearance on back roads where limbs may be low, or for that matter in a garage, is no problem. The one we used and liked immensely had a permanently raised roof. Even then it was lower than other motorhomes, both standards and minis, and we found that for a "back in" vehicle it took us just about anywhere we wished to go.

Gas mileage, even with the one-ton chassis, big tires, and a 350 engine, was just great. It averaged about 12 miles to the gallon. Driving comfort was superb, visibility exactly as in any passenger car, and the unit handled identically. The interior was carpeted, there was a small bathroom, small butane stove with oven, small electric-gas refrigerator, modest closet space, and the lower seats made into a double bunk. There was also an overhead pull-out bunk at the rear, and overhead storage (not an overcab of course) up front.

In my estimation the misconceptions about van conversions are sparked by manufacturers who advertise that their units will "sleep a whole family." Some claim five or six. Now there may be families who wouldn't mind packing into such a small space. But the overhead bunk, at least in the model we had — built by one of the largest U.S. builders of RVs, Open Road — was a real claustrophobia special. The rear portion — before the rest was pulled forward to make the bunk, would have served well for extra storage, always badly needed in small interiors. But even for youngsters it would have been a snug fit.

The van conversion in my opinion is a virtually perfect miniature motorhome for a couple, for two fishing or hunting partners, or in a pinch for three people. Certainly it is possible to add on a room by using the van with a tent set up outside for extra sleeping quarters. However, that means stowing a tremendous amount of gear and people inside on the road, and brings the whole concept actually back to a kind of station-wagon type of camping. And that isn't the idea of the van conversion at all. Fundamentally this tiny motorhome was conceived to allow all the comforts of the larger units while one camped and roamed at will, with a minimum of restrictions on where the unit can be taken, and with no feeling whatever of even handling a motorhome as one drives.

We checked out the models with raise-&-lower tops. The permanent top suited us better. A passenger can get up and walk around while the unit is traveling; there is full headroom the whole length and not just in one spot. Further, some of the up-and-down tops with canvas wear rather quickly. The permanent top restricts one so little as to where the unit can be driven that I see little point in the others.

Compared to the builders of mini motorhomes, the van conversion manufacturers are few. But they are represented in several parts of the country — California, the Midwest, Florida, the East. An advantage for the buyer is that almost all equipment is optional. Thus a van can be ordered that has spartan accommodations, or "the works," or anything in between. Prices thus cover a rather broad span. All told, however, the van conversion is not only the most compact of the motorhomes, but also the most economical.

On the average a new, unconverted one-ton van, with cab air conditioning, power steering and brakes, automatic transmission and the varied options most owners will want will cost between $4000 and $4500. Paring options brings it down below $4000. The conversion, with comfort items most generally desired, will add on between $2000 and $3000. This cost can be modified by cutting down options — for example an ice box instead of a refrigerator. Thus, depending on what options you want on the van, and what you want inside, the roof type desired, etc., the total cost span will run from around $5000 to $7500. By careful planning and perhaps foregoing a few conveniences, or modifying the type in some cases, you can set yourself up in this mini-mini motorhome for not much more than the cost of a fully equipped station wagon. In any event the well-appointed van conversion costs less than the most stripped down standard or mini motorhome. All the prices given here are those that were current in mid-1973.

But as I said earlier, this is a rig for rather specialized purpose. So cost isn't all of it. If you want to go light and fast, get good gas mileage, roam tougher country than the larger units can handily take, and are willing to do without spaciousness, this may very well be an excellent choice. Particularly for only two people.

By the time we had used both the van and the mini-motorhome on tours, I was torn. What I'd really like, I knew, was to have one of each — a not very sensible idea, and also too expensive. One feature I want in particular to mention regarding the van is the door arrangement. Most vans have vertical double doors at the rear. By adding a broad step-type bumper so the doors open outward above it, a kind of mini back porch can be arranged. There are of course the two standard cab doors. But vans differ in placement and type of the side, or cargo doors. Some have double doors. The one we used, however, had a broad, sliding side body or cargo door.

We liked this feature immensely. There were no open doors to get in the way when one was outside. The big door simply glided on its track to the rear alongside the body. It was easy and positive to operate. Often we set a table up outside for meals, right in front of the big sliding door. By opening rear and side a breeze blows through nicely on warm days or evenings. There is only one disadvantage. To date, so far as I know, the matter of screens for rear and side has not had the attention of the conversion people. In mosquito country with warm weather this could be a problem.

We gave the van our "ranch test," too, putting it up some rough hills and into a few spots the larger higher mini couldn't go. It passed easily. For general camping travel the more spacious Diamond is of course far and away the most enjoyable. Regardless, all these motorhome minis are my all-out favorites among modern camping rigs. They lack the ponderousness of the larger outfits, yet pack in all the conveniences.

HOW TO CAMP WITH A MILLION PEOPLE AND ENJOY YOURSELF

by JIM TALLON

Families that camp in town can find parks and zoos where wildlife collect.

The in-town camper has the best of two worlds. Here, in the in-city world, good restaurants are available.

PICK A CITY. It may have the virtues and vices of any city, even a million people. But it should: (1) Have boundaries that end fairly abruptly rather than a girdle of suburban areas that straggles out to the next city. (2) It should be strategically placed in a scenic slice of North American real estate. (3) And if at all possible, it should have at least two of those controversial freeways, one running north and south and the other east and west. These demands automatically eliminate most of the cities east of the Mississippi, maybe *all* of them, and quite a few west of it. But with a little effort and planning, a camper can find such a city, station himself in it, literally capitalize on the outdoors and the indoors, and very likely cut

way back on his usual camping expenses.

The city that I live in, or rather a complex of cities— Phoenix, Arizona, nuzzled by such smaller cities as Mesa, Scottsdale, Glendale, and Tempe—conforms to the above requirements. This complex centers in a picturesque sweep of cactus-studded desert within easy range of other coveted landscape types. It has two freeways; and, except for a narrow belt running due east and due west, its metropolitan limits drop off quickly into relatively unpeopled outdoors. Therefore, I will pull from it examples on how to camp with a million people and enjoy yourself.

Perhaps I should emphasize here that if your camping plans consist of making nothing but one-night camp stops

Henry Mancini and camping? The big city camper has such shows at his convenience.

across the land, then re-fill your beer glass and go on to the next story in this issue of CAMPER'S DIGEST. For this article is aimed directly at the camper who wants to spend two or more weeks at a specific locale; rather than skim over the top of a camping experience, he wants to dig deep into it.

Some years ago I spent a three-year period split up between bases at Grand Canyon, Phoenix, and Tucson. Any camper can go only as far, and see only as much, as his budget allows. Not exactly endowed with unlimited funds, I quickly learned that overall it cost less to camp in Phoenix and Tucson than at Grand Canyon. Even though an extended stay as I made at the latter seems far more inviting, it has its limitations, some unprintable here, some physical and some financial. In Tucson, which has over a quarter-million people, I parked my aged travel trailer in a small trailer court on East Lee Street for about $25 per month. (I understand that monthly rates at the same court are only slightly higher today.) Weigh that against the cost of camping at most of our major scenic and recreational areas, or in commercial campgrounds. Last week my wife and daughter and I spent a night in a dustbowl of a commercial campground where undisciplined children and

dogs screamed and barked (respectively) until past midnight. Cost was $3.65. Multiply that by 30 and you get $112.50 per month for camping. Most national parks now charge you $2 per night plus entrance fees. On a monthly basis that comes to $60, but generally the NPS (National Park Service) seldom allows you more than two weeks in one of its campgrounds. Of course the commercial campgrounds will give you a monthly rate, but I'll bet that it in no way approaches the low cost of staying in a trailer court or mobile home park that *does not* cater to the camper per se. They have their rules oo, but offer far fewer restrictions to patrons in many cases. Some limit their spaces to RV's and tenters may have to look a little harder to come up with courts that will allow them to drive their tent-pegs.

By now perhaps you have deduced that camping with a million people and enjoying yourself is hinged to economy. It makes even more sense when you figure other costs of camping as well. At Grand Canyon village, for example, the price of food has been known (and probably still does) to exceed that of remote cities in Alaska. If the camper has to replace an automotive part while there, he can expect to pay three to four times as much for that part

Delightful places to cool off can be found in easy range of big cities.

as he would in a big city. It seems unfair, yet these prices are controlled by the National Park Service. No one can accurately predict when his vehicle will break down, so often he is forced to pay such costs. He can cut the cost of his groceries and other camping needs by as much as half in some cases, providing he has the storage space for them, by stocking up at a big city. (Once I bought a water cooler at Grand Canyon for $18. In Phoenix a few days later, I found they sold for $9. Same brand!) I have chosen Grand Canyon as an example, not to crucify it, but after camping there periodically over 29 years, and working there eight years as a guide, I have come to know it well. Other concessionaires in other national parks (again with price ceilings set by the NPS) have prices on the same level. Too, some towns near major recreational attractions are hardly above reproach.

Okay. So big city camping costs you less. But are you really camping when you park your rig or put your tent up within it? "Camping" is really a broad term individually interpreted by each and every camper. Some feel they must be alone in the wild before they are camping. Others believe if you own a tent that makes you immediately a camper. Still others think they are camping if they can hit

another camper with an underhand throw of a badminton bird. One friend of mine believes he is camping anytime he cooks out, which may be on a hibachi in his backyard. However, my own answer to the question is that I feel that big city camping is camping only in the broadest sense of the word—a compromise. Remember that I have been referring to a city camp as a "base." This base represents an economical and convenient location from which to commute to the outdoors, and offers certain "fringe" benefits as well.

The keys mentioned in the first and second paragraphs of this article are mandatory for the total city camping experience. The freeways and abrupt geographical city limits —not a sign saying "City Limits"—permits quick escape from town. Item number two provides for someplace to escape quickly to. In Tucson I didn't have the "luxury" of a nearby freeway, but lived on the east side of town and three mountain ranges were easily available to me—the Santa Catalinas, the Rincons, and the Santa Ritas. In Phoenix I parked my old trailer far enough from the freeway to eliminate the noise, but close enough to expedite my departure. Only one traffic light winked between me and Flagstaff, Arizona, 150 miles away; and Tucson 135

Almost every city has historic shrines available to the in-city camper, or at least nearby. This is Tumacacori National Monument, a few miles south of Tucson, Arizona.

You will find some trailer courts where you can camp that are less crowded than this campground in Organ Pipe National Monument.

Very often you'll have less trouble finding a camping spot in town than at our major national scenic and recreational areas.

miles to the south. Because the city limits were so defined (true of many western cities) I found solitudal landscapes 15 or 20 minutes from my city campsite; only a little longer is necessary today. I rarely made long trips, concentrating on the nearby desert and its flora and fauna. In addition to the small trailer, I also owned camp gear such as a bedroll, a pump-up gasoline stove and lantern, battered pots and pans, and a small tent. Some of these forays were for one day—I returned to my city camp for the night. Others took me overnight and longer.

One month I spent so little time at the trailer court that my kindly landlady cut my rent to $15 for that particular month. Most of these trips had a certain commercial connotation as I was trying to make a living from doing outdoor articles and photographs. (What really kept me alive was human interest photographs and stories that I did for the local Sunday newspaper magazine section.)

The camper who tries city camping finds his activities aren't confined to the interiors of an RV or a tent during bad weather. Neither rain nor snow stays your enjoyment of museums, aquariums, and art galleries, etc. Or, maybe "Deliverance" is showing in a theater just a few blocks away. How about a culinary experience? No realistic camper will deny that once in awhile he'd gladly trade what's over the cookfire for a nice restaurant dinner cooked by a talented chef. Then on nice in-town days, how

This is camping as generally recognized. You can use your big city camp for a base to carry on this kind of camping.

Some campers never see javelina in the wild, but in town, just a trip to the zoo will show you what they look like.

Big city campers will also find cultural activities available to them while camping with a million people.

about a trip to the zoo—most have examples of wildlife found in their region—or to a botanical garden where you can bone up on the growing things of the area. Doing this in your home town, which may also have a million people, may not sound exciting. With a fresh million people, its a whole new ball park. The airlines and travel bureaus depend upon sales pitches like this for a living. Unlike their customers, though, you are never caught afoot and your costs are sliced to a fraction of theirs. Yet you see the same attractions and probably a lot more.

This is camping? Big city camping can sometimes be no worse than "country locales."

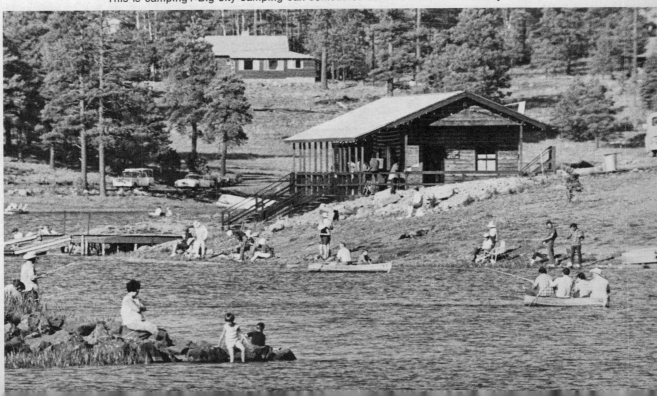

Beautiful to see, great to hike, but expensive to stay at, is the Grand Canyon.

If the thought of camping with a million people still sounds appalling, consider that you are less likely to feel city pressure in a city designed for moving traffic swiftly which allows you to get out of town in a hurry. In our national wonders, again using Grand Canyon for an example, summer people-pile-ups often exceed those in big cities during the to-and-from-work rush hours. As far back as ten years ago, I have seen traffic come to a bumper-to-bumper, horn-blowing standstill in Grand Canyon village. Too, in your big city camp you won't have to worry about being edged out of your campsite by another camper or hustled out of it at the end of two weeks by a National Park Ranger.

One of my most enjoyable outdoor vocations is creeping at about five miles per hour down backroads looking for and photographing wildlife. In my search for more remote backroads, I have become something of a "map freak." I even own a road map of Australia and get a kick of studying it even though I have never been there and have no plans to go there in the immediate future. Of course the best maps for my purposes are topographical, those that show, in addition to the backroads and trails, such details as old cabins, dry lakes, or wet ones that may have some fine fishing, elevations and contour lines. If you think there's something to this camping with a million people, your first move should be to start your own map collection of the areas you like.

Once you narrow it to a state (meaning also Canadian provinces and Mexican states) a road map will help you select potential cities. Letters to their Chambers of Commerce will get you a stack of brochures and lists of things to do. No doubt this information will include the nearby hunting, fishing, camping, hiking, and exploring possibilities. Then you can pick up the topographical maps to help you see in extreme detail just exactly what kind of outdoors you might be missing.

If you're a family man, your wife is going to start being a lot nicer to you because of city camping; I can count the number of 100 percent camping gals I know on one hand and still have a couple of fingers left over (and I suggest these may be lying a little). They like the conveniences of the type of city I have suggested, including good restaurants, shops and culture. In the long run, you'll get a lot more days afield.

Camping with a million people is hardly a new angle. During the winter months in the southwest, and the summers months in the more northern states, a tremendous migration of people with every conceivable type of RV and tent (and even backpacks) move into cities—some large, some small—for extended stays. During that time they get deeply involved in all the activities I have mentioned here plus a great deal I haven't even thought of. They've been doing it for decades, but you know, you can't find one of them that will admit that he has camped with a million people.

the BICYCLE
—newest "recreational vehicle" on the outdoor scene

by MIKE MILLER

The camper on a bicycle can stop at any point en route to admire the scenery. Many tourists driving mobile homes or pick-up campers bring bikes along too for day-long excursions from the camp site.

The cyclo-tourist enjoys the forest beauty in silence. He burns no fossil fuels, adds no hydrocarbons to the atmosphere, and he can even hear the birds sing.

I CAN STILL RECALL (vividly, painfully, my leg muscles going into a minor spasm at the memory of it all) my first experience at bicycle camping. Gad, it was awful; the whole affair a flat-out miserable failure.

The place was Kansas. The time was mid-summer, 20 years ago. And the idea was as simple as it was ill conceived.

Four of us, my wife and I and a neighbor couple, thought up this wonderful plan. We would bicycle about 30 miles from where we lived to this lake we knew and had previously enjoyed. It was a lovely spot, this water hole, an oasis of sorts on the Kansas plains, set with elms and cottonwoods. There were fish to be caught there. And the swimming from sand beaches was grand. The lazing beneath the shade trees was superb. Our plan was to take tents and sleeping bags plus cooking gear, and we'd stay for two or three days.

Now actually there was nothing wrong with our goal. What was wrong was: Our bikes. Our gear. Us.

For bicycles we salvaged four heavyweight old clunkers—dusty, even rusty in places, in need of lubrication—which none of us had even pedaled around the block since high school days. To haul our supplies and gear we simply planned to utilize wire baskets on the fronts of three of the cycles. We would carry everything else in canvas "Boy Scout" packs on our backs.

To "get in shape" the four of us rode all of one mile a couple of days before our departure, to pick up a few six-packs for the trip.

In my mind's eye I can still recall our departure. Each bike, decked out like a junk peddler's vehicle in some comic opera, was loaded fore and aft with strapped-on, tied-on supplies of food, camp stoves, fuel bottles, sleeping bags, clothing and the beer. Strapped to our backs were additional loads of pots, pans, more food, more clothing . . . believe me it was ridiculous.

But, ridiculous or not, thus we departed that hot Kansas morning . . . overloaded . . . unconditioned . . . huffing, puffing, sweating from the first moment . . . weaving back and forth across streets and roads like drunken sailors . . . the immense loads on our backs threatening to topple us at every turn.

Without going into the horrors of the trip, suffice it to say that somehow we made it. But not in the two hours we had estimated. It was more like six. And, certainly we did not arrive at the lake exhilarated, stimulated, anxious to sample the fishing and swimming joys which the lake held in store. Instead all four of us fairly collapsed from our vehicles upon arrival. We lay panting, sweating, cramped, dizzy on the ground. An hour passed before we could even think of setting up camp.

I will say that getting home was a lot easier. Because I hitched a ride back to town with an acquaintance and came back with a station wagon.

So what is the moral of this tale of woe? That a person who enjoys being out-of-doors, who savors the joys of living beneath the stars should nonetheless discount the bicycle as a means of getting to camping places and enjoying them more?

No way. Today, in America, bicycles are selling literally by the millions. And most of them are being sold to adults—many of whom plan to use them for trips which may stretch many hundred miles and many days or even weeks. For great numbers of these Americans—my wife and I among them—bicycling has provided a new zest, a new dimension to the camping experience. If the story of our initial try at bike camping has a moral it is simply this: When you try bike camping, *do it right, from the start,* and your initiation to cyclo-touring as it's sometimes called, will be as successful as ours was absurd.

In order of absurdities, these then are the blunders which we made that first trip out but which you can easily avoid.

First, our bikes. It was nonsense for us to undertake a 30 mile trip on 40 or 45 pound bicycles which, even when new, were never precision machines. I'm not sure that anything quite like today's ten-speed, high-performance, lightweight touring cycles were even available two decades ago, but definitely they are available everywhere in the U.S. today. And to ride one is pure, almost effortless delight. So rule number one, if you're at all serious about bike touring, is to buy a decent ten-speed machine. More about this later.

Blunder number two was our loads. Both couples had done some camping out before—but from automobiles. Our tents, campstoves—almost everything we had—were three times heavier than necessary. When you plan your first bike camping excursion, do as the backpackers do; go light and compact. The total weight of everything you carry should come to no more than 25 or 30 pounds, and this poundage should be carefully stowed, heavy stuff to the bottom, in panniers which hang on each side of your rear wheel, on a handlebar bag mounted on the front of your machine, and on a saddlebag hanging from the seat.

And, finally, blunder number three was the matter of our own physical condition. We had assumed, since we were active, healthy, young adults that we were reasonably in shape for a trip of "only" 30 miles. Oh, wow . . . We wouldn't have thought of trying to swim a mile, or of trying to run three or four miles, without breaking in first, gradually. Why we thought we could undertake a major trip without training for it I can't imagine. On *your* first few times out, ride only a mile or two, then later you can try three or four, finally eight to ten. After that you can extend your trips to 12, 15 and 20 miles. It's amazing how easy it really is if you work up gradually to longer length tours. It's equally amazing how devastating it can be if you overdo.

There are a number of ways you can utilize a bike when you go to the out-of-doors. Our family favorite, I suppose, is what you might call "pure" bike camping. That is, using our bikes as our only means of transportation, we pedal to some place in the woods or along some mountain stream and set up camp for a day or a week or whatever. Our stay completed, we travel home by the same method we came, by footpower.

The author's wife, Marilyn Miller, leaves her tent-camp to explore the woods and trails of a national forest.

Here's one good way to bring the bikes along. Careful how you back up, though.

Thus, for us, the bicycle has become the newest (and most economical) recreational vehicle on the outdoor scene.

An increasing number of our friends, outdoor enthusiasts who enjoy traveling by rec vehicles such as campers, trailers and motor homes, have taken to mounting bikes on the backs and tops of their vehicles then using their cycles for day trips once they arrive in national parks, forests, or wherever their fancy leads them.

There are several advantages to this sort of arrangement. You can cover a relatively large number of miles per day on a bicycle, yet because you are outdoors, not shielded by the frame and windows of your vehicle you feel an intimacy with your surroundings which previously only the hiker could enjoy. Too, there's the environmental thing. Your contribution to air and noise pollution, on a bike, is exactly zero. And of course there's the practical matter of holding on to a camping space in a crowded campground. If you've managed to secure a good camping place, and can leave your vehicle there during the day while you pedal around on your bicycle, you're obviously assured of your same campsite when you return in the evening.

There is, of course, another alternative for the biking traveler. This is simply not to camp out at all, but instead to ride from point to point during the day, absorbing the pleasures of the out-of-doors, then stay at motels in the evening. If you do this, it's still pleasant, and economical, to cook some of your meals around a campfire along the way. If you don't want to go to the trouble of cooking, an inexpensive wine, chilled in a mountain stream and served with bread, cheese, and some kind of fruit, makes noon an especially satisfying time of day.

Let's emphasize again, however, that no matter what kind of camping or traveling you plan to do, your experience will be no better than the bicycle you select to do it on.

And—let's be blunt about it—this means laying out a fair sized bundle of cash.

Eugene A Sloane, in his excellent *The Complete Book of Bicycling,* advises his readers that, "if you intend to get serious about cycling, for health, for the pure pleasure of getting out of doors, or for family trips and touring, you will eventually wind up paying *at least* $120 for a new ten-speed machine. I recommend therefore that you seriously consider this purchase now." I concur with Mr. Sloane.

So, let's talk about the machines—what kinds are available, what sizes, what styles.

First, let's eliminate the bikes you do not want. Unless you want to duplicate my Kansas fiasco of 20 years ago, you don't want to buy a balloon-tired conventional one-speed, no matter how new and sleek and shiny it appears in the dealer's show window. And unless you plan to limit your cycling to toodling around the neighborhood, you don't want one of the so-called "English racer" three-speed models either. They are easier to pedal, perhaps, and they are lighter than most one-speeds, but they're not all that much easier, and not all that much lighter. "Racers" they definitely are not.

Getting into the lightweight field, you don't want to purchase a racing bike (track or road model) either.

Your best bet, and best buy I'm convinced, will be either a ten-speed "sport" model or—if you feel you'll be doing a great deal of camping—a "cyclo-tourist" or "camping" model equipped with ten or even 15 speed gears. (The advantage of the 15-speed bike is that it can climb steep hills and mountains even easier than a ten-speed model.

The sports cycle will likely have 27 by 1¼-inch high-pressure tires. (And if you're going to do much camping

Getting into shape gradually before the first genuine bike-tour is important. So is packing the gear properly.

and touring, be sure to specify you want clincher, not sewn-on tires. The latter are lighter in weight and more responsive for city and short-haul use, but usually they are too thin and hard to repair for camping purposes.) The camping cycle, in anticipation of heavier loads, will likely have semi-balloon type tires 26 inches by 1⅜ or 1½ inches. Another difference between sports and camping bikes will be the addition of permanent, brazed-on carriers, both front and rear, for carrying bags and panniers on the cyclo-tourist. If you buy a sports model, you will have to add this equipment whenever you take an overnight trip.

Choosing between the two models is something of a tossup. Let's put it this way: if you plan to limit your cycling to camping and touring, the camping model will probably be best for you. If you plan to do some over-night touring, but plan to do a lot of recreational afternoon and one-day riding, the sports model may be the way to go.

In either case, when you order your machine be sure to specify, *emphatically* that you want a *wide range of ratios* in your gear selections. What this means, without going into a great deal of detail, is that in your low, hill-climbing gears, the pedaling will be easy.

Both sport and touring models come in four or five frame sizes, thus assuring you a more-or-less customized "fit" regardless of your height or leg length.

Let's talk, incidentally, about fitting your bike to you. Even an expensive cycle, when mismatched to the rider, is no fun to ride; it's hard work. So it is vitally important to ascertain the right frame size for you before you make your purchase. It is for this reason that I strongly recommend that you buy your bike from a reputable bike shop if there is one in your community. A specialist in bikes can "fit" you to the right machine, and the right frame size, from the beginning. Equally important, he can set saddle and handle-bars to the right height and make other adjustments which are so important for comfortable, easy riding. Most department stores, discount houses, and hardware shops simply do not have the specialized, trained personnel to help you make these important decisions. If you order your bike from a catalog you are at even a greater disadvantage.

As a general rule, the proper frame size is one which will allow you to straddle the top tube of your bicycle snugly but not uncomfortably. If you are ordering a bike, and cannot "try it on" for size, you should order a frame size that measures nine to ten inches less than your inseam, measured barefooted.

Finally, let's assume you have made your purchase and now own a sleek new ten-speed fitted nicely to your height and your needs. Let's talk about how those "speeds" work. Again without going into a great deal of detail, suffice it to say that by manipulating two little levers, usually located just behind the handle bars on the top tube, you can adjust gears and "derailleurs" (French for "derailers") in such a way that ten different "speeds" or "ratios" are possible on your bicycle with any given turn of the crank.

In the lower gears, the crank will turn quite easily—but you won't make any speed to speak of. In the top gears it's harder to pedal your bicycle—but with every revolution of the crank you cover considerably more ground, and you do it much faster. In the middle range the pedal effort on level ground is neither easy nor difficult, and the speeds are similarly average.

Here's how the gears will work in actual practice:

You're on a bike-camping trip, touring through scenic forested country. It's been level traveling up to now, so you've set your gears in the upper middle range—your left hand lever pulled back, toward you as far as it will come; your right hand lever back to about the middle position. Then, a few miles further, looms your first obstacle. A hill, a tough one, the kind cars might have to be shifted down for. You shift too, into progressively lower gears as the going gets steeper, until finally you are in the lowest gear on your bicycle. Your right-hand shifting lever is now in the full back postion, towards you.

Now here's the interesting thing about gear-shifting on a ten-speed bike. If you've done your shifting properly you are now going up the hill without a great deal of exertion. And your legs are pedaling the crank at about the same rpm that was required to propel you along on the level road a few miles back. True enough, you're not making much speed

—but so what? You're still enjoying a smooth, relatively effortless outdoor ride.

Finally you reach the top of the hill. Time to start your decline. But it's not a sharp decline. It's very gradual. So, still pedaling at the same rate of speed (or "cadence" as it's called) you shift into high gear, your left lever full back, your right one full forward—and you fairly well zoom along toward your destination and a comfortable night's camping.

Sound easy? Sound like fun? It *is* easy, after you've spent a few hours getting the hang of it. And it *is* fun, from the very first moment you take off on your ten-speed, through the city park and home again.

If you want to know more about ten-speed bicycling, I'd suggest you get a copy of Eugene Sloane's book ($9.95, Trident Press, New York) or *Bicycle Digest* ($5.95, Digest Books, Inc. Northfield, Ill.) And if you are especially turned on by camping and touring by bike, a number of organizations which specialzie in such outings may be of interest to you. Among them are the League of American Wheelmen, 19 South Bothwell, Palatine, Illinois 60067; The American Youth Hostels, Inc., 20 West 17th Street, New York, New York 10011; and the International Bicycle Touring Society, La Jolla, California 92037.

No question about it, bike riding and especially bike camping is a grand way to see and enjoy the great outdoors. It's health building; it's scenically rewarding; and once you're over the initial expense of buying your bike and gear, there's one more big advantage to this kind of camping— the cost of your excursions, even the cost of transportation, becomes practically zero.

Many bike routes are well marked as this one is, the trails firm and, at some places at least, level.

YOUR NATIONAL FORESTS

What do they offer?

by MARV LINDBERG

... who gratefully acknowledges statistical assistance from Barbara Myers, Div. of Information & Education, U.S. Department of Agriculture, Forest Service.

NAME YOUR PREFERENCE in outdoor recreation and you are sure to find it somewhere or everywhere in our vast system of national forests. Best of all, nearly everything is free of charge except for commercial public-service facilities such as resorts, hotels, cabin camps, ski lifts, stores, gas stations and similar services under special-use permits.

Public Law 93-81, which went into effect on August 1st, 1973, specifies the facilities which must be provided before fees may be charged. No fees may be charged for access to, or use of, any campground not having flush restrooms, showers reasonably available, access and circulatory roads, sanitary disposal stations reasonably avail-

able, visitor protection control, designated tent or trailer spaces, refuse containers, and potable water. Nor can a fee be charged for boat launching unless mechanical or hydraulic equipment is available.

What does this mean to you? Prior to this law, user fees had been charged at 2235 family campgrounds within the National Forest System. Under the new law, fees will be charged at only 37 campgrounds. Previously, fees were charged at 99 boat launching ramps, but the new law eliminated practically all of these.

Where else can so many obtain so much in the way of outdoor recreation for so little!

There are 154 national forest units (some forests are

Relics of the past abound if you seek them out in the back country.

comprised of two or more separate parcels of land) located in 40 of the contiguous United States, plus Alaska and Puerto Rico. Together, they contain over 180 million acres of land—nearly an acre apiece for our total population.

Some states are blessed with considerably more national forest land than others, with the western states having the most. Alaska, Idaho and California have roughly 20 million acres each. Montana has over 16 million acres, Oregon over 15 million and Washington nearly 10 million. The smallest acreage is in Maine, with about 50,000 acres. However, in the 48 contiguous states, you are within a day's drive of one or more national forests no matter where you live.

For a map showing the location of all the national forests, write the United States Department of Agriculture, National Forest Service, Washington, D.C. 20250 and request a copy of "Field Offices of the Forest Service." This guide lists the addresses of all Regional Offices and the headquarters for each national forest.

How can you take advantage of your national forests and all the recreation features they offer? First, decide where you might like to go and what you might like to do. Then, write for information and a map(s) of the forest(s) you wish to visit. Be precise about the type of recreation that interests you. They may have additional information they can send on specific subjects.

There are presently 4880 family type campgrounds that will accommodate well over 400,000 people at one time. (This does not include picnic sites of which there are nearly 1500.) Such campgrounds vary from those with space for only a few people to those that can accommodate over 1000. Some are off the beaten track, but accessible by car on forest access roads. Many are located right off major highways.

It is the nature of the Forest Service to develop these campgrounds in such a manner as to preserve the natural setting. Even on the highways, the only indication of the existence of a campground may be the sign at the entrance road.

Nearly all campsites will have tables, fireplaces, toilets,

garbage receptacles and approved drinking water. Most sites are so spaced as to leave some trees and underbrush between campsites to provide a degree of privacy.

Some national forest campgrounds may not accommodate extra long motorhomes or trailers—these may not fit in the parking spurs or they cannot be turned around within the campground. If you have any doubts, contact the Forest Supervisor or District Ranger in advance for further information on any specific campground.

You can expect competition for the more popular and accessible campgrounds. In 1972, there were over 36 million visitor-days recorded in the campgrounds, and over 5 million in the picnic grounds. Naturally, weekends produce the most crowded conditions. Where necessary, due to the demand for campsites, some campgrounds have limits on the length of time you may stay.

Most campers have some additional type of recreation in mind. Some national forests offer a greater variety than others. Obviously, you can't go mountain climbing where there are no mountains, but you can go boating in the desert regions. You'll have to study the information available to find an outlet for your particular desires.

Hiking? That's easy. Statistics change as quickly as new trail construction is completed, but the combined total of existing and proposed trails includes over 120,000 miles of foot trails in your national forests. Some merely take you for a short stroll along a self-guided trail with interpretive signs or leaflets to acquaint you with the flora or geological features of that particular area.

If you *really* want to stretch your legs, you can do so in either the west or east coast mountain ranges. Along the 2313 mile long Pacific Crest Trail stretching from Canada to Mexico, 1599 miles are in 19 national forests. Over 500 miles of the 2000 mile long Appalachian Trail from Maine to Georgia are routed through eight national forests.

Only a few hardy souls have made it in one prolonged hike, but roads or trails provide access to all segments of these trails where you can hike for a day or a week or two.

Thousands of people have come to recognize the need for more intimate contact with nature on her own terms. On foot, horseback or by canoe, they are traveling into areas not accessible by automobile. To accommodate these

people and generations to follow, the Forest Service has set aside over 14 million acres of wilderness in 84 areas in 73 national forests in 14 states. In these Wilderness Areas, no development, no roads, no mechanized vehicles, no timber cutting or other commercial uses, except existing grazing permits, are allowed.

Wilderness lands may range from desert country to lofty mountain peaks. They range in size from a few thousand acres to over a million. They contain countless fishing streams, rivers and lakes. Wildlife in all manner of birds and animals abound.

Parts of the present Boundary Waters Canoe Area in Minnesota were given special protection. Here, by canoe, you can cast off the burdens of civilization and lose yourself (or get lost if you don't go well prepared or have a guide) in this primitive land. There are 887,000 acres you can explore by portaging from one lake or stream to another.

For those who enjoy the thrills and rewards of rock or mountain climbing, the national forests offer an abundance of opportunities. You may settle for the rock cliffs of a canyon or strive for the lofty peaks with fields of glacial ice. Such sport is not for the amateur. The skills required must be learned under the guidance of experienced instructors.

Many foot trails are also used for horseback riding—some exclude such use. However, the combined total of existing and proposed horseback trails exceeds 110,000 miles.

The Forest Service has a number of trails for handicapped visitors, including those who enjoy the sound and scent of the outdoors but cannot enjoy the sights. On some such trails, markers are done in Braille.

If you prefer a mechanized steed, something over 40,000 miles of trails for trail bikes are in the offing. Where such trails combine with horseback trails, the conscientious bike rider will defer to the people on horseback as some horses still do not take kindly to the advent of the internal combustion engine.

With the advent of the snowmobile, trail riding became a wintertime activity as well. Trail mileage is next to impossible to estimate because snowmobilers utilize the

A mountaintop affords a bird's-eye view of the valley and lakes below.

Not all national forest roads are recommended for conventional vehicles.

countless miles of logging or access roads that weave a network of wintertime trails. The Forest Service has many such trails clearly marked with signs and some areas posted as closed to snowmobilers to protect the winter ranges of deer and elk.

There are also a few hardy souls who accept the challenge of winter on cross-country ski trips or seek solitude on snow-shoes.

Although winter, with heavy snowfall, precludes access to many areas except by snowmobile, there are over 200 ski areas located entirely or partially on national forest land with access by automobile. They are operated under use permits by organizations other than the Forest Service. To insure the safety of skiers, Forest Service Snow Rangers are assigned to many of the more popular ski areas. They inspect the lifts, watch for dangerous snow buildup and precipitate controlled avalanches before they develop spontaneously.

Understandably, some of the best big or small game and bird hunting is to be found on national forest land. Estimates indicate over one-third of all big game animals exist in the national forests. Through good game management, herds of deer and elk far exceed the population of yesteryear.

Upland birds of forest and grassland provide the hunter with a challenge and a choice. Waterfowl are to be found on lakes and rivers within the national forests.

Rabbit hunting and plinking for varmints is a very popular pastime and offers a father a chance to introduce his son to the proper use of a gun.

There are some 80,000 miles of streams and 2¾ million acres of natural and man-made lakes in the national forests. Needless to say, the fisherman willing to put forth the effort to reach a remote lake or stream doesn't have to depend on luck for success. Some such areas are so seldom fished, a strike at every cast is not uncommon. Hunting and fishing regulations are governed by the states in which the forests lie.

Hikers pause to admire the superb view above Glacier Lake in Mission Mountains Primitive area at Flathead National Forest in Montana.

Most national forest campgrounds and access roads are open to the new breed of wintertime enthusiasts.

THE NATIONAL FOREST SYSTEM

MINN.
SUPERIOR
CHIPPEWA
OTTAWA
HIAWATHA
HIAWATHA
CHEQUAMEGON
NICOLET
HURON
MANISTEE
WIS.
MI-21
MILWAUKEE
MI-22
MADISON ✳
MI-23
MICH.
NORTH CENTRAL ▲

IOWA
ILL.
CHEQUEST
KEOSAUQUA
EASTERN REGION
OHIO
IND.
IN 21
HOOSIER
WAYNE
MO.
MO-21
SHAWNEE
MARK TWAIN
CLARK
KY.
DANIEL BOONE
MONONGAHELA
W. VA.
ME.
VT.
GREEN MOUNTAIN
WHITE MOUNTAIN
N.H.
N.Y.
NY-21
MASS.
CONN.
R.I.
ALLEGHENY
PA.
UPPER DARBY ▲
NORTHEASTERN
N.J.
MD.
WASHINGTON ◉
DEL.
GEORGE WASHINGTON
VA.
JEFFERSON
CHEROKEE
YADKIN
PISGAH
NANTAHALA
SOUTHEASTERN
CHEROKEE
PISGAH
UWHARRIE
N.C.
CROATAN
SUMTER
SUMTER
TENN.
S.C.
FRANCIS MARION

OZARK
OUACHITA
ST FRANCIS
HOLLY SPRINGS
WM B BANKHEAD
CHATTA-HOOCHEE
ATLANTA
OCONEE
OUACHITA
CADDO
ARK.
SOUTHERN   **REGION**
TOMBIGBEE
TALLADEGA
MISS.
DELTA
TALLADEGA
TUSKEGEE
GA.
KISATCHIE
BIENVILLE
SABINE
DAVY ROCKETT
HOMOCHITTO
DE SOTO
CONECUH
ALA.
ANGELINA
...STON
LA.
SOUTHERN ▲
APALACHICOLA
OSCEOLA
OCALA
FLA.

Legend

U. S. DEPARTMENT OF AGRICULTURE
FOREST SERVICE

NATIONAL FORESTS AND FOREST SERVICE FIELD OFFICES

MILES
0   50   100   150   200

- NATIONAL FORESTS
- PURCHASE UNITS
- NATIONAL GRASSLANDS
- LAND UTILIZATION PROJECTS
— REGIONAL BOUNDARIES
◉ REGIONAL HEADQUARTERS
• SUPERVISOR'S HEADQUARTERS
▲ FOREST AND RANGE EXPERIMENT STATIONS
✳ LABORATORY (MADISON, WIS.)
□ AREA DIRECTOR STATE AND PRIVATE FORESTRY PROGRAMS

Everyone participates in and enjoys camping in the Monongahela National Forest in West Virginia.   U.S. Forest Service Photo

If you want solitude, winter camping is the answer.

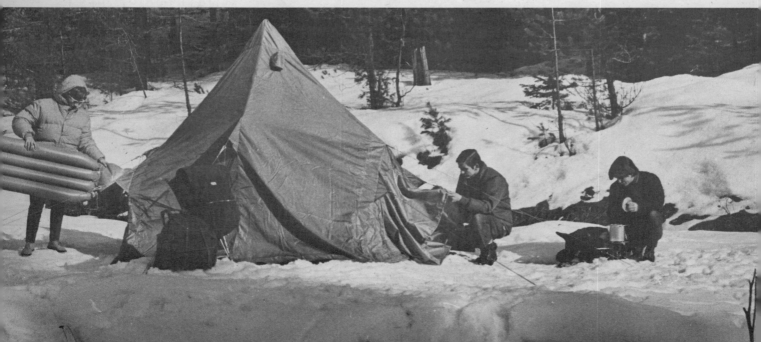

Inyo National Forest in California offers cross country skiing at the Mannoth Winter Sports Area.

Lakes with access by boat are popular. Some have restrictions regarding the use or size of motors, others are unrestricted. You have a choice of a quiet lake "cruise" with canoe or row boat or you may enjoy sailing, speedboating or water skiing.

Perhaps you would rather enjoy your national forests in the comfort of an automobile. Over 150,000 miles of access roads afford you the opportunity to do so. They vary from paved to low class "proceed at your own risk" dirt roads. Most are graveled, and quite passable in good weather if you drive at the speed you should in order to enjoy the scenery. A map of the forest is most helpful to avoid dead ends and to allow you to schedule your time. Places of special interest are often marked on the map. It will indicate the type of roads and the elevations so you can choose a route that suits you.

National Recreation Areas are those that lend themselves particularly to family enjoyment of the outdoors. In these areas, the Forest Service puts more effort into development in order to take full advantage of what it has to offer.

There are also numerous formally designated special interest areas with specific historical, archeological, geological, botanical, memorial or scenic value.

Following is a brief indication of the scope of such areas adapted from information furnished by the United States Department of Agriculture, Forest Service.

The Bee Branch Scenic Area in the Bankhead Forest in Alabama has a deep box canyon with sheer sandstone cliffs and a yellow poplar tree 80 inches in diameter. Alaska has the Kasaan Totem Park Archeological Area in the South Tongass Forest containing restorations of artifacts made by the Haida Indians.

. Arizona's C. Hart Merriam Scenic Area in the Coconino Forest includes rare (for Arizona) Arctic-Alpine life zones. The Hurricane Creek Natural Bridge Scenic Area in the Ozark Forest of Arkansas has a typical hardwood forest.

The world's oldest living trees are in the Ancient Bristle-

Most national forest campsites are spacious and made secluded by natural underbrush left between each site.

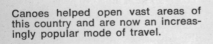

Canoes helped open vast areas of this country and are now an increasingly popular mode of travel.

Ancient suspension bridge offers a unique thrill.

cone Pine Forest Botanical Area in the Inyo Forest of California. The Lost Creek Scenic Area in the Pike Forest has some of the most spectacular granite formations in Colorado.

Florida's Bowers Bluff Archeological Area in the Ocala Forest has three Indian Shell Mounds 2000-5000 years old.

Joyce Kilmer is honored by a Memorial Area of hardwood forest in the Nantahala Forest of North Carolina. The Hell's Canyon Seven Devils Scenic Area in the Wallowa-Whitman Forest in Oregon is the deepest canyon in the North American continent. Pennsylvania's Hearts Content Scenic Area in the Allegheny Forest features northern hardwoods. Cane brakes reaching a height of 30 feet can be seen in the Long Cane Scenic Area of the Sumter Forest of South Carolina.

Eleven waterfalls flow through a rugged gorge in Tennessee's Rock Creek Scenic Area in the Cherokee Forest. Texas has its Big Thicket Scenic Area in the Sam Houston Forest, characterized by various hardwoods.

The awesome power of nature is represented by the 2000 foot land slide in the Gros Ventre Slide Geological Area in the Teton Forest of Wyoming.

The foregoing are just a few of the 130 such sites scattered over 29 states. The others are all of equal interest.

Because all this land belongs to each of us, you are expected to treat it accordingly. Some people evidently throw their mealtime leftovers on the floor at home; dispose of their tin cans, bottles and trash in their own back yard; flip a burning cigarette away at random; vandalize their own property; and don't mind living in such a mess. That's their own personal affair and they're welcome to it.

However, when they subject their neighbor's property to the same abuse, it's a different matter. On national forest land, *everyone* is your neighbor—from the family living next door to those living clear across the country from you. It shouldn't be necessary to say more. Mother Nature made it clean and green—let's keep it that way.

Following are the addresses of the 9 Regional Offices of the Forest Service:

Northern Region
Federal Bldg.
Missoula, Mont. 59801

Southwestern Region
517 Gold Ave. SW
Albuquerque, New Mexico 87101

California Region
630 Sansome St.
San Francisco, Ca. 94111

Rocky Mountain Region
Federal Center
Bldg. 85
Denver, Co. 80225

Intermountain Region
324 25th St.
Ogden, Utah 84401

Pacific Northwest Region
319 SW Pine St.
P.O. Box 3623
Portland, Oreg. 97208

Eastern Region
710 North Sixth St.
Milwaukee, Wis. 53203

Southern Region
50 Seventh St. NE
Atlanta, Ga. 30323

Alaska Region
Federal Office Bldg.
Juneau, Alaska 99801

A New Way to See the West: the Pack-Hike Trip

by PEGGY PETERS

IT WAS OUR SECOND DAY OUT. Early, single beams of sunlight nuzzled their way past our tent flap and somehow found, as they always did, a not-quite-closed corner of my eye lid. My nose felt cold and I slid down farther in the sleeping bag. This warmed my nose and managed for another few minutes to keep the light from my eyes but it was no good. No good at all. I was awake. Stretching out in the almost sinful luxury of the warm bag I felt an unfamiliar tightness in my calves and remembered yesterday's climb. That first day my husband, Joe, and I and the rest had travelled only about six miles, but we had gained 1500 feet in altitude and we had done it all on foot.

The aroma of camp coffee filled our frosted tent and we shoved arms and legs into every available piece of clothing and clumsily lumbered toward that coffee and the breakfast Pauline McCarty, the camp cook, was preparing. Blue-gray smoke from the wood fire had risen to fill the fly overhead and was now edging out into the stillness of

the morning air beyond. Morris, Pauline's husband, and boss of the wranglers, was alert and smiling over a mug of steaming brew. Some of "the boys" were giving their breakfast orders ("three over easy and three hot cakes") while the others were on the near ridge collecting our string of pack horses. Meals were consistently delicious and abundant.

Foot locomotion, yes. Pack horses, yes again. For this was a pack-hike trip, perhaps the best way for most of us to experience the Western wilderness. This kind of trip combines parts of back-packing with counterparts of pack-tripping.

Back-packing is an inexpensive, exhilarating, fast-growing way to explore beautiful out-of-the-way areas, but this requires the muscle tone and stamina usually found only in the young. The longer the trip and rougher the terrain the truer this is. Then there is pack-tripping. This requires less in the way of endurance, but can be an

Each morning after the hikers have assembled their gear the outfitter and his hands pack the horses for the day's journey.

expensive undertaking, especially if it is to be a family affair.

In pack-hiking the group, and ours numbered a dozen plus one or two from ages 14 to 60, goes afoot from one camp site to the next. Each can proceed at his own pace and each carries only a rucksack containing what will be needed for the day: a camera, bag lunch, tissues, insect repellent, etc. After breakfast the hikers set out across country in twos and threes while the wranglers pack the horses with the tents, bedding, duffle bags, kitchen equipment and paniers of food. Later, somewhere along the trail, the line of horses passes the hikers at a fast walk and winds its way ahead through the roadless country. By the time the group straggles into the new camp by late afternoon the fly is up, the fire is well along to coals and dinner underway.

On our ten-day adventure we explored the Gros Ventre Range in the back country of Teton National Forest in northwestern Wyoming. Although the first day's journey was only six miles, the second was longer and each day found us able to hike farther with more ease and loving it. By the end of our tour, a 12-mile hike left us exhilarated and ready to "set awhile", but certainly not exhausted. The outfitter supplied everything but our sleeping bags and personal items and the cost was a modest $260 each.

The first day began on the north side of the range and we hiked southward and upward along Big Cow Creek trail to Sportsman's Ridge. The second day's journey took us to a lovely, green, rolling meadow in an area called Six Lakes. As we walked along the narrow trail we saw first one lake and then as we rounded it and the path arched upward, the second came into view. Finally the promise of the other four in the necklace. It was magnif-

Part of the pack string pauses for rest enroute to the new campsite. Hikers have left earlier, but will arrive after the faster-moving horses have reached the new area.

icent. The meadow grass was a rich emerald dotted, and in places splashed with wildflowers—yellow balsamroot clumps the size of bushelbaskets; masses of scarlet Wyoming paintbrush and when we took time out to lay on our backs, puffy clouds punctuated a cornflower blue sky. On one of the lakes we saw a goldeneye hen with 14 chicks. As we approached she swept her brood together and herded them from the shore to the center of the water. As our scraggly line wove along the path to the southward end of the lake the chicks were edged northward, always a safe distance from the featherless invaders.

Nor were ducks all we saw—elk cows migrate to the high country to drop their calves in early spring and we saw several herds on the tops of towering earth masses opposite us. The cows, colored with the same palette used for Siamese cats, merely gazed at us when the distance was great, but as the space narrowed their chins would jut upward in that peculiar elk-fashion and they and their incredibly leggy offspring would bound away.

We watched a band of bighorn ewes and their wooly lambs through binoculars and came as close as yesterday's paw prints to black bears. Once a mule deer came to see us. At the end of the day's trek Joe and I found a secluded loop of a cold creek not far from our tent and sat down to soak all remembrance of rocky trails from our feet. We were silent, just enjoying the surroundings, when a twig broke off to our right. Looking up we exchanged a long look with a slightly surprised deer. I guess mulies don't often stand in cold water for the pure comfort of it.

Grey-capped rosy finches and Audubon's warblers populated the wooded areas and comprised the majority of the 33 species we counted. Yellow-bellied marmots whistled to each other—or was it at us—from rock slides. The marmots are close relatives of the groundhog who can

This is one of the beautiful Six Lakes. We pitched our tent toward the very best view.

scamper over, under and, I sometimes believed, through rocks with speed and agility uncommon in a creature so round and furry. They look as though they'd be thoroughly at home in the hollow of a tree rather than in a den beneath a boulder.

We camped for two days at the headwaters of the Gros Ventre River, a major tributary to the Snake, and expectantly unsheathed our fishing rods. The plan was that we would take Morris' advice and follow the rivulet which trickled past our camp down stream. As other threads joined the flow and bound themselves together and then tiny streams entered from here and there, Joe and I were soon paralleling a healthy, rolling current. Our instructions were to just keep going until we reached Ouzel Falls and in the pools beneath we would see trout "as long as your arm and probably thicker". Well, it may well be true that such creatures did and do exist but I can't really say for sure because we never did get to the falls. Although the sun warmed our backs as we hopefully strode from camp, clouds soon rolled in and then a rain began to add moisture to the already soggy mass underfoot. When we were several miles away from the protection of camp, thunder boomed from hill to hill and lightning pierced the clouds. As we raced for an abandoned hunting camp, fishing tackle snagging the scrubby brush, the rain turned to hail. We couldn't put our hands in pockets because we were carrying the fishing gear, and we couldn't avert our faces from the stinging stones because we needed every one of our senses to negotiate the most direct route to shelter.

Pauline McCarty and her assistant, Mary Ann Schwartz, begin preparations for another flavorful, robust dinner. Open "cabinets" in background have panels which seal them completely and they are loaded on each side of a pack horse each morning.

I find that a good foot-rub feels marvelous after the long day's hike.

All exposed skin was pink and smarting by the time we dodged inside.

The day before our last the landscape changed more dramatically than it had on any of the previous days. Once again the main direction we took was upward and we ended the day at 10,000 feet. Although it was near the end of July by now, the spring snows stubbornly remained on the shady sides of jagged points of land. Melt water trickled from beneath the crust and meandered over and around small rocks lining embryonic gullys on the hillsides. Gone was the flower show of earlier days; here were only the earliest of all the western wildflowers, the marsh marigolds; white waxy, daisy-like petals radiating from a fuzzy yellow hub. Thousands bloomed at the icy edges of snow patches. We gingerly crossed ice bridges over larger flows, then gained confidence and leaped from boulder to small cliff and finally cliff to cliff keeping generally to what we hoped was the trail while avoiding wet, chill feet as much as possible.

It was cold that night—no doubt about that. A heavy frost covered every blade and leaf the next morning and a thin skin of ice lidded the water bucket. Our breath was a cloud in the air. Fortified with a massive hot breakfast on that last morning we began the final upward push—this time over solid ice and snow. On most days the hikes began with a brisk pace which slowed here and hurried there throughout the day. This time we all sensed that our reserves of energy must be husbanded carefully and parsi-

Joe has described some camp-coffee as, "too thick to drink and too thin to plow," but this early-morning cup couldn't have tasted any better. ▶

We all enjoyed widerness scenes like this at Six Lakes. On our entire trip, lasting ten days, we saw only two people other than those in our group.

On some days fishing gear was part of the day's necessities.

After meals the hikers scraped and pre-rinsed their own plates leaving only the pots and pans needing real work. Each day the routines became easier and faster leaving more time to explore or just loaf.

moniously doled out as circumstances demanded. Up and up we went, the wind increasing in intensity. We were more aware of our fellows than we had been and hands were frequently extended to steady the person behind, or voices to call encouragement to those below: "it's easier right here and out of the wind". About mid-morning we reached the highest point of our entire journey. On a wind-blasted ridge where even the snow couldn't lie we found a U.S. Geological benchmark. It read 10,675 feet.

From here on the path was downward. Steeply downward. From that point we dropped 4,000 feet to reach bottom and the end of the adventure by late afternoon. En route the snow vanished, mud slicked the path for a period, and then dried, flowers we had seen earlier reappeared, birds hopped in the brush and ground squirrels raced across the path in front of us.

Over the ten-day period our group had walked, climbed, jumped and scrambled over a hundred miles of wilderness and more. We emerged tanner, healthier and happier than we had begun and we had something else—a wonderful sense of accomplishment.

A GOOD NIGHT'S SLEEP

Half zipper on Coleman mummy bag is fine for total cold weather use. I recommend full zipper for all around bag and different temperatures.

by CHARLES J. FARMER

WE HAD no way of being positive, but my bighorn sheep hunting partner, Allan Sicks and I knew the temperature was below zero. At dusk, a strong wind blew and flurries of snow flakes sifted through our natural, scrub pine windbreak.

It was our ninth day in the mountains. With backpack camps on our shoulders, we had been roaming prime sheep habitat in hopes of getting close to a legal, three-quarter-curl ram or better. So far, we had counted 62 ewes and kids. The rams were nowhere to be found.

The November weather in Wyoming's 11,000 foot high Beartooth Range had challenged us every day. Snow, below freezing temperatures, wind and dampness marked the nine days. And it did not get any better.

One of the real highlights of that hunting trip, aside from the fact that Allan shot a nice three-quarter-curl ram on the last day of our hunt, was knowing that we had slept warm and comfortable, despite the bad weather. The ability to stay warm, regardless of season or temperature, can be mastered by any outdoorsman, provided a few, basic guidelines are followed.

Allan and I slept warm on the sheep hunt because we had selected the right sleeping bags for the occasion. As fly fishermen match the hatch for trout, the sportsman can match the proper bag for various areas and temperature situations. This is not to say that campers, hunters and fishermen need a variety of expensive bags for different parts of the country. But rather the purpose of the statement is to emphasize the importance of purchasing a good sleeping bag . . . one that can meet the demands of the coldest weather a person can expect from his or her brand of camping. Selecting the right bag is simple when you keep a few important points in mind.

For the sheep hunt, my partner and I had selected good down filled bags that weighed about 4 pounds each. Weight was an important consideration to us since we wanted to keep our packs around 30 pounds. Any more weight than that would have pooped us out fast in the rugged terrain and thin air.

Equally as important as weight was warmth. We knew temperature conditions would be severe around November in sheep country. So for the maximum in warmth, Allan and I chose mummy bags filled with 3 pounds of prime white northern goose down . . . the best insulation going in my opinion. The outer shell of the bags consisted of 1.9-ounce Ripstop nylon. Foam sleeping pads, long enough to cushion shoulders and hips, and a fine insulation against ground cold, rounded out our sleeping gear.

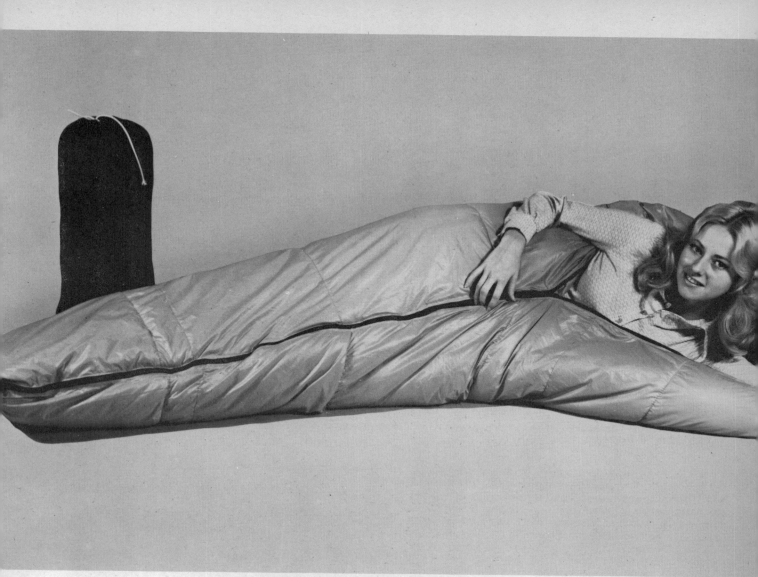

Here is Dacron II Coleman bag that features full length zipper.

The Right Bag for You

There are sleeping bags on the market today that perform every function a camper or hiker expects from a good bag. The best all-around bags are those that effectively trap dead air. Good bags are thick enough so that there is a sufficient amount of dead air all around a camper's body. Thickness of insulation, and the ability of that insulation to fluff . . . and stay springy, is more important to the sportsman than the weight of the insulation in the bag.

For example, prime goose down has a springy quality about it. Although a bag may be tightly compacted in a stuff sack for a month, it will retain its original thickness when taken out of the bag and fluffed. It is this thickness, with its built-in dead air trap, that provides warmth.

Now, if that same down bag were laid flat and used merely as a mattress, its insulating qualities would be nullified. The reason? The down, whose main function is providing dead air from its thickness or loft, would be compacted to such a degree that most dead air space would be eliminated. This is the reason that a good, foam pad is used for insulation under sleeping bags these days. Pads provide dead air insulation. Among backpackers, the pads are far more popular than air mattresses. There is always the chance of puncturing an air mattress. And, within the chambers of the mattress, air is alive and circulating—not dead. Although the packer gives up a degree of compressibility when he chooses a pad over an air mattress, the choice is a good one nonetheless.

O.K. . . . so what is the right bag for you? I have talked, so far, about goose down. This insulation is best for me. But there are other fillings that do the job. The Coleman Company has a Dacron II line of bags that have good loft, and are still light enough for backpacking. Included in this line, are two mummy type bags and two rectangular models. The comfort range within this line can cover a variety of temperature ranges. And this is an important consideration for the camper.

For example, one of Coleman's Dacron II mummy bags has a comfort range of 25 to 45 degrees. It is filled with 3 pounds of Dacron II and covered with rip stop lining. Construction is the overlapping tube-type and the bag weighs about 4½ pounds.

The other Dacron II mummy bag has a comfort range of 10 to 30 degrees . . . a good range for average, cool or cold weather camping. This bag is filled with 4 pounds of Dacron II; weighs about 5½ pounds and is constructed in the same manner as the first bag.

This is the "Backpacker" bag by Eddie Bauer. It features slant box construction—and has comfort range from 15 to 60 degrees.

Although mummy bags are preferred by most backpackers because of their weight, compressibility and tapered, body fit (which means better and faster heating due to less circulated air space) rectangular bags are popular with most other campers. Although there is more space for the body to heat, and cold spots are more common than with mummy bags, many campers like the freedom of movement of the rectangular bags.

The good, rectangle bags can be warm when the proper filling is used and a suitable loft is obained. Coleman has two such bags in their Dacron II line. One bag has a comfort range of 25 to 45 degrees with 3¾ pounds of Dacron II. The other bag has 2½ pounds of Dacron II filling that yields a comfort range of 40 degrees and above.

By listing a specific sleeping bag manufacturer, and a certain line, I am trying neither to promote the bags nor that manufacturer, but rather my intention is to list important features that make up the worth of bags by all manufacturers.

Last year, Coleman had 22 other sleeping bag models. Some were filled with Polyester fiber, Acrylic fiber, and Dacron 88. I call most of these bags "limited use" sleepers. By themselves, they are not warm enough for fall or winter hunting. And in the mountains, in the summertime, their insulating qualities are marginal. They are too big and heavy for backpacking. So, their use is limited to certain periods in the summer when temperature conditions are ideal. Unfortunately, most campers cannot predict ideal conditions. An untimely cold snap, a spell of rainy days . . . brings out the best, or worst in sleeping bags.

The majority of bags sold in discount stores fall into the "limited use" catagory. This is unfortunate because so many novice campers, or those outdoorsmen looking for a bargain, shop the discount sporting goods department. "Bargain bags" are bad deals all the way around. I have never seen a good bargain bag . . . and probably never will.

Backpack mummy bag by Gerry features northern white goose down insulation.

Here's what I mean. Pre-summer sporting goods sales . . . the bargain sales, great savings—types usually hook most of the unwary campers. I have seen bags on sales for as low as $12. The average sale price is around $15 or $20. Limited use bags. Rarely does the manufacturer list a comfort range on the bag. Insulation or fill, and the amount contained within the bag, is usually not listed. And furthermore, the camper is buying a bag that will not do the job intended. A couple of wool blankets, with a ground cloth and a nylon or canvas cover on top would do a better job of keeping a camper comfortable.

Where Can You Find a Good Sleeping Bag?

Good bags can be found in discount sporting goods departments. Usually though, these bags are in the minority and must be scouted out. Look for top sleeping bag manufacturer names first. Ignore bags that do not display manufacturers' labels, the exact weight and content of filling and the comfort range. That narrows down the choice considerably.

Gerry; Eddie Bauer (Seattle, Washington); Alpine Designs (Boulder, Colorado); Recreational Equipment (Seattle, Washington); Outdoor Leadership Supply (Lander, Wyoming) and Powderhorn Mountaineering (Jackson, Wyoming) are all reputable manufacturers of top line down and Dacron bags. The Coleman Company (Wichita, Kansas) produces top quality Dacron II bags, plus a good prime northern goose down bag.

Retail sporting goods outlets, ski shops, backpack outfitters and climbing supply stores usually stock good bags. They carry a minimum of limited use bags since their business is ordinarily geared to top quality sports specialty items. Their prices usually run higher. But in selecting the right sleeping bag, cost should be secondary to comfort range, thickness, weight, compressibility and durability. You can expect to pay from $40 to $110 for a suitable bag depending on your specific needs.

Mail order houses often carry a top quality line of sleeping bags. When ordering by mail, make sure the supplier or manufacturer has listed appropriate information such as length and width of bag; carrying weight; type of fill— and this should be specific (for example, duck down is not as good an insulator as goose down and prime white northern goose down is best).

Federal trade regulations do not require advertising to state the color of down used in sleeping bags. The name "waterfowl down" is sometimes used. However, the bedding tag required by state law, to be attached to every sleeping bag, must state the color and type of down. Most reputable sleeping bag manufacturers, although not required by law to do so, will advertise the exact filling they use for their bags.

Choice of mummy or rectangular style is based on needs of camper. Mummy conserves body heat and is easier to compact. Rectangular model gives more foot and leg room.

Here is a Gerry bag that looks comfortable because of good loft.

Stuff sacks come in a variety of sizes and material weights. They protect sleeping bags from the elements and compress bags to carryable size.

Here is a Gerry foam pad with built in pillow pouch. Foam pads are more comfortable and less trouble than air mattresses.

Color of bag, type of stuff sack (if any), loft, washing instructions, guarantee and comfort range are of vital importance. If a catalog has left out one or more of these points of information, write to the manufacturer directly for the information, or choose another bag that lists all appropriate qualities.

In regard to the price of a good sleeping bag there is a consolation. Under normal use, a bag that is kept clean and treated as a valuable piece of camping equipment, can easily last 15 years. While a poorer quality bag, which does not serve its designed purpose in the first place, may last only five years. So, in the long run, a camper will probably save money by purchasing the best sleeping bag. The good bags are versatile. They are warm enough for cold weather. They can be ventilated (by good, bag-length zippers) for warm weather.

There may be no such thing as a perfect, all-around sleeping bag that fits every climate and camping situation— but from practical camping experience, in just about every type of condition, I can tell you that a good down or Dacron II bag is the most important camping investment you can make.

Remember flashy colors, animal picture linings, sexy models and good salesmen often detract from your ability to select a bag that will keep you warm and comfortable. So, I have organized a pocket guide to *good* sleeping bags that you can take to the store with you. It will give you everything you need to know for choosing the bag that's right for you.

CHOOSING THE BAG FOR YOU

Versatility—You may, at the time of purchase, not consider that a year from now, you may be in northern Canada fishing for lake trout, or hunting moose in Quebec. Purchase a bag that has built in flexibility. You can never go wrong with a bag that is "too warm."

Price—Expect to pay over $40 for a good bag . . . and $80 is about the norm for a top quality sleeping partner. But, look for more than the price tag. Some shrewd merchants have taken advantage of the "you get what you pay for" theory.

Good Names—Gerry (Denver, Colorado); Eddie Bauer (Seattle, Washington); Alpine Designs (Boulder, Colorado); Recreational Equipment (Seattle, Wash.); Outdoor Leadership Supply (Lander, Wyoming); Powderhorn Mountaineering (Jackson, Wyoming), Woods (New York City) and the Coleman Company, (Wichita, Kansas) are reputable manufacturers. Within their lines of sleeping bags, you still must choose the best bag for you. Important though, is the fact that these companies back their claims and their merchandise.

Construction—Here's some technical terms. Don't let them scare you. They are described, usually with illustrations, in the brochure or on the tags of the best bags. Slanted Gusset, Slant-Box Tubes, Inverted Vee Tube and Quilt Stitch. These names describe how various manufacturers keep the down or Dacron fill in place. If there was no method for keeping fill in place, lumps of insulation, usually at the bottom of the bag would result. Cold, thin spots in the bag would result. I'm sure many of you have had experiences with bags whose filling seemed to disappear.

The main object of various types of stitching used on good bags is to keep insulation in place—evenly and uniformly—without sewing the inner fabric directly to the outer fabric . . . thus producing cold spots. The type of stitching can be detected only by close observation. Manufacturers usually advertise their particular style because they are proud of it. Personally, I feel the Slanted Gusset style, used by Gerry is the most reasonable. It permits good thickness for good dead air insulation. (See attached illustrations of various styles.)

Zippers—Boy, are they important! Have you ever felt trapped inside a bag when the zipper jammed? Technically speaking the best zippers for bags are called YKK —big, heavy duty plastic zippers that don't freeze in extreme cold. Double zippers, inside and out, are standard on good bags. I prefer bags that zip the entire length, although some manufacturers use half zippers to save on stuffing room. Ventilation is better with full zippers that zip around the bottom of the bag . . . making it possible to spread the bag completely flat for airing.

The Right Size—This is important. Good bags come in small, medium, large and extra-large. They are usually measured in inches. A small man or boy would find a large bag unsuitable. But a six-footer, or better would be defeating his purpose by purchasing a five-foot bag.

A bag that is too big for a small man means unnecessary air space. The bag takes longer to warm up and cold spots result. Proper fitting of the bag is as important as a good fitting coat.

Bags That Mate—Two bodies, in one bag, especially in cold weather, can make sleeping cozy, warm. Many top manufacturers produce bags that mate a right bag to a left one. It is practical. And when considering a bag for husband-wife, or children, this option is one to give serious thought to. The bags, of course, can still be used separately.

Under the Bag—Foam pads, for all practical purposes, have replaced air mattresses or should have. They are more comfortable and less trouble. All the major bag manufacturers now have their own pads. They all serve the same function basically . . . to cushion that part of the body from shoulders to hips. Materials differ a little, as does the size of pads.

Gerry features a Shortie Foam Pad (about $7.50) that measures 36" X 20" X 1½". It weighs approximately 1 pound, 2 ounces. They also have a full length pad that measures 72" X 24" X 1½" and weighs about 3 pounds, 2 ounces.

Coleman, Eddie Bauer, Recreational Equipment, Woods, Alaska Sleeping Bag Co., Outdoor Leadership Supply, and other manufacturers also produce similar pads.

I recommend any foam pad, with a top covering of breathable, ripstop nylon and a bottom of urethane-coated nylon that protect the bag and the sleeper. The length of the pad should be a size to cushion the camper's shoulders and hips. Some persons can use short pads; others must purchase longer ones.

An addition to some pads is a pouch to stuff a pillow or a jacket to be used as a pillow. The additional pouch is practical and the extra weight negligible.

Stuff Bags and Covers—Lightweight backpack bags come with nylon stuff bags that enable the hiker to compact the bag into a small, easy to pack container.

Larger, more conventional bags also come with stuff sacks or covers that compact the bag for easy storing, and handling. Stuff bags protect the sleeping bag from moisture and dirt.

Backpack bags that compact small enough to be carried inside a pack compartment can be stuffed into a light, nylon sack. Bags that are carried on the frame of the packs, and are subject to moisture and abrasion are best covered by a heavy-duty nylon stuff bag.

Summary—How important is a good night's sleep to you? Think about it. If it is the sound, soft, warm, uninterrupted type you like . . . under the stars or under canvas, then purchase the best bag you can afford. A good bag is a good bag because it was built that way. No shortcuts in quality and material.

Tube Construction

Slanted Gusset

Quilt Stitch

Inverted Vee Tube

Slant-Box Tubes

CAMPERS on the INTERSTATES

by GEORGE LAYCOCK

THE BIG WHITE travel trailer was rolling along the interstate outside St. Louis, behind a family car filled with vacationbound citizens who had no idea that their trip was about to be cut short. The traffic was building up. Trucks were moving along at a steady pace, mostly in the outside lane.

The vacationing driver overtook one of these rigs and began maneuvering into the lane to his left, preparing to pass. The problem might have begun with the wind. Or it might have been pilot error, but a corner of the travel trailer swerved over and touched the rear corner of the commercial rig and that was all it took to set the sequence of events in motion. The collision was not much of a bump, but the travel trailer never came under control again. Instead it weaved across the road, and car and trailer both rumbled into the median strip where the trailer bounced on the culvert and came apart. The people came out undamaged, except for a bad case of nerves and a vacation trip gone sour before it was well underway. But the trailer, as well as its contents, was scattered widely over the grass between the lanes of speeding traffic.

Accidents with recreational vehicles on the big superhighways that crisscross this land occur frequently enough to encourage vacation drivers to give full consideration to the best ways for staying out of trouble with their motor homes, camper trailers, travel trailers, vans, and pick-up coaches. As a class, the drivers of recreational vehicles fare well indeed on the big interstate highways. But today's traffic is heavy and getting heavier, the vehicles are big, and high speeds permitted. The potential for trouble is always there waiting for the vacation driver who is inexperienced, careless, or no longer alert. Our system of interstate highways is the finest anywhere. These roads are engineered to move large numbers of vehicles at high speed. They are the fast link between home and vacation lands which helps account for the hundreds of thousands of new recreational vehicles merging with the existing traffic on the interstates every year.

Any time a driver climbs behind the wheel of a vehicle new to him, there is a period of adjustment during which he has to come to understand his equipment. In this critical time as he is learning the controls of his vehicle and how it responds at various speeds and under differing conditions, he should if possible be away from the heavy traffic. Whether it is his own new vehicle or a rented one there should be a test drive. The interstates, with their wide lanes and infrequent stops are good places to get the feel of a new vehicle, but it's best to choose a time when the traffic is light for these first hours of driving.

All but the smallest of trailers should be equipped with brakes and load equalizers. Dealers as well as experienced highway travelers can help advise the beginner on how to start out with a safe outfit. One rule (which I learned the hard way some years ago) warns the recreational vehicle driver on the interstate to inspect his outfit frequently. Because I had picked up a new camper trailer from a rental agency, I assumed that the small tires were properly inflated with the 65 pounds of pressure which they should have carried. At high speeds these small tires, when underinflated, take a beating and often are quickly ruined. Scarcely an hour out of town a rumbling, bumping, and swerving warned me of trouble. The right tire had blown

on the little trailer. After inspecting the damage on that side I looked at the other tire and found that it also was coming apart. Right then I determined that it is a good idea for the driver of a recreational vehicle to carry a tire pressure gauge and to use it frequently. It is a good plan to make a practice of checking the outfit at every gas stop. See that hitches and chains are in order, tires in good condition and everything secured and riding well.

The experienced driver who knows the feel of his outfit senses the slightest difference in how it is handling and notices new sounds which might tip him off to approaching problems.

This matter of anticipating trouble and avoiding it is particularly important on the busy interstate highways. From some early days of camping I recall trips where gear was stowed away on the cartop rack, covered with canvas, then tied down in what we took to be a secure pack. But wind and highway motion can loosen ropes and change the shape of things with disturbing speed and persistence. Do a poor job of such packing, and a few miles down the road you are almost certain to become a member of the "flapping canvas club." Those early experiences taught us something about the importance of securing a load properly in the beginning.

When carrying a cartop pack or boat, bicycles or motor bikes on racks, or towing a boat, be certain before leaving home that all is secure, road-worthy, and capable of riding the interstates at legal speeds. The load that works loose might cause an accident or at least make it necessary to risk a hazarous stop where traffic is heavy.

Another precaution calls for the driver of every recreational vehicle to acquire a proper fire extinguisher and keep it in a handy spot. Some months ago I talked with the driver of a pick-up coach who was depressed at the moment because a fire had burned most of the wiring on his engine. "Ordinarily," he said, "I would have had a fire extinguisher handy. And I did have one. The only thing was that it was in the wrong place when I needed it. It was back in the coach by the stove. We had the door locked to the back and by the time we found out who had the key, opened the door, found the fire extinguisher in the cupboard with the pots and pans, and got it around to the front of the truck, the damage was done. I have learned one thing the costly way," he said, "keep a fire extinguisher in the front of the car where you can find it. We should have had two; one in the front and one in the back. And another thing is that the fire extinguisher should never be all mixed up with the toys, pots and pans, magazines, and other items that are sure to be hiding it when you really need it."

One of the early lessons learned in towing a trailer, especially a small two-wheeled camper trailer, is that the balancing of the load in the trailed vehicle plays a major role in how well it tows. When the load is not balanced, such a trailer can swerve badly at high speeds, a definite hazard. The answer at this point is to slow down, pull off, and reload the outfit with attention to balancing the weight. These small trailers, in cases where the equipment may not include an equalizer, can also cause serious problems by directing the headlight beams upward into the eyes of oncoming traffic. This matter of proper adjustment of headlights with the load attached should be investigated and if need be, corrected before leaving home.

The first hazard, and one of the biggest, in driving recreational vehicles on the interstates comes at the moment when you enter the freeway. The engineers who designed these roads built them for speed and the idea

America's Interstate Highway System was built for swift transportation—and not necessarily for large recreational vehicles. Drivers must be doubly cautious when traveling interstate roads anywhere.

Because interstates normally traverse the most open country, high winds can be a factor when driving a vehicle or pulling a trailer with a large silhouette. Best advice is to proceed with caution.

is not to stop or slow down other traffic but to move gradually into the lines of vehicles while gaining speed and fitting your own vehicle into the flow of traffic. The responsibility here is on the driver entering the freeway. He acts with a sense of decision, studies the traffic in the lane he intends to enter, has his turn signal blinking and remembers that it is going to take more space for him to move his recreational vehicle into the flow of traffic than it would if he were driving only the family sedan. Good driving on the super highways calls for the oncoming traffic in this outside lane which you will enter, to lay over if possible, leaving you room to join the happy throng. This is not, however, always possible, nor do all drivers possess the experience or inclination to be so cooperative. The driver of the recreational vehicle, no matter how big his rig, must judge his timing and available space with the full knowledge that the responsibility for avoiding a collision is his.

Once your recreational vehicle is committed to the interstate and becomes part of the surging flow of traffic, the three driving practices most filled with hazard are moving too slowly, driving too fast, and changing lanes. Many interstate highways have minimum speeds posted. There is

sound reason for this. Drivers of commercial trucks are always alert for the slow moving vehicle in front of them. Their heavy loads are not easily stopped when moving at legal highway speeds. Consequently the slow moving vehicle that suddenly looms into view in front of them is in danger. This is less a problem during the day than at night because the interstates are so engineered that drivers in most places have long sweeping views. The driver of the recreational vehicle who does not feel confident of maintaining respectable highway speeds in the hours of darkness should not, say the truck drivers, drive at night.

The vacationer with his big recreational vehicle has to take special care when passing others on the interstates. The motor home or the typical pick-up coach is no "bug" that can be whipped in and out of lines of traffic casually. The driver with experience on these super highways always tries to anticipate the need to pass a vehicle being overtaken, and never waits until the last possible moment. He switches on his turn signal then awaits his opportunity and eases out into the available space in the next lane giving everyone around him full opportunity to know of his maneuver. Then, only when well ahead of the other vehicles, does he switch on his other turn signal and begin moving safely back into the slower lane. The secret here is to cast ahead, trying never to sneak up on trouble without anticipating the possibility of it. Police, commercial truck drivers, highway engineers, as well as anyone else who has driven much on these modern highways agree that the good driver never erratically moves in and out of lanes no matter what kind of vehicle he is driving.

This erratic driving is frequently encountered where interstate highways pass through cities and cross-country traffic must mingle with local drivers. Trembling parents enter uncertainly onto the interstates transporting their children to school or into town. Members of the day shift attempting to save 20 seconds on their ten mile homeward trek, or seeking release for the day's frustrations, exceed speed limits and move from lane to lane. Understandably there are slower speed limits posted where the interstates lead through large cities. The traveling vacationer also faces more confusion because of a greater abundance of exits and entrances to the highway within city limits. This city driving, even on the interstates, is high risk. The most alert drivers can become confused by the signs and occasionally boxed in by the traffic. Perhaps the most important rule of all for those about to move a recreational vehicle through a large city by way of the interstate is to study the city map in advance, not wait until they are in the heart of the city traffic to do so. Check the various interstate highways coming into the city and know which one you will follow in and out and where you will have to change from one route to the other. Anticipating these changes and knowing which signs you are searching for can save time, nerves, and possibly avoid accidents.

The secret to making good time on the open highway, and commercial truck drivers can verify this, is not always speed but moving along at a steady pace hour after hour. Try to pace your day so there will be a minimum of stops between those necessary pauses to refuel and eat.

These magnificent highways with which we live today have made it possible for vacationers to drive much far-ther in a day or on a two-week vacation than they might have gone previously, and to do so safely and comfortably. There is however a daily limit for every driver of a recreational vehicle beyond which it is neither safe nor comfortable for him to be on the highway. Even the pressured executive, accustomed to putting in long days, would benefit by slowing down on his vacation trip and limiting the number of hours he will push his recreational vehicle. It is good planning to stop well ahead of dark and get your family established for the night. Even so, a full day of driving, followed by more full days of driving can take the edge off a vacation trip. One answer is to switch drivers and most modern recreational vehicles are so easily handled that the women or competent teenage drivers in the family can take their turns at the wheel. Driver changes are best made at fuel stops or rest areas where there is little hazard from fast moving traffic.

Before you have driven a recreational vehicle many weeks, you come to understand the risk that the elements can add to your adventure. Rain, snow, wind, fog, and smoke bring their own problems. These are problems enough for the family sedan but the hazard grows as the size and number of axles of the vehicle increase. The number one rule to remember when confronted by these hazards of the elements is to reduce the speed. A rain following a long dry period can create a slippery highway from dirt and oil on the road. Autumn leaves falling on the road can also set up a situation causing a vehicle to slide.

Some years ago recreational vehicles were seldom seen in the months when snow and ice could be anticipated on the highways. But recreational vehicles became more comfortable, winter vacations more common, and free weekends for young and old alike more frequent. Today's recreational vehicles are on the highways winter and summer. Of all the slippery highways I have encountered, the most memorable was on Tennessee's Jellico Mountain a few years ago. Not even the salt trucks should risk being out on a day like that. One Florida bound travel trailer, two

Remember when entering the flow of traffic that a camper accelerates slower than a passenger car and that a greater interval between other cars is necessary for safety.

Winding roads with S-curves are scenic, but call for special alertness on the part of the driver.

Taking the super-long camper onto the highways is not to be a task undertaken lightly. Practice turning, backing and other maneuvers carefully before the start of the trip.

days out of its home base in Michigan, topped a hill, went into a slide, jack-knifed and ended up with the front end against the guard rail and the back out in the traveled highway. Other vehicles were scattered over the mountainside in various angles of repose. Down the road some miles we stopped for lunch. Two elderly ladies headed northward asked for advice and were told that the best answer would be to check into the motel next door and stay there until conditions improved. This they did, proving themselves perhaps wiser than all those who crossed or tried to cross Jellico Mountain in that icy blizzard.

Wind is an enemy of the recreational vehicle. These vehicles with their broad sides exposed to the gusts are vulnerable in the high winds. Some highways have warning signs telling drivers that they have reached areas where high and dangerous winds are commonplace. The wise drivers take these signs seriously. There have been incidents where high winds have blown travel trailers off overpasses. In other cases winds have broken the bolts loose on pick-up coaches, and frequently upset trailers or made motor homes swerve dangerously. There is one way to cope with high winds: slow down.

Fog, smog, and smoke are other hazards that confront drivers at certain times and in various localities. Here too, reduced speed is the key to safety and perhaps survival.

Remarkable perhaps is the fact that so many recreational vehicles are driven so many millions of miles across the interstates of this land every year with no more accidents than there are. This testifies to the skill, experience, and common sense of this army of vacation-bound drivers and to the quality of their vehicles. The careless driver of a recreational vehicle is quickly noticed by his fellow drivers in that unending flow of traffic moving along the interstates toward beaches, mountains, and national parks.

by BILL BROWNING

UNDER THE blue-black canopy of a giant sky, its glittering stars flashing like a theatre marquee, our horses made interesting noises clattering over rocks, hollow ground, and sucking bogs. We were returning to camp from a side trip to Crescent Lake in Montana's Pioneer Mountains, when the yellow glow of our lighted tents loomed ahead, looking ever so good.

We had just fished the alpine lake through the exciting "witching hour", and now "Cookie" would fry up our catch of rainbow trout, some too big to fit a skillet in one piece.

"Wash up while Jim and I put up the nags, and supper will be ready before you know it," announced outfitter George Smith, who with his partner-son was showing us a deluxe way to see a slice of Montana's beautiful wilderness, just four miles in from their Canyon Creek guest ranch. It had been a short trail ride to one of several almost virgin trout lakes and our day couldn't have been more delightful.

Base camp itself, just feet from a goat lick, was a place of beauty, set beside beautiful Canyon Lake on an alpine meadow floor, with towering granite peaks surrounding our Shangri-la. As the last of the horses nickered his thanks for a feed of sweet pellets, "Cookie" slid a mound of browned trout, hot biscuits, and a fresh salad onto the rustic table and hands and food became a blur of motion making the rounds. It was a day and night to remember for a lifetime.

Pack tripping is unique, but only one of many camping experiences found in the Big Sky recreation area of Montana, and it is certainly one of the most enjoyable. For here in one of Montana's 11 national forests are combined the thrills of remote fishing, alpine scenery you can't imagine, horseback riding, photography, and superb camping — wholly conducted by capable outfitters. Wrangling, cooking and tenting are all provided for you and your family. You simply tend to your fishing, enjoy yourself under a virgin sky by day and relax at night to a warming campfire where song and stories go on and on. From ranch

BIG SKY COUNTRY CAMPING

Raw camping by foot, horse or four-wheel drive in Montana's 11 national forests is one of Bryon Dalrymple's favorite activities. The writer comes to Montana from Kerrville, Texas; is seen here on the left.

to camp, and back, you're guests on a package trip, within a price range of most vacationers.

Hiking will also put you into this same wild domain. I remember one idyllic day in Montana's Beartooth Plateau, northeast of Yellowstone Park, we were at Star Lake, the end of the 4-wheel trail. Gene and Dennis Wade, Cooke City outfitters suggested hiking to Goose Lake for fishing, and to the unique Grasshopper Glacier. Loading up packs for overnight we sighted Goose Lake before noon, lying among snowbanks, and a hollow ring of rocky peaks.

My friend Erwin Bauer, and his two sons Bob and Parker, were first to cast flies into the waters, and by strange happenings the three were all fighting cutthroat trout at once. Three 14-inch trout soon lay on the flower-strewn grass, and with another trio that followed we had our supper entree. Bending barbs we had a ball for another hour before they quit catching and releasing active trout in a primeval setting.

Pitching two two-man tents, burying our fresh trout in a snowbank refrigerator, and stowing packs, we hiked on

to Grasshopper Glacier, only 30 minutes farther on. Topping a boulder-strewn ridge we saw below us a huge bank of "pink snow." Descending a steep hill we walked across the snowbank and left curious deep-red foot prints bleeding into the snow. It is thought to be wind-blown algae or red dust.

Only a few preserved insects are now seen in the Glacier. Scientists think millions of migratory grasshoppers, or locusts, were chilled or caught in a storm several centuries ago and fell onto the forming glacier, to be buried and preserved in snows until 1914 or later, when a hot summer melt exposed them on the surface.

The boys found a handful of insects, and that night at our Goose Lake camp we talked into the night, under a full moon, of the natural wonders so many road-locked campers miss.

Montana just has to be at the top of the list of a camper's great vacation places. It's a happy mixture of badlands, prairies, and mountains, threaded by hundreds of streams, most of them unpolluted, and is dotted with

A fishing pack trip into the Absoraka Mountains
can be a memorable, primeval experience.
This is Fossil Lake, northeast of Cooke City.

Canoe floats are easy and interesting
camp potentials in Montana.

Boating, fishing and camping at Bighorn Recreational Area in one of Montana's most scenic areas.

Clark's Canyon Reservoir, Dillon, Montana, one of many state impoundments yields lunker trout for campers.

scores of scenic lakes; hundreds if you count alpine bodies. Its natural splendors, though touched by man here and there, are relatively preserved and, mixed with manmade facilities offer easy access to great outdoor adventures.

Over 50 per cent of the state's land is public; most devoted in some way to recreation, with camping playing a major roll. In the 11 national forests are nine wilderness areas, accessible by foot or horseback, without any permanent structures. Thousands of trails, many maintained, cross these areas.

(If you are interested, the Montana Wilderness Society conducts some three-dozen annual guided walks from one to four days each, open to the public.)

Forbidding badlands are found in several areas of eastern Montana, notably around Glendive's Makoshika State Park, called by Indians "Hell cooled over"; Carter County's Indian ceremonial grounds of Medicine Rocks State Park; and Ft. Peck Reservoir areas. All provide camp facilities and much potential for finding fossils, rocks, and even giant pre-historic animal remains, as well as for good hunting.

Several national and state refuges, and many historic landmarks dot the rolling plains from the eastern border westward through most of the state to the mountains. Along the lower Yellowstone River famous moss agates are found, and in the entire area moonstone and many other worthwhile rocks and minerals attract rock hounds.

In the several mountain ranges dotting the western prai-

Annual Indian pow-wows are held on Montana's seven Indian reservations.

ries and covering ⅓rd of Montana are giant opportunities for recreation and camping. Here green-clad mountains and valleys fold and unfold revealing top fishing streams and lakes. Hideaways and campgrounds lie at the ends of the many county, forest and mining roads; scenic lakes, falls, and rushing waters are there as are unusual natural attractions. Great stands of timber, ghost towns, interesting villages, cities, hotsprings, and a whole raft of resorts, dude ranches, and other vacation and camping potentials abound.

Take ghost towns for example: some 100 relics of former mining towns and the mines, (many restored), plus Virginia City and Nevada City dating from the early gold rush days are accessible even to big rec-v's. At Alder Gulch prospectors are again "scratching for colors" (gold). You can search for rubies and other gemstones and view Americana of the 1860's in the two restored gold camps. Nearby are commercial and public campgrounds, some with hookups, and some barely developed.

Although a dry country, Montana offers lots of quality boat camping, by canoe, raft, power or even by conducted tours. Along its glorious waterways, fringed with conifers, softwoods, and colorful brush, you may rough it or find developed public campgrounds. Or you can have resorts and other recreational facilities, plus the big fishing.

In the mountains swift waters often require special gear and precautions, but as the waters reach the prairies they slow and meander. Try both kinds.

One of the best float camping trips in relatively easy waters is the lower Missouri River between historic Ft. Benton and Ft. Peck Reservoir. By power boat this 150-mile float can be made in about three to four days, or stretched indefinitely. (Floating on down to Ft. Peck Dam is another 150 miles.)

Along the first section which is being studied for national park status, are Lewis and Clark expedition sites and other historical sites, forts, and Chief Joseph's famous retreat route, and great scenery. Fishing is for warm water species like big channel cat and paddlefish.

Canoes can be rented at Ft. Benton or you can take a deluxe conducted cruise with local Ft. Benton outfitters on big powered, canopied flat boats. You can camp in the rough or at any of six developed public recreational areas.

Another beautiful float is in the Gates of the Mountains on the Missouri River near Helena, where Lewis & Clark saw the now extinct Audubon sheep on thousand-foot walls

Some 40-50 rodeos perform throughout Montana's summer travel season.

lining the river. Public and raw campgrounds are available; a few hiking trails intersect. Wildlife photography including goats and bears is possible. This can be for a day or two, or for your whole vacation.

Perhaps the greatest camping done, however, is the general camping by rec-vers or tenters using the thousands of miles of paved and back roads to state parks, national parks, national forests, and other camping areas.

Some 30 state parks offer such attractions as excellent lake fishing, historic sites, a giant colorful cavern, and even a buffalo jump.

A whopping 200-plus campgrounds are offered by the national forests in Montana. Among them you can find practically anything which interests you. Most larger campgrounds are by fee but many are free and far away from crowds. Most are located near trail heads, some on scenic boating spots, and there is even a fly-in spot or two. Most are readily available to modern cars or rec-vs but check the ranger's office to be sure. Take a shovel, axe and bucket as required by regulations.

At least seven major national attractions should be on every Montana camper's vacation list:

1. How better can one describe Glacier National Park than the way one scribe put it: "God sat here while He created the rest of the world." For here you will find dynamic mountain scenery; 1000 miles of trails to remote lakes, rivers, and to two chalets; beautiful flora and wildlife including rare bighorns, mountain goats and grizzlies; superb, developed campgrounds; and a host of other facilities and potentials.

2. Yellowstone Park at the southern border is noted for its thermal and scenic attractions and wildlife display but is less well known for its camping possibilities. How about a canoe or boat campout around a gigantic lake, or at the bottom of its Grand Canyon, or to a remote fishing area? There are fine commercial camps near Montana's three park entrances. A trip over the 11,000 foot high Beartooth Highway on the N.E. entrance and camping in its rare atmosphere is an unforgettable experience.

3. Custer Battlefield Monument on the Little Bighorn River, and the Big Hole Battlefield Monument in southwestern Montana are both related to Indian engagements which were turning points in our history. Both have fine museum displays while "Custer's Last Stand" event is an open-air reenactment of that gigantic encounter. See this early in July annually, at the Crow Agency.

Montana has scores of float potentials, great scenery and top fishing.

Yellowstone National Park's thermal attraction ranks tops with millions of visitors.

A state park on Flathead Lake's west shore, in Western Montana.

4. Several dams—Yellowtail, Hungry Horse, and Libby, to mention a few—with their recreational facilities, scenery, boating and fishing offer ideal camping areas.

5. Beautiful Quake Lake is the legacy of the violent Madison River Earthquake. Its visitor center, campgrounds, boat ramp and nearby Hebgen Dam also offer superb camping opportunities.

6. Not to be missed are our national refuges, topped by the enormous C.M. Russell near Ft. Peck and the National Bison Range. Both have do-it-yourself tour-drives and the latter boasts one of the U.S.'s best buffalo herds. Other wildlife to see and photograph is there too, including elk, deer, antelope and bighorns.

7. Seven Indian reservations are open to visitors and each has some sort of pow-wow, with the North American Indian Days in July hosted by the Blackfeet at Browning one of the best.

Local attractions and special events round out the long list of Montana offerings to campers. Museums, historic buildings and collections, parades, celebrations, fairs and rodeos all are wide open to the camper in Montana. If our cool, invigorating summer climate doesn't get you, the great camping certainly will.

INFORMATION SOURCES
For Further information write:

Fishing, hunting, parks, fishing access camps and guides lists:
Montana Fish and Game Department.
Helena, Montana 59601

Campgrounds, accommodations and services, and travel info:
Montana Chamber of Commerce
Box 1730, Helena, Montana 59601

Annual wilderness walks lists:
Montana Wilderness Association
Box 548, Bozeman, Montana

National parks and recreation areas:
Glacier National Park,
Superintendent,
West Glacier, Montana 59936

Yellowstone National Park
Superintendent,
Mammoth, Wyoming 82190

(recreation areas)
National Park Service
U.S. Dept. of Interior
Washington, D.C.

(refuges, including National Bison Range etc.)
Bureau of Sports Fisheries and Wildlife
U.S. Dept. of Interior
Washington, D.C.

Local information:
Any local Chamber of Commerce in a specific city.

You Can Camp with Your Mother-in-Law

by JIM TALLON

THE FALSE DAWN had barely pried open the morning at Wahweep Campground on the Arizona side of Lake Powell when someone knocked on the side of our van conversion camper. With no little effort, I forced my eyelids up, pulled on my pants and slid the door back far enough to let in my Brittany spaniel if he had been wet. What came through, though, and nearly cracked me on my ample nose was a cup of steaming coffee. On the handle end smiled the 73-year-old mother of four, grandmother of five, great grandmother of two, and mother-in-law of me, Thelma June Chanslor.

"Here's coffee for you, Jim," she said. "Heavy on the cream, light on the sugar. Just like you like it."

That woman. She was at it again. I've been in the camping business for 30 years and I've never seen a camper to match her. I took the coffee, and thanked her, somewhat embarrassed that it wasn't *me* serving her. She scooted off in the dim light and I knew that others of our group were about to get the same treatment; the only way you can beat this camping lady up in the morning is not to go to bed the night before.

"Mom" Chanslor had organized this particular camping trip and put it into motion. For her, it belonged under the heading of "family reunion." Mom lives at Logan, Utah, north of Salt Lake City. She tries to pick central meeting places for family camping reunions since her sons and daughters and their husbands and wives and children are scattered across Utah, New Mexico, and Arizona. Let me say here that Mom is of Mormon descent and family reunions are big with these people. Her folks forged westward with well-known campers like Brigham Young to help pioneer Utah. (Another avid camper in Mom's family did most of his camping just ahead of the law — Butch Cassidy. But Mom says he really wasn't a bad guy at heart.) So you can see that Mom comes from a line of capable outdoor people who weren't afraid to deal with the environment on its own terms. Perhaps partly because of this she is a better camper than most women half her age.

"When Bert (her husband) died, I just sort of waited around for the end myself," she told me. "But there is so much to see and appreciate in the outdoors that I'm now planning to be around for a long time to enjoy it."

Knowing a camper like Mom has added certain new dimensions to my own camping experiences. I like to think of her as an inspiration to others of her age group, but at

Trying to find a central locale for a family reunion, Mom Chanslor picked this spot, Wahweep Campground, on Lake Powell, Arizona-Utah.

With temperatures in the high 90s, Mom Chanslor goes wading in Lake Powell with our Brittany spaniel, "Britt."

the same time, she inspires me as well. How many 73-year-old camping ladies do you know, and if any, how many of them will go camping on their own? Mom has played a part in improving on my own personal set of outdoor values, but perhaps even more interesting, she has taught me that you *can* camp with your mother-in-law.

When I married Mom's last eligible daughter, Vicki, over eight years ago, she nodded with approval at the fact that I was a gung-ho outdoor-type guy. And right off the bat she suggested that perhaps we ought to plan a trip together. I'm going to admit it here for all the world that I then belonged in the group that believes all those mother-in-law jokes and I had even invented a few of my own. This stemmed largely from knowing friends with mothers-in-law who, without making an effort, fit those jokes perfectly. But then, none of them camped; not a single one, and all of them turned up their noses at the thought. Putting Mom down as probably relative to that mother-in-law syndrome, I smiled my best mother-in-law smile, then stalled for five years. Well, I'm making public apology right here and now for being such a short-sighted boor. I started wising up at a campground on the north side of Hermosillo, Sonora, about a day's drive from Phoenix.

Mom claimed Phoenix as her residence at that time and

had popped into our place one afternoon with the suggestion that Vicki and I join her for a trip to Guadalajara, Jalisco. Her original plan had been to fly to Guadalajara, then rent a small place there for a couple of weeks. "But I'd enjoy it more if I had company while in Guadalajara," she said. "And a whole lot more if we drove there and camped along the way." We owned a telescopic cab-over camper on a pickup truck then and three adults living in its small confines for two weeks represented something of a challenge, especially when you consider that one of them would be my mother-in-law. Two days later, we cranked up the telescopic camper in Hermosillo on the first leg of the trip. And Mom Chanslor and Vicki got in a squabble right away . . . over work.

"I want to do my share," said Mom. "I can start by cooking."

"Mother, you just sit down and enjoy yourself," said Vicki, "I'll handle the cooking."

"Let Mom cook, let Mom cook," I jabbered under my breath. Mom and I hadn't been camping before but I'd been at her place often enough to sample the fine cooking she dishes up. (This is not to say my wife isn't a fine cook too, because she shows definite Chanslor cooking traits. But a change of cooks is often welcomed by the stomach.)

At Hermosillo, Mom and Vicki rotated on the dishes and cooking meals. Our telescopic camper served as home for us for two weeks.

Vicki finally strong-armed Mom into the camper's dinette seat, but a new fight ensued after dinner when it came time to do the dishes. Mom won that one. Meanwhile, I sat outside on a slump block wall, enjoying the warm Mexican night, the sweet smell of tropical plants, and a cold bottle of *cerveza* (Spanish for beer). It was a nice change from *me* doing the dishes.

The next morning the girls traded jobs while I reflected on Mom pitching unhesitatingly into camping chores. As we "professional" campers know, a person that willingly does his share of camp work without being asked earns a certain respect and the odds are in his favor of being invited on future camp trips. Mom qualified on this count,

camper an "advertisement neatness" than any camping rig I have seen in genuine use. Of course I chalked up some more camping points for Mom, but all this began to make me feel like I was *not* really on a camp trip. My chores dwindled to driving; and occasionally the gals would let me crank up the camper's top to assure me I wasn't losing my masculinity. My main fear, though, was that we might get the Good Housekeeping Seal of Approval and I could never live it down with my camping buddies.

Mom Chanslor's tidiness doesn't end with campers. She keeps herself the same. A gust of wind may blow a lock of hair out of place but it is pushed right back. Her clothes always look freshly pressed, and when she walks through

On a bridge spanning an estuary near Topolobampo, Mom tries her hand fishing for snook.

not only in Hermosillo but for the entire trip.

At Wahweep now, with a gas lantern aiding the scant daylight, I watched Mom busy re-straightening our big family camp table (actually several folding tables placed end to end) which she had straightened up last night and once or twice after that. On the trip to Guadalajara it was the same. No matter how hard Vicki and I try to keep things in place in our camper, It still seems cluttered. You see those classy camper ads with a lovely young lady sitting in a decorator-perfect interior, but you never see a camper so neat in real life once it is off the sales lot. Now mind you, the three of us had clothing, grub and other necessities to make us look good for two weeks. But Mom, with the touch of a miracle-worker, came closer to giving our

a campground, she looks a housewife that has stepped out of her home to do a little shopping. Mom is a helluva camper, but she never looks the general image the public has of campers.

By the time we reached Mazatlan, I found that Mom had another most admirable trait — an affinity for nature. She found beauty in a gray sunset that had just a sliver of orange in it. She rarely misses a bird or an animal, and nearly jumped out of the moving camper in an attempt to get a picture of an iguana sleeping on the limb of a tree. She delighted in the way the Mexican jungle undulated over rolling hills, festooned with flowers. In fact, not even the tiniest of blossoms escape her appreciative eye. At a seaside campground, she bent so long over the multitude of plants that laced it, that I swore it would take a quart of liniment to straighten her up again. Not so, though. No doubt this love of growing things comes from her farming background. When we go to visit her, no matter where she happens to be living at the time, we don't look for a house number, just the house with the most plants surrounding it. I make part of my living through nature photography and have a reputation for pumping film through my cameras, but this time, Mom out-did me with her Instamatic. The way I see it *all* campers should have an affinity for nature, for without nature, there is no camping. Again, Mom meets the requirements.

All of the above points discussed are necessary to qualify

invited to go into town with a newly-married couple who knew Guadalajara well, but Mom refused to go along on the grounds that she would be a burden. Several times along the way, she had insisted on staying in motels to give Vicki and me some time to ourselves. Again we couldn't change her mind. That evening we bought a bouquet of Mexican roses and gave them to her when we returned. Her natural pleasantness was tuned to a lightness because of this simple gift.

A day later, this situation made a total reverse. I felt "down at the mouth," and Mom cheered me up with a gift of a bottle of tequila, fresh limes, and a small cutting board. She knew that once in a while I like to sip South

On a street in Tlaquepaque, near Guadalajara, and with Jim and Grace Cooke (who met and were married in Mexico), Mom Chanslor brings up the rear. Unusual for her, since she is normally way out in front.

as an "honorable" camper, but perhaps the most important virtue or quality that a fellow camper can have is being good-natured and uncomplaining. On a camping trip that spans a week you can learn more about a friend or acquaintance than you can in a lifetime of living next door to him. During that time, both probity and negative traits will invariably surface, and that first trip will largely determine whether you will ever camp together again. You find great respect for the person who appears to be having a great time and can accept and shrug off sour notes along the way, even if he has to lie to himself a little. I'm sure that both Mom and I lied a little in Mexico.

In Guadalajara, she seemed pleasant enough, but I sensed that underneath she might be depressed. We were

of the Border style, a taste of tequila, followed by salt (usually on the back of the hand), then a wedge of lime. This exchange, though unnecessary to keep us on an even plain, had its merits. Mom and Vicki had some good laughs on me when, after sipping a little tequila, I started to forget which came next, the salt or the lime.

The basic camping rules for good fellowship on a camp trip hinge directly on the enjoyment of all on that trip. Mom Chanslor has these rules built in: She works harder at camping chores than any other camper I have ever known. She continues to be pleasant when situations are hardly peaches and cream. She feels the flow of nature through sight, sound, scent and touch, realizing the value of a single blade of grass. She keeps a neat but unvarnished

At La Quemada Ruins, Vicki and Mom are guided by local Mexican man and his son.

appearance of both herself and camp. On top of that, unfortunately, she worries and wonders if she is giving *enough* effort.

Mom Chanslor generally keeps her station wagon ready for camping at all times — plenty of grub, sleeping bag and other camp gear. She never knows when she might want to spend an extra day at Bryce or Zion canyons, or some place else when the notion strikes her. At Lake Powell, when she saw all the comforts and conveniences of our new van conversion camper, she said that maybe

that was the answer for her, too.

Do you suppose Mom Chanslor is going soft? Well, maybe she has a right to. She has proven she is just as rugged as most of today's campers. She has proven that people in their "golden years" can get a helluva lot out of camping, perhaps more than the younger folks. She has proven that she knows the rules of good camping fellowship.

But for me, most of all, she has proven that you *can* camp with your mother-in-law.

S·T·R·E·T·C·H your camping $$$

Beautiful spots to stretch out your tent can often also stretch out your camping dollar. Plan ahead to stay at no fee or low fee areas such as this.

by JIM RUTHERFOORD

Goose Neck State Park in south Texas is a state-owned park of great beauty and right on the water, too.

EVERYBODY LOVES a bargain. The feeling of having made a good buy—whether it's a food bargain, a new car, or a low cost campsite—seems to bring out the Scotch in each of us. And the money saved gives us a little "left over" for bourbon or some other personal whimsey.

Not long ago, a rather respected recreation magazine published an article on how to camp free. It can be done if you happen to be a hobo, are willing to mooch all you can and even cheat a little—like checking into a campground late at night and leaving early so you don't have to register or pay. Mooching and bumming are not practices I recommend, and you can save many dollars playing it straight, anyway.

Choose your travel or destination campground with care, paying particular attention to the extra cost services such as swimming pool charges, added fee for air conditioner hookup; even for basic electrical hookup. You may not want the swimming pool or some other extras while overnighting along the way to your destination. Once there, however, it may be cheaper to select a park that charges a flat fee for all hookups and services.

TRAVEL COSTS—If you drive a recreation vehicle (truck camper, motorhome, or tow a travel trailer or camping trailer with the family car) it will save you money to have a thorough check-up of the RV and its prime mover *before* you start your vacation. Your local dealer or custom mechanic will probably charge you less than you will pay for road services, particularly in case of a breakdown that could have been avoided by such preventive maintenance.

If your vehicle's gross weight rating will allow, by all means install extra fuel tanks. This way you can travel with an easier mind in these gas-short days. Get as much as allowed at every stop.

Most truck and motorhome engines are warranted for use with regular gasolines. The use of premium fuel does not improve their performance. So, if you've been using the high proof juice, switch back to regular and save a few more bucks on a trip.

Driving below the mandatory 55 mph saves valuable fuel and lets you enjoy the scenery, too.

There is a wide variance in the price of crankcase oils with no difference in engine life or performance. Just stick to the weights and grades recommended by your owner's manual. Single viscosity is less expensive than the multi-ones and may be used whenever ambient temperatures are within the limits shown in your manual. Drug and grocery stores often offer oil and antifreeze specials that will save you even more if you do your own servicing.

My El Dorado chassis mount camper carries a 25 gallon (not pounds) propane tank for cooking, heating and refrigeration gas. The tank is permanently mounted under the chassis. Some campgrounds are not equipped to service the big tank, but it will last and last, and refilling at bulk gas plants results in savings. If you use small propane bottles, the installation of a sight gauge, such as a Rochester's C-Level Gauge, will save you money by letting you refill the bottles only when nearly empty. Most service facilities have a flat charge or a minimum charge for filling these smaller containers and it may cost just as much for 10 pounds of gas as for 20 or 30.

Know the loaded weight of your vehicle and the recommended tire air pressures for the weight on each tire. Tire manufacturers or authorized dealers will give you this information. It can also be had from a free booklet, *Guide to Tire Care and Safety,* from Rubber Manufacturer's Association, 444 Madison Avenue, New York, New York, 10033. The owner's manual that came with your vehicle also contains other valuable tire information. Keep inflation pressures at those recommended and, over the long pull, you'll be pleased at the savings effected by a few pounds of free air and the greater ease with which the vehicle handles.

Cover your spare tire and shelter others as much as possible from the sun when your vehicle is parked. Sunlight causes premature cracking and checking of the sidewalls. If you must have a front spare tire carrier on your truck or motorhome, forget the tire cover. The restricted airflow through the radiator may cost you more than a new tire from engine damage due to overheating.

TRAVEL CAMPGROUNDS—Always carry a good campground and recreation vehicle park guide. It will tell you the location of facilities and services offered and ads usually show the base rates for comparison. If you are merely traveling through an area and plan no side trips or other longer stays, minimal facilities are all you will need. If your vehicle is self-contained with a 12-volt power supply (battery) there is no need for electric, water or sewer connections, either. A propane or gasoline lantern or a rechargeable electric lantern will provide ample illumination for station wagon-tent camps, or you may prefer to use a plug-in type extension light around camp.

A few states allow overnight stops at interstate rest areas where sanitary facilities are available and there is no charge, but most states do not. You can, however, catch a few hours sleep and get on your way before a trooper runs you off.

Recently, many states are adding "CAMPING" to interstate signs where camping areas are within reasonable distance (3 miles or so) from the interchange. The signs are fine, but won't tell you whether the subject campground is public, private, luxurious or minimal. That's why you should have that campground guide along and use it.

I know of several national forest campgrounds that are only a few yards off well-traveled highways. Their cost? Only the Golden Eagle Passport, or $1 per night if for some reason you don't have the bird ticket.

I have found a number of enterprising service station operators who operate small travel parks on their unused land. Some are free; others charge a minimal fee. You don't need luxuries for a single overnight stop and the money you save will come in handy at your destination resort campground.

Camp free? Sure you can, relatively speaking, of course. If you're in a big hurry or are caught between campgrounds, stop at a shopping center or supermarket lot and ask permission of one of the businessmen to park overnight. A small purchase will often assure permission if your vehicle is self-contained. It would be wise to get permission in writing or have the business notify the police that you have such permission. Be sure to leave early the next morning so your rig won't be in the way of paying customers.

The big truck stops frequently welcome overnighters at low or no charge. Frequently they set aside an area as far removed as possible from the idling sounds of the big diesel engines.

The Pet Dairy-owned Stuckey's chain of food shops and service stations is now going in for overnight stops. Where facilities do not yet exist, most Stuckey's operators allow use of their parking lots after normal business hours.

The excellent franchise chain of KOA (Kampgrounds of America) travel campgrounds offer complete facilities at reasonable fees. Base charges are usually about $3 to $3.50 for the average family, including water and electricity. KOA publishes its own directory of travel and destination campgrounds throughout the United States, Canada, and Mexico. There are more than 700 KOA's at this writing (Spring, 1974) and there are more to come. Their directory is free at all KOA's and it contains in addition much useful information in feature articles.

The Holiday Inn chain is also in the campground business with their franchised Trav-L-Parks, some of which are operated in connection with established inn locations.

With more than 4 million recreation vehicles on the road and an ever increasing number of parks for their use, the traveling tenter is almost the forgotten camper these days. It is pretty hard to drive stakes into the concrete paving of a supermarket lot or the asphalt surface of a truck stop or service station. Some RV parks will not accept tenters. It's wheels or nothing.

The tent camper will find overnight accommodations in the national forest and national park campgrounds. In the forests it is usually permissible to pitch a tent almost anyplace there is room without cutting trees. Often minimal sanitary arrangements are thrown in at no cost. Usually the free campsites are those away from the established campgrounds and those cleared for use by hunters, fishermen, and hikers. They offer quiet and solitude unavailable elsewhere.

Corps of Engineers lakeside campsites and Bureau of Reclamation recreation areas are likely spots for the tenter; again these frequently are some distance from the planned travel routes.

FOOD AND COOKING—Much has been written about camp cooking but anyway you slice the roast or grill the hot dog, food costs should be no more than what you would spend at home. More often they'll be less.

Take advantage of roadside stands that offer fresh fruits and vegetables in season without the profits extracted by truckers, distributors or supermarket advertising. Small

Bringing your own "room," lighting and cooking facilities means you don't have to pay to use someone else's. Note also the inflatable boat and light-weight plastic oars securely tied to the pack board on the left.

Getting away from the heavily-traveled highways means less expensive accommodations and not having the disappointment of finding all available spaces taken.

town grocers may sell for less than high-overhead city stores.

Shy away from specialized, specially packed "camp" foods unless you need them for a particular purpose such as backpacking where weight and space are important. You may be able to find comparable products on grocery store shelves. Repack them yourself in suitable portions to suit your personal needs and pocket the difference.

ATTRACTIONS—If you're planning a few days in Disney World, Williamsburg, or Opryland, U.S.A., you'll just have to face the fact that attractions cost money, a *lot* of money, to build and admission fees are very steep. But there are scads of almost untapped free attractions just waiting for someone to come and see them.

Stroll along the waterfront of old Savannah, Ga., or other port cities. Take a free tour through a brewery, often with the fringe benefit of free beer. Look up interesting free museums in some cities or on college campuses. I even found one once in a hospital in Quebec.

Industrial plants, aircraft factories, automobile factories, shipyards, offer free family tours and experienced guides make the trips interesting for the kids while they are getting an education.

Most state travel and tourism bureaus offer free calendars of events to take place during the year. Many of these are free; and chambers of commerce are also a great boon to the thrifty tourist. Write for these before you leave home and plan your schedule accordingly.

Above all, resist the urge to buy useless overpriced souvenirs offered at most "tourist trap" shops. Their cost can skyrocket your trip expenses while adding nothing to its real value.

OFF-SEASON BONANZA—You can save a pile by doing your camping during the period between Labor Day and Easter. Many campgrounds offer winter rates that are only about one-third seasonal rates. Some national parks and national forests don't even bother to collect fees, claiming it is cheaper than maintaining a staff for that purpose. Of course, if you wish, you can buy a condominium site at one of your favorite vacation areas and let it help pay for itself by renting it out when you're not using it. Often several individuals or an organized group will purchase a single site or a series of sites to be used by members on a scheduled basis but offering them for rent to others at slack times. It could be another way of getting your camping dollar's worth. Investigate such condominium enterprises as Venture Out in America, Outdoor Resorts of America, Inc., and others. Their ads are to be found in most camping and RV magazines.

Saving money can become habitual—as can taking more frequent trips than you thought you could!

Rec-vehicle Camping in the 49th State...

The Old And New— camping equipment has changed drastically for "do it yourself" Alaska visitors since the days of the gold rush. In 1898, when this unidentified trio had its picture taken in Skagway en route to the Klondike, the self-contained traveler carried his bedroll, his gear, and his food supplies literally on his back. The self-contained traveler of today—and this type of visitor accounts for nearly half of Alaska's motor tourists— comes via pickup camper or pulling a trailer. Frequently, equipment includes lightweight canoes or skiffs in order to take advantage of lakes and streams within many of Alaska's public campgrounds.

Campground near Glennallen, Alaska, provides a forest-rimmed setting for this camping couple. Alaska and the federal government have located camping facilities throughout the road network of the nation's biggest state.

HOW TIMES

by MIKE MILLER

THERE WAS a time, and it wasn't all that long ago, that to say you were going to take a camper or a trailer to Alaska was to be greeted with stares of dumbfounded disbelief and no small measure of concern over your sanity. Heads would shake solemnly, as if to say, "Well this time the old boy has really flipped . . ."

To think in terms of driving a recreational vehicle to Alaska was to conjure up a picture—rather accurately—of a vehicle crammed to the rooftops with supplies and spare parts. Strapped above the roof would be at least four, and possibly a half-dozen, spare gas tanks. Tales were told—again, accurately—of such vehicles en route to Alaska being mired in, or being bulldozed out of, seas of thick gushy mud in places where roads were supposed to be.

That's the way it was, not long ago. But no more.

Today's typical Alaska visitor drives his normally loaded camper, motor home, or trailer onto a big ocean liner-sized ferryship at Seattle or Prince Rupert, B.C. End of driving chores en route to the 49th State.

While the vessel's captain navigates northerly, the vehicle driver enjoys a never-ending view of islands and mainland covered with lush, thick forests and towering snow-peaked mountains. He has, at his disposal aboard ship, one of Alaska's finer dining salons, at least one (sometimes two, depending on which ferry he's riding) cocktail lounge, a stateroom if he wants one, plus observation lounges, snack bar or cafeteria, and the considerable pleasures of the open deck. When the visitor arrives in Alaska waters he can drive his rig ashore at any one of several Alaska seacoast communities for a day (or a week, or a month) secure in the knowledge he'll find adequate if not posh camping accommodations. After a time of sightseeing or fishing or hiking in one community, he can board another ferry going his way and travel further.

Nor is ferry travel the only option which the rec-vehicle traveler has for getting to Alaska. The Alaska Highway (Alaskans never call it "the Alcan"), though still unpaved for more than 1,000 of its 1,500 miles, is nonetheless an adequate, reasonably well-maintained road. It can be dusty, true, and slippery and muddy when wet, but taken at moderate speeds it is not the least bit unnegotiable. Single women, college kids, even unescorted grandmothers make the trip without mishap every year. The highway originates at Dawson Creek, B.C. and ends in Fairbanks in the Alaska interior. Campgrounds, grocery stores and service stations are to be found at frequent intervals along the way.

Many (in fact most) rec-vee visitors to Alaska take the ferry system one way on their trip to the North country, then take the Alaska Highway the other.

But enough about just getting to Alaska. What is it like? you wonder, the camping and the fishing and the travel, once you're on the scene.

In brief it's wide open, wild, and wonderful.

Wonderful, that is, if you accept Alaska for what it is—still a frontier of sorts. Wonderful, if you don't expect all the frills and finery that has come to typify so much of camping in the "lower 48" states.

Campgrounds, for instance, do not for the most part have water wells on site. (For that reason, you should always "top off" your water tank whenever you get the opportunity.

A family of campers relax in a campground on the Kenai Peninsula.

HAVE CHANGED!

Trailer and camper visitors in Mt. McKinley National Park arise in the morning to the sight of North America's tallest peak. This picture was taken, incidently, about 2:30 A.M.

You might even want to carry an extra five-gallon jerry jug of the stuff.) Toilets in public campgrounds are almost always privy-types; flush johns are all but non-existent. Dumping stations are equally rare at campgrounds, but quite a number of service stations have them. Showers are available at an occasional municipal campground near the larger cities, but none of the state or Federal campgrounds feature them. In the private sector there is only one KOA campground in the state and all but a few of the other private facilities are "add-on" areas adjacent to mobile home parks, motels or service stations. Some of these are quite nice and are situated in wooded, scenic settings and feature showers, laundries, and other facilities. Others, most in fact, are simply wide, flat, relatively dry places which are okay for a night's stopping place—but they contribute little to the excitement of a trip.

Most of the above sounds pretty negative. On the plus side, Alaska's public campgrounds as well as its private ones are located fairly frequently and conveniently along the various roads of the state. The Federal agencies and the state government do a better-than-adequate job of keeping wood cut and stacked near each camping place. Grounds seem to be pretty well maintained and cleaned, though at the peak of the season the work understandably gets ahead of the crews, especially at the much-used campgrounds near the big cities. There's little theft or other crime in the campground areas. And Alaskan campers, as well as their non-resident visitors, seem to be among the world's friendliest and most gregarious camp colleagues.

Best of all, a great number of Alaska's public campgrounds are located in superlative scenic settings:

. . . alongside pure, tumbling freshwater streams;

. . . overlooking salmon-filled ocean bays and inlets;

. . . facing great mountains, or great glaciers, or sometimes (joy to behold) facing both;

. . . or beside lakes that fairly teem with trout, char or pike.

The thing, then, that makes Alaska camping one of the great outdoor experiences of a lifetime is not the state's network of campgrounds. It is instead the big, beautiful entity of Alaska which surrounds such camping places.

Alaska, in the language of the natives who first populated the Aleutian Islands, means "Great Land." It's easy to see why they thought of the place in those terms. Everything about the state is on a great, grand scale. Mt. McKinley, North America's highest peak, is located here, in a national park named for the 20,320-foot mountain.

The world's biggest bears stalk the woods and tundra of the Alaska bush country (though, fortunately, they rarely invade campsites or other grounds heavy with the scent or sound of man). The biggest, most heavily-antlered moose on earth likewise call Alaska, and particularly the Kenai Peninsula, home. There are herds of literally tens of thousands of caribou, plus mountain goats, Dall mountain sheep, deer, wolves, foxes, and hundreds of species of birdlife. Alaska is the last state in the union where the great bald eagle soars in anything like its original numbers—unmolested, uncontaminated by DDT and the other pesticides, sought after only by photographers and scientist-observers intent on preserving his life and life-style.

There are great rivers in Alaska that the kayaker or the canoeist can spend whole summers exploring. For the backpacker, trails exist virtually everywhere and they vary from the historic well-trod old Chilkoot Trail of goldrush fame to game trails in true wilderness where few if any men have previously gone before.

Huge glaciers, remnants of the last "little ice age" abound throughout Alaska. Many a visitor has filled his camper or trailer ice chest with chunks of ice that are centuries old.

Comfortable A-frame cabins, like this one at Mallard Slough, on the Stikine Flats near Wrangell, Alaska, have been built by the U.S. Forest Service for the use of visitors to Tongass National Forest. The cabins, located at more than 100 locations in the southeast Alaska panhandle are accessible by safe low-cost "bush" aircraft.

One glacier, Malaspina, is bigger than the state of Rhode Island.

The biggest superlative of all about Alaska is of course its own sprawling size. One-fifth the land mass of all the rest of the U.S., containing four separate time zones, the state comprises 586,000 square miles—and that's a lot of mileage to consider when you're trying to plan a camping vacation trip to the place.

Here, to make your planning easier, are a number of questions which prospective Alaska visitors frequently have asked over the years. The answers are based on the writer's two decades of traveling, camping, and reporting the Alaska scene:

How long a trip should we plan, many ask, in order to see most of what Alaska has to offer?

The answer has to vary, of course, with each family's particular style of travel—driving speed, how long they like to spend in each locale they visit, etc. But, realistically, one should not plan to spend *less* than three and a half to four weeks *within* Alaska, that is, if you really want to see much of the panhandle, the interior, the southcentral gulf region, and perhaps take a short flying jaunt up to the Arctic. Even four weeks is cutting it pretty thin. Six weeks will allow a more leisurely look-see and many spend eight weeks driving the highways and ferryways of the state. If you have less than 25 days or so to spend within Alaska, it might be wise for you to limit your visit to one region of the state. One way to make the most of your time is to fly direct to Anchorage and there rent a camper or even a car and tent.

Another frequently asked question concerns clothing.

Campgrounds in Alaska often adjoin good angling lakes (like this one, not far from Anchorage) or near streams and even glaciers. All facilities offered at Alaska state camp grounds are free.

What kind should you bring? Unfortunately, in a state this big, you may need several weights of clothing before you're through. Summers can be hot or they can be cool and moist or, in any given month, they can be both. So prepare accordingly. By all means bring rain gear, a sweater or jacket, and most importantly—pack-along comfortable walking or hiking shoes. Because Alaska is an informal place, you don't need much in the way of fancy garb. But if you do want to take in an occasional night of dining and dancing at the swishier night spots, a cocktail dress for m'lady and a suit or sport coat-slacks combination will do nicely for dad.

A lot of would-be visitors ask about prices in Alaska. No question about it, prices are higher here than elsewhere in the U.S. Plan to pay *at least* 25 percent more for most store bought items.

What, others ask, about border crossings, into Canada then into Alaska? Is there any hassle?

Not really. The Canadian authorities will want to see some proof of your U.S. citizenship. And they'll want proof of ownership of the vehicle you're driving. That, plus evidence you have enough money or credit cards to get where you're going, is about all there is to it. U.S. Customs is generally about as brief.

How about Alaska guidebooks? Are there any written with the camper in mind?

The best single source of information for anyone traveling the highways and byways of Alaska is *The Milepost*. (Alaska Northwest Publishing Company, Box 4-EEE, Anchorage, AK. 99503, $3.95). It lists virtually all the communities, attractions, accommodations, tours, and campsites along the roads of the state. Although it lists campsites it does not rate them. The only guide which actually tells which campground in Alaska are great, and which ones are lousy, is *Camping and Trailering in Alaska* (Alaskabooks, Box 1494, Juneau, AK. 99801, $2). Rajo Publications (Rt. 1, Box 877, McCourtney Road, Grass Valley, California 95945) has announced that *All About Camping in Alaska* will be off their presses soon.

Finally, many visitors ask if there's one "best buy" the camping family should take advantage of when they come to Alaska. There is, indeed. It has to be the unique system of cabins in the wilderness which the U.S. Forest Service maintains in two national forests in Alaska.

The cabins, more than 150 of them spread throughout the Tongass National Forest in southeast Alaska and the Chugach National Forest in southcentral, are first-class, fully enclosed weathertight accommodations. They come furnished with four to eight bunks per unit, table, chairs and benches, and either a wood stove or an oil burner. There's a privy toilet out back at each unit, as well as a garbage disposal pit. At most locations the Forest Service or local sportsmen's organizations have provided a skiff and oars which visitors are free to use.

The cabins are located for the most part on prime fishing lakes and streams. In season there's often excellent hunting for deer, bear or moose. One cabin, located facing the tumbling surf of the Pacific Ocean not far from Sitka, sits adjacent to another cabin which is, in actuality, a big bath house. For through the second unit flows a never-ending stream of hot water, the product of a hot spring that bubbles up from beneath the surface.

Prices for these accommodations are an incredible $5 per

No question about it—the Alaska Highway can raise a lot of dust, as evidenced by this trailer's back end.

Typical U.S. Forest Service cabin in the wilderness of national forest in Alaska.

night per party. And "per party" means per group, not per person. This has to be one of the nation's top travel bargains.

Naturally, you have to provide your own groceries, bedroll, cooking utensils and fuel oil. (The latter only if you've selected an oil-heated cabin.) If your cabin is heated by wood stove, the Forest Service and local sportsmen's groups usually have wood cut and stacked for burning.) To get to your cabin, it's usually necessary to charter a float-equipped light aircraft. Costs for such charters run in the neighborhood of $60 an hour for an airplane which will carry at least four passengers. An hour's charter is often sufficient for a flight in to a lake and the pilot's flight out. Another hour's flying time will take care of your pickup on the day you designate for the pilot to come and get you.

It's a satisfying, exhilarating feeling, cabin-camping in the Alaska wilderness. Depending on where you are you may well see black bear, brownies, deer, moose, or mountain goat. There are rainbow, lake trout, cutthroat, and Dolly Varden in abundance. Around you, and towering high, high above you are sky-piercing Sitka Spruce, hemlocks, and cedar trees some of which were alive when the Danish navigator Vitus Bering came exploring these shores for the Russians back in 1741.

History records that immediately after Bering saw the Alaskan mainland he ordered his ship to change course and set sail for home. His supplies were running low. His men were sick with scurvy. The natives of the place were feared to be inhospitable.

There's no need for modern-day Alaska explorers to depart in such haste. Supplies are easy to come by . . . Alaska is a healthy, happy place to be . . . and it's been absolutely centuries since the homefolks hereabouts have sacrificed a visitor by tossing him into the hole of a soon-to-be erected totem pole.

A Camper's Food for Thought

by PEGGY PETERS

OUR JEEP MADE another one of those impossible maneuvers. With my husband at the wheel and me, white-knuckled in the passenger seat, it tipped sharply downward while at the same time the rear swivelled to the right on a non-existent axle joint. The sun was lowering over a tiny lagoon on the eastward shore of Baja California as Joe persuaded our hot, dusty vehicle to a hard packed area of sand where it made a sound between a gasp and a sigh as the ignition was switched off.

It had been a marvellous day of touring this area of the world, but undeniably hot under the cloudless skies. No growing thing afforded more than a stick of shade and a fine dust covered us and every exposed surface in and on our car. We were spoiled by this point of our journey and weren't surprised that this exquisite area and all that surrounded it for miles was ours. Our bright orange and blue tent was erected in jig time; the process speeded somewhat by our experience but even more by our great desire to plunge head-long into the clear, cool water of the Sea of Cortez.

Our swim was pure delight. After the first exhilarating plunge and leisurely paddling Joe and I floated on our backs watching brown pelicans dive from rocky heights at the entrance of our cove about a quarter mile off. Bliss. Perfection. A tough act to follow—especially when the next item had to be a meal.

We had several adequate but uninspiring tins of meat with us which would fill the growing emptiness in our stomachs but which in truth didn't match our surroundings or our mood.

Slowly, slowly we elbowed and toed our way shoreward tacking slightly toward the rocks nearest our tent. The tide was on the ebb so when we reached the beach hollowed, tidal pools pocketed in ancient lava slabs were visible. Seaweed strands swayed with the advancing and retreating water and Sally Lightfoot crabs ran this way and that, their cardinal shells like animated polka-dots on the charcoal stone. Watching, I realized that one part of the picture remained stable. Studding the bottoms and sides of the pools were what appeared to be collections of radiating spines, a rich burgundy color beneath the lime of the maiden-hair seaweed. Sea Urchins! A half-bushel of these delightful morsels plus some locally-grown vegetables steamed barely tender-crisp and a cool bottle of cervesa (Mexican beer) provided Joe and me with a meal we won't soon forget.

This is, or should be, the essence of camping meals. It has always seemed to me that if the touring camper eats as he does at home, only the locale has changed; the taste is repetitious and the preparation time could be better spent some other way—swimming in your private lagoon for instance.

This time Sea Urchin was the basis of our menu; it could

Your own fresh-caught fish foil wrapped and baked with flavorful additions makes a memorable meal.

just as easily have been clams—small ones to steam just until they open, or larger types for a chowder. The addition of freeze-dried vegetable soup and water would do for basics. Wild potherbs could add a new flavor.

The snorkeler could, with luck, break the water's surface with lobster or crayfish for the pot, and anyone who can walk can pluck mussels from wave-splashed rocks. Almost the only way to ruin seafood is to overcook it. This is true not only for shellfish, but for fin-fish as well. The camper who is near either fresh water or the sea can eat deliciously with (usually) little time or effort expended. Caught by you, the creatures are the freshest, least expensive tidbits possible. If your luck is poor, but the area rich, do the next best thing: find the busiest fish market in town and make your choice from the case or bushel baskets. You needn't spend much money here either; prices in a fish market are governed by supply and demand only. Because one variety is in short supply and high priced doesn't make it any better than another species which may be "running", widely available and low in cost. There is little waste here, so the per pound price can be considered lower than it would be if attached to something at the butcher's.

The availability of locally grown produce is another boon to the travelling camper. I submit that there is nothing more delicious than vine (or stem-) ripened fresh-picked ANYTHING.

It has been truly said that for the very best corn one should grow one's own, set the water to boil before picking it and race back to the kitchen to cook it. This way the sugar has no time to make the chemical transition to starch. Since this is not possible for most of us and certainly not for the camper on the move, the best move is to buy it just as fresh as possible, and this means from a roadside farm stand, not the local supermarket.

Fortunately, when the corn is ripe for the pickin', the tomatoes are ready too and so are the eggplants and zucchini. Any one of these, fresh from the warm soil, is a delight and happily any two or three combined are a summer's treat. It is unlikely that there will be any left-overs but just in case—don't throw them out—serve them again, chilled with the addition of some chopped onion and sprinkled with wine vinegar.

Early last spring Joe and I drove our camper through Yuma, Arizona and bought oranges and grapefruits by the carton from a sunny display by the side of the road. The proprietor insisted we try each variety: pink meat and white; seeded and very sweet; seedless and not-so-sweet etc, etc. Decision was impossible so . . . we just bought them all! We ate them between meals and even for meals during the long drive to our Rocky Mountain home. Each night as we got farther north the cartons had to be carried into our motel room to avoid being frozen. They were heavy and bulky,

but we never minded. After all, they were our treasures. If there is such a disease as Vitamin C Poisoning, we must certainly have had a touch of it by the time we finished that batch. We wouldn't have missed it for anything.

What is even fresher than that from the farm stand? Wild foods you've gathered yourself. It seems possible that they taste better than the usual varieties because you've put yourself (or the kids) into the equation. Not so. They really are better and better for you too. Did you know that some greens lose one third of their vitamins within one hour of picking? True; and with the vitamins, goes some of the flavor.

Fortunate is the early spring camper for this is the time to harvest the most delectable leaves in nature. Consider the dandelion greens—not those picked later in the season when the flowers are blooming, and the leaves are bitter and tough, but those tiny, early tender leaves. I confess that since those we use are collected in areas where no insecticides are used I just never wash them except to remove any dirt. They are best in a salad. Just cut them in smallish pieces, mix with chopped onion, green pepper, hard boiled egg and splatter with an ordinary oil and vinegar dressing.

A soup can also be made if you are the sort of camper who will spend a little more time over the fire. Cut the leaves in small pieces, bring to a boil and drain. In another pot make a roux of flour and butter, add bouillon cube and

Fish filets grilled over a campfire are a treat any time.

If weight is not a consideration, consider the cast iron utensils. Long, even, slow cooking brings out the best in many foods.

The Dutch oven lets the cook play while it spreads the heat evenly and bastes the simmering viands inside.

water. Season with onion salt, white pepper and salt; simmer 10 minutes and then add the dandelion leaves. The addition of a bit of heavy cream just before serving makes it extra delicious, if you just happen to have such luxuries along.

There are countless other wild greens free for the picking during the spring and numerous books available to initiate the novice.

During the mid-summer, the camper can look for berries. These are produced in great abundance and some species will be found growing at almost any altitude and some variety in almost any soil conditions. Look for grapes, prick-

ly pears (Opuntia), cherries, blueberries, gooseberries and cranberries which every year produce literally thousands of tons of fruit. What's more, picking these does nothing detrimental to future supplies, in fact it may even increase next year's yield by strengthening the plant. Its energies are put to growth rather than to producing seeds from unpicked fruits. Use the bounty in muffins & pies; over cereal or ice cream; just as is or, if the fruits are truly found in very great amounts and you can get them home quickly, do consider making jam with them. How delightful this bit of summer will taste on a hot biscuit on a snowy January day.

Lightweight, easily carried products are the basis of delicious meals and can even be meals in themselves.

I am almost afraid to bring up the subject of mushrooms —but the edible varieties are so delicious no camper should miss them. With the aid of a guide you can reliably distinguish between those which are safe and delicious and those which should be left where they stand. Certainly, if there is even the slightest doubt, pass them up. Do not rely on tests like a silver knife turning color etc; that would be foolhardy. Once you recognize the snow mushroom, puff balls, morels and shaggy manes your menus will take on a new and delightful facet. Use the mushrooms in salads, making soup, sauteed or, if they are a bit past their prime, in a stew.

In late summer and during the fall anyone roaming the North American outdoors may find himself in an area of nut trees. Species such as the black walnut, butternut, hazelnut and hickory abound. Don't pass these up. Finding and gathering them on a crisp day under red and yellow leaves could be an unforgetable experience for anyone.

I cannot leave this discussion of wild foods without noting what an early expert on the subject, Henry David Thoreau, had to say of wild apples. "This noblest of fruits must be eaten in the fields, when your system is all aglow with exercise," Thoreau said, "when the frosty weather nips your fingers, the wind rattles the bare boughs or rustles the few remaining leaves and the jay is heard screaming around. What is sour in the house a bracing walk makes sweet. Some of the apples might be labelled, 'To be eaten in the wind'."

The camper who procures his own viands is no doubt the best off of all, but when this is not possible we must consider alternatives. Much has been written about what can and should be carried along by a family of campers, by those in plush motor homes, by back-packers and by pack-trippers so we will note these only briefly.

There are the special-for-campers-freeze-dried foods: those small bits of dry, almost weightless particles which, when soaked or cooked in water miraculously swell up to become a hearty stew or whatever. It is my personal opinion

Let the kids pitch in; experience in all aspects of camping for each camper should be the rule.

that these packets are indispensible for the serious back-packers and can play a small role in the more usual type camping, too. They can round out otherwise skimpy meals and are a kind of insurance that one won't actually go hungry (Heaven forbid!) no matter what. Joe and I were glad to have them in the back of the Jeep that trip to Baja. However it must, in truth, be noted that they are rather expensive, tend to taste rather alike (except for the fruits which are the best product) and for some reason most are very salty which might be a consideration for those with special medical problems.

Canned goods are an obvious choice—nice to have along, especially meats,—but heavy.

There are also packets of freeze-dried products not nec-essarily for campers which we find a great help. These are seasoning mixes which give variety to the usual fare. Taco mix for instance, or Sloppy Joes.

Don't overlook those uncooked tortillas. For a quick hot meal these can be heated or fried and filled with almost anything: canned chili, canned meat in instant gravy, sea-food or just cheese with tomatoes. For the adventurous, drip some "salsa" over the top. That removes any fuzz from the alimentary tract.

While the camper can do a great deal of pick-and-choose-as-you-go so far as the selection of foods goes, a choice of utensils, plates and tableware must be made before the camper leaves his home grounds.

Unless you are a backpacker, bring the heavy Dutch oven. And don't forget the lid. A light-weight pan gets hot spots over a flame, and you may find the contents in the center scorching while that at the edges remain stubbornly luke-warm. You can leave the heavy pan to its own devices while you do something more interesting and it will spread and hold the heat evenly. Cleaning the Heavy Helper, especially if it's well-seasoned, isn't so bad as you might think. Pour in water (even cold water is alright) to cover the bottom

"Real" cutlery and crockery rather than the disposable type are worth the extra trouble they require.

Camping in the autumn has rewards like these delicious hazel nuts, usually free for the taking.

and as far up the sides as the contents reached. Just let it soak and then rub off the softened debris with a loosely woven, metalic pad made for the purpose. Rinse, and dry with a paper towel.

There are two schools of thought on the paper plate question. One side states, and rightly so, that they are available, convenient and sanitary. They feel similarly about paper cups, bowls, napkins, and towels and a host of other disposable products. Joe and I feel that to a large extent these conveniences are an unnecessary extravagance and a waste of a national resource—timber. We do use paper towels to some small extent, but have our plastic camping plates and mugs along on every trip. It *is* more trouble to wash them than it would be to throw them away but we do it anyway.

Plastic tableware, even the best, is a poor investment. The inexpensive variety is too small to serve its purpose and infuriatingly loses what little shape it possesss with only moderate heat. The more durable type is too expensive to throw out after one meal and if you're going to wash cutlery anyway, why not wash stainless steel?

An evening campfire is one of the finest things under the stars. It is warm, beautiful, and oddly active while at the same time quiet. It encourages shared confidences, and ghost stories. It dries damp socks and keeps the Wild Ones at bay. A campfire is one of my favorite things. But — the only thing it cooks really well is a frank on a stick. It is the unromantic truth that a small propane-fired stove (such as those manufactured by Coleman) does a far better job of cooking than an open fire. If you are not in a kitchen-equipped camper, bring one. It is a camping necessity. (By the way — so is a good pot holder.)

A final word on cooking and camping must concern the environment. No can burns. Don't throw it into the fire; put it where it belongs even if that means carrying it back to civilization. For some reason the plastic holder that binds six-packs together is attractive to wildlife and causes untold harm. Don't leave it around. And those metal rings from the tops of soft-drink and beer cans — where do they belong?

On our last camping excursion I shocked the neighbors. They couldn't believe what they saw. I had picked up some litter that wasn't mine. Imagine.

No luxuries, few amenities; but beauty and solitude are all these campers require from life at this minute.

WHAT'S CAMPING ANYWAY?

by CHAS. F. WATERMAN

ABOUT THE ONLY thing I know about the word *camping* these days is that it means something generally done away from home. Since the lean-to lovers sometimes say caustic things about the motor home pilots and since residents of travel trailers often find it desirable to stay upwind from perspiring backpackers you have to be careful when talking to strangers who claim to be campers.

Of course the funny parts happen when a camper gets into the wrong neighborhood by accident. There was this business about my old friend Dan Bailey who figures a campground is a place near a trout stream and a long way from a post office. Well, Dan and his wife Helen took off on this trip to a Montana spot where they knew only the more stalwart fishermen would be present. They knew the Forest Service had a couple of trash cans there and that there was a sort of a road to the spot but it was quite a piece from the asphalt. They had a very small travel trailer (an insult perhaps to some nature lovers) but it was pulled by a four-wheel-drive Bronco that will head up a steep incline on its own if you give it its head.

The road was just what Dan loves and he clenched his pipe happily and threaded between the trees, slipped cautiously down into the deeper holes and eased his rig over boulders. It was just as Dan had hoped and the little campground was empty, grass getting a new start where tents had stood and the ashes long cold in the makeshift fireplaces. The creek gurgled and muttered with its snow water from the high peaks.

It was after Dan had found his parking place and was sorting out his waders and custom-built rod that the other rig arrived. It was a big trailer and Dan starred at it in sur-

prise, wondering what steering-wheel genius had managed to bring this rolling home into the wilderness. But it was all a mistake, I guess, for a neatly dressed lady got out of the tow vehicle and approached him.

"Pardon me," she said, "but could you direct me to the electrical outlets?"

The best stories generally concern the users of highly civilized equipment who find themselves in rustic spots by accident, but now and then there is a vehicle camper who figures four wheels are four wheels and if they have power enough other features are incidental. Although I have seen station wagons and sedans that were abandoned in high country with the arrival of late fall storms, I recall with awe a few campers who just didn't give a damn and got away with it. There was the Rocky Mountain elk hunt of several years back—

My wife and I had a four-wheel-drive carryall and we took to an uphill Forest Service trail on the day before elk season opened. There had been a high-country snow followed by a thaw and the road was terrible. There were several times when I worried about our considerable length and wished for a bobtailed outfit but we made it to our preselected campsite early in the afternoon and set up a skimpy camp only a few yards from the "road."

Our location was poorly chosen because that road was the sole route into a vast area of elk country and as evening came on we heard the growls and thumps of an assortment of high-clearance trucks, their lights flickering on and off our camp with distorted shadows from the pines. There was some especially nasty going near our stop and an outfit would become mired now and then to be pulled out by

It's a happy circumstance that not all campers like the same type camping. Some on the beach and some at the cabaret thins things out.

someone who could find better footing. It was no place for amateur drivers or lowslung trucks.

It was about bedtime when I heard a new sound, a scream of tortured machinery, rapid-fire thuds as somebody seemed to hit only the high spots of the trail, and the slap of high-thrown sheets of water striking trees and cliffs. There were headlights coming up the road, their beams darting right to left as they made short, fast turns, and then going up and down jerkily in a dizzy dance. This I had to see, and I grabbed a flashlight and hurried to near the road, crouching behind a boulder to avoid showers of stones or cold water. The rig came by at what seemed terrific speed but I could make out a hunched figure at the whipping wheel. As it went past I turned on my flashlight to make out any detail possible. I saw a gleam of wet chrome inscription—*Chrysler New Yorker,* it said, and the car was gone in a curtain of water, stones and mud with whirling tire chains and crashing contacts with the chuckholes.

Now sheer velocity can carry a sedan through a little messy going but how it got that far from civilization I'll never know. It would be excellent advertising for the manufacturer except that I have no idea whether it ever got back down that muddy mountain or not.

People in the state and national park business and in fish and game conservation are confronted constantly by the fringe between those who want untouched wilderness and those who want street lights and concrete parking pads. It's even a question for owners of commercial campgrounds, although it's less troublesome for them, even though they *do* have to please both users of complex hookups and the tent campers in many cases.

Now park and forest personnel, national or state, are greatly concerned with safety. Spunky though it was, the performance of the Chrysler-mounted elk hunter is exactly the kind of thing that ruins sleep for public officials con-cerned with back country of any kind. Remember this when you find chains across roads you thought would take you to secluded nature. The problem is in that nebulous fringe between the nature lover and the traveler who loves push-buttons and asphalt.

The Florida State Parks, for instance, have a problem no one anticipated a few years ago. When the swarms of tourists arrive with their travel trailers and motor homes they are happy to accept the state parks as low-cost parking areas although they may spend their days at the racetrack or in the cities. Despite attempts at limiting their use of state campgrounds (there's been talk of minimum charges to cover two or three days' camping to discourage overnighters who couldn't care less about flora and fauna) there are still visitors who get lodging instead of camping.

A Florida State Parks naturalist, Joe Kenner, deplores the colonies of folks who arrive in motor homes and trailers, cluster about the electrical outlets and don't even glance along the nature trails he feels are avenues to a "true outdoor experience." That problem certainly isn't confined to Florida and there's the question whether state funds should be spent for the lodging of such visitors. To the naturalist, a *camper* is someone who wants to commune with nature. He finds it difficult to understand the tourist whose primary interest is in the comfort of living away from home and whose hobby is in the assembly and operation of wonderful gadgets that make it possible for him to tour the country without ever stepping on earth or grass. In fact, except for plugging in the electricity, it would be possible to tour the nation without even stepping on asphalt or concrete.

But although he may have no interest in the outdoors as such the owner of a motor home has become a "camper" by modern designation—and his contribution to the camping industry (which is responsible for many of the good things enjoyed by the tent liver) is substantial.

For the camper who wants more luxury while away from home than when at home, there are places to fulfill his desires.

Backpackers never have to worry that all the sites with electrical outlets will be taken when the sun sets.

One of the really difficult puzzles for anyone making a backwoods study of the camping business concerns the nature study groups, made up of some of the most learned ecologists and most energetic environmentalists. It is these people who are so often found in the front ranks when a river, forest or mountain must be saved and they are willing to contribute money or time to worthwhile projects that most others would ignore. Yet, they speak of solitude, silence and communion with nature, but they often travel in mobs.

Grubby, unshaven and thinking of a warm bath (mentionable in a CAMPER'S DIGEST providing it follows several days in the outback), a pair of us were coming down from a high mountain fishing trip when up the narrow trail wafted the unmistakable sounds of infantry on the move and hikers by the dozen came up, most of them young, athletic and sharp looking. Such organized groups study nature (what hasn't departed ahead of their rhythmic steps), learn of survival methods; they could tell me things I never dreamed about natural foods and could outwalk and outclimb old fuds like me—and that goes for the pretty young girls in the short shorts and the Italian climbing boots as well as for the handsome young men.

But why do they bunch up like winter starlings? Their camps are like small cities, and even when they carefully destroy or carry off their own trash (and some left over by sloppy types that may have preceded them) they can't help leaving some sign of their passing. On that occasion in the mountains the two of us watched them start to make camp and then went trudging on toward the highway, wondering how it would feel to camp in peacetime with a party of 25 or 30.

Now some nature lovers will say it is better to go in a bunch for the shock to nature is brief whereas little groups are always pestering the flora and fauna. I don't even argue that, but the organized hike of large numbers of adults has always been a mystery to me except for the old explanation that man is a herd animal. And, although I hold the nature organizations in respect—even with some awe—I don't know why they flock, for that's what I leave town to avoid.

Although large parties of guided backpackers are wondrous things that wouldn't appeal to me personally I can't help thinking how much less space they would take if they scattered.

So "camping" breaks down into many facets and as the numbers of campers grow there's going to be more and more need for tolerance. You should be glad to see diversity of camping interests because you'd be in big trouble if everybody took up your pet procedures. Now most of my camping is for hunting or fishing purposes and if all campers went hunting and fishing there wouldn't be much of that left.

And most of us like the entire picture to fit our personal choices in method. For example, in Florida's Everglades National Park I spent a long time learning routes to fishing spots, often camping in areas where there wouldn't be another boat in a week's time. Then the Park Service marked the routes and there may be a hundred boats a day on some of them this year. That's a matter of getting the Park used by more people and I have no legitimate beef but I dislike

The backpacker-fisherman and the mobile home jockey will have the least friction of any parties—they probably won't ever see each other.

it for purely selfish reasons.

In mountain country where horse pack trains are an efficient means of travel there is the recurring problem of where motorized vehicles should be allowed and where they should be excluded. Now all-terrain vehicles have torn down some beautiful mountainsides and in the innocent days of long ago I guess I did my share of damage—but the horse-packing trip is confined to those who can afford horses themselves or can afford to hire outfitters, and, despite what you may hear from horse exponents, the use of gasoline vehicles under proper regulation can contribute greatly to enjoyment in much rough country without doing damage. This isn't to say there are *no* areas where power vehicles should be excluded.

If there are two groups who should strike no sparks at all

they are the backpacker and the user of the large trailer or motor home. The backpacker isn't going to hog the power outlets and the motor home isn't going to jostle anybody on the Appalachian Trail.

An acquaintance bought himself a nice big travel trailer and he and his family hied themselves forth to a scenic national park where they found a sylvan spot by a musical stream with a background of murmuring pines. Ah, solitude!

Then along came a somewhat frazzled character with a dusty pack and worn shoes. He brought forth a sleeping bag and sacked out by my friend's rear wheel.

"What *is* this?" asked my acquaintance, peering out apprehensively.

It's a campground, friend. It's a campground.

BOAT CAMPING IN SUB-TROPIC FLORIDA

Upper Nest Key is one of the Florida Bay Islands which permits camping. Here the boat camper wades ashore to enjoy the comforts of solid land for a little while.

The Only Way to Cruise a Vast Water Wilderness

by JIM MARTENHOFF

THE SOUTHERN MOST TIP of Florida juts downward toward the tropical trade wind zone, an arm of America extended into island-dotted, emerald seas. It is small boat country, huge shoal areas laced with narrow channels and a tattered fringe of mangrove wilderness along the mainland.

It is fascinating small boat country, too, for much of the area by its nature bans larger craft. You can cruise much of the region only in an outboard, or modest sterndrive hull, and never have to worry about tangling wakes with a 60-footer.

And cruise it you can, for a week at a time, for a tent set up ashore at night can be your "cabin" and a charcoal grill your "galley."

Not that campsites are common. They aren't. The Florida

Keys and southern mainland area are mostly mangrove—a many-legged plant that grows in the shoals, indistinctly and vaguely separating somewhat soggy land from the sea. There are some beaches, nearly all appropriated years ago by private interests. You can't plan a boat-camping vacation haphazardly, cruising aimlessly during the day, hoping to find a suitable beach at dusk.

But you can enjoy the unique boat-camping advantages offered by parks in the area—and don't think the word "park" means a crowded canvas city, as it does in many parts of the nation.

The Everglades National Park is mostly water wilderness, still pure and unpolluted, still very much as the good Lord made it. Around the southern coast, where the Park stands

Fishing is excellent in many of the Florida waters and this gentleman hasn't far to travel from his tent to his sport. Note typical Florida sub-tropical trees.

at the edge of the sea, the only means of transportation is by boat—be it outboard, or a canoe.

There are 600 square miles of water "out front," as the local folks describe open Florida Bay, with scores of islands. And on the "inside," the park is a patchwork of broad bays, some of them a puzzling maze of islets—Hells Bay is aptly named, and anyone can lose himself within an hour.

But the park has meticulously marked the waterways, opening them up to visiting boatmen and their families. They even created what is known as the "Wilderness Waterway," a 99-mile stretch of interconnected bays, rivers and creeks. It links Flamingo, the main access point in the park, with Everglades City far to the north and west. It is solidly marked, easy to follow, absolutely pure wilderness, and virtually unique in the American park system.

The park has been assiduously developing campsites exclusively for boatmen. There are no fewer than 19 on the inside, with three more out front. All but one, that on Cape Sable—a wild and lonely stretch of sandy beach that is the southernmost tip of the continental United States—have one or more charcoal grills and picnic tables. Eleven have toilets, most of them chemical; six have docks for boats; six are uniquely native. Located in pure mangrove country, they are "chickees" which is the Seminole Indian word for a platform shelter covered with thatch.

You can spend a month just cruising in park waters, and if you want to get away from it all, this is the place. You will share your days with manatee and porpoise, fish and birds; your nights with (depending on where you are) alligators grunting nearby, and the mysterious sounds of a

Florida Bay is fine fishing area. You may camp from your boat on several islands or on mainland beach at Cape Sable.

tropical jungle the likes of which you haven't heard since a Tarzan movie.

And this is the time to mention that you may also share your evenings with mosquitoes. This is on the edge of the tropics, and the bugs can be big and mean after the sun goes down. There's an unconfirmed report that a pair of particularly husky Everglades mosquitoes were once observed flying away with two alligators and a school teacher from Iowa. They were said to have surrendered their victims after a brief battle with bigger bugs from the backcountry.

So how do you venture into this strange mixture of paradise and challenge?

Assuming you can trail your boat to South Florida, in these days of limited gasoline supplies, head for Homestead. This is a town some 30 miles south of Miami, and is

the gateway to both the chain of islands known as the Florida Keys and to the Everglades National Park.

Opting for the park first, just follow the signs. You can halt at the Visitors' Center some 12 miles from Homestead, gain information about the sights to see on the road ahead. It's 38 miles to Flamingo, over the most level landscape you'll ever see on earth. At Flamingo, there's a campground, motel, marina, and more; but if you want to go boat-camping, check in at the Ranger Station.

You must have a fire permit to go camping. And you must file a "float plan." This would include a description of your boat, number of people aboard, a rough schedule of your trip, and don't be disturbed if the Ranger asks you about safety gear aboard. After all, this is a wilderness, and you are on your own—like Columbus. You'll need plenty of

Boaters on Wilderness Waterway pause on Onion Key.

fresh water to drink, and some sort of signal device in case of engine failure—more about that later. You'll also receive a poop sheet full of useful information, backed by a base map.

This is a water wilderness, remember, so you will need government navigational charts. Let's list them all right now:

No. 598 and 599 SC, Whitewater Bay-Flamingo, and Lostman's River-Whitewater Bay; No. 642-SC, Wiggins Pass to Lostman's River. These are a must. You will also find others helpful: No. 1253, Alligator Bay to Lostman's River; No. 1254, Everglades to Alligator Bay. And if you decide to venture out front in Florida Bay, you can use No. 1249, Fowey Rocks to Alligator Reef; No. 1250, Alligator Reef to Sombrero Key; and even 141-SC, Miami to Marathon including Florida Bay.

Why list them all in detail? Because you can order them by mail in advance. Nos. 141, 642, 598, and 599 are each $2; the others $1.50. Send a check or money order to the National Ocean Survey, Department of Commerce, Distribution Division C44, Riverdale, Maryland 20840. Studying the charts in advance can prove very helpful. You know the area before you see it.

To cruise the wilderness waterway, you need a guidebook entitled, to no one's surprise, *A Guide to the Wilderness Waterway of the Everglades National Park*. This is sold at Flamingo, and you can pick it up on the spot. It's a spiral-bound booklet, with full-page maps facing each page of text, and it simply details the 99-mile route linking the two western ends of the park. It is indispensable, however.

You do not have to be an expert navigator to cruise-camp this area. The route is very well marked indeed, and you cannot go astray. But these points are important: Your boat cannot be too large. About 18-20 feet is tops, no high windshields; no cabins. Some creeks are very narrow and tight. You must carry everything you need. Gasoline, water, food, insect repellent, mosquito netting, tents, charcoal, whatever. You must carry everything out again. All trash, litter, garbage. The park tried installing garbage cans at campsites, but it didn't work out. Few people used them. Now they all but beg you to preserve the wilderness purity of the region, and not to litter. So tote plastic bags, bring your trash back out with you.

Binoculars will help you pick up consecutive waterway markers. Run them in order. In some bays you may spot a marker far ahead, think it is the next in line, then run hard aground on an oyster bar. Make sure there isn't another marker in between, slightly to one side. When in doubt, stop and look and check your charts and the guide book.

If you have a compass and know how to use it in conjunction with a chart, you can constantly orient yourself at

Do youngsters like camping? Early morning smiles of Claire and little Dave provide a clue.

How to Camp with a Large Family

by **DICK DIETZ**

Camping with a large crew can not only be successful but a vacation necessity at today's resort prices. Here's how a family of eight solved the problem.

Our camping condominium lined up on a woodsy site—van with canoe atop, trailer and wall tent.

REMEMBER the old circus act where a tiny car about half the size of a stunted VW pulls into the arena, the doors pop open, and an unbelievable succession of people start pouring out? One, two, four, six, eight, maybe more.

"Holy smokes," everyone laughs, "how do they do it"! The first time I saw the act I can remember trying to see underneath the mini-ark because I was sure there was a hidden trap door in the arena deck feeding all those clowns up through the chassis.

Today, I occasionally get the same sort of reaction when I mention that we camp with our large family of six children. "How in the world do you do it," I'm asked, as if I had accomplished some modern-day miracle.

Now, I'm not going to tell you that camping with such a large family group doesn't create some additional problems. It definitely does. But the problems aren't all that large and there are ways to surmount them.

As a matter of fact, camping is about the only way any large family with a limited budget can afford an away-from-home vacation today without taking out a second mortgage on the old homestead to pay the cost.

First off, let's define a large family as one with at least four children (or more), all of whom will be included in the trip. With both parents, that means six or more in the camping group.

Our experience has indicated that some special thought and planning becomes necessary when the size of the family group exceeds five. Each extra person after that (and, in most cases, it will be an additional child) can cause potential difficulties with available space for both transport and camping shelter, as well as potential difficulties from the resulting spread in ages, interests and activities.

In our case the situation was complicated a bit further by my activities as a free-lance outdoor writer and hunting and fishing buff. Any equipment I obtained would have to double in brass, serving for hunting and fishing trips as well as family camping jaunts. It would also have to be adaptable to trips involving anywhere from two to eight people.

I realize that not everyone will have as many and as varied demands on their camping gear as do we. However, the system we've worked out offers, I think, interesting benefits of economy, versatility and practicality to many families, particularly large ones. For want of a better term, one could call it a "modular" system of camping—because it consists of a series of add-on units. Each of these units serves more than one purpose. Each one can be included or left off as the need dictates.

The major units include a Ford Club Wagon van with seating capacity for eight, a Coleman Model 580 camping trailer that can sleep from four to six, a 9 x 12 ft. wall tent that can sleep up to five comfortably and a lightweight, 14-foot Sportspal canoe that goes atop the van.

To begin, we ruled out any vehicles designed primarily for camping only. We need two fairly standard vehicles at home —both capable of carrying a number of passengers. Mine had to get me to work daily, as well as take me on trips to locations ranging from the middle of a large city to the northern Maine woods. This eliminated any consideration of motor homes, van conversions or pick-up truck campers. We needed wheels that would carry people and pull something else behind.

Normally, a regular station wagon would fill the bill. And we already had one of these—an eight-passenger job. So, the first time I attempted to take the whole group camping,

Lise, Ann Marie and Claire get ready for a canoe trip. Camp sites on water can keep children busy and happy all day long. Sportspal canoe and Aquabug motor (combined weigh under 50 lbs.) are easy for youngsters to handle.

I simply had a Class 1 hitch attached to the wagon, rented a small camping trailer, brought it home and started packing. At that point it occurred to me that maybe I should check the weight-carrying capacity of the station wagon. It turned out to be 1200 lbs. That means an eight-passenger wagon loaded with eight adults averaging 150 lbs. in weight can't carry anything else. Luckily for us, the children were not too big, and my wife and I are not too heavy. So we used up only 650 lbs. of our limit. But, with the addition of the tongue weight of the trailer, and extra gear crammed inside the wagon, we landed right on the 1200 lb. limit— with too much of it distributed over the rear of the wagon. Result—we and the gear were packed into the wagon like sardines and we wound up blowing a rear tire.

Obviously we needed heavier springs, shocks and tires for the wagon. But this still wouldn't solve our space problem inside the vehicle. I found a better solution. My ten-year-old smaller wagon, used previously for my personal trips, was finally beginning to show signs of serious fatigue after 100,000-plus miles. I replaced it with the van.

The Club Wagon we chose has the long, 123-inch wheelbase, heavy duty springs and "D" load range truck tires. This gave it a GVWR of 6700 lbs. or 2300 lbs. of carrying capacity over its curb weight of 4400 lbs. There was no way we were going to overload this baby. The long wheelbase provided plenty of comfortable, non-crowded seating capacity for eight with an extremely generous amount of space for additional gear behind the third seat.

After two years' experience with the van, we've discovered that it was a wise and highly useful choice. On family camping trips, it provides roomy seating for all eight of us, ample space for necessary gear and sufficient, if not out-standing power in its 302 cu. in. V-8 engine to climb hills and travel at highway speeds when fully loaded and towing the trailer.

On some of the back-country hunting and fishing trips I take with just my son, we remove the two, three-passenger rear seats and sleep right in the van. For other trips, involving part of the family, from three to five, we take either the trailer and the 9 x 12 ft. wall tent or two small tents. Finally, the van is superior to any current station wagon for week-end hauling chores and serves as my drive-to-work transportation.

Let me make one more comment on the choice of a van for the outdoors-minded family. To me, the van offers the kind of utility and transport for which the station wagon was originally intended. But as station wagons became popular with the suburban and country club sets, they fell prey to Detroit's competition for the mass market. The result was a product overstuffed with plastic interior decoration, soft sprung for the mushy ride that robs weight carrying capacity and low-slung for the preferred silhouette that seems to bounce off every exposed rock on a back road. I made the mistake of taking my current wagon into the Maine wilderness once. We managed to get back out, but I had to replace a muffler, a set of shocks and a tire. For the camping family a van makes a lot of sense.

Having ruled out "all-in-one" camping vehicles, we were left with but one choice for our movable shelter—a trailer. A big, self-contained trailer was beyond our budget and not in keeping with our style of camping or the rough country we intended to visit.

It's quite true that there are large trailers which will sleep eight. To us, it makes no difference. We just do not want to

One growing family's unique solution to camping transport and shelter—a retired school-bus they converted themselves.

get by with one camping bedroom, no matter how big. When you have to use the same quarters for a large family that includes age levels of adult, teens and pre-teens—with the resulting variety of interests, activities and sleeping habits—you're bound to run into problems and conflicts. Camping trips should be a source of fun, recreation and relaxation for all. Often this requires separating adults from children or children from children on the basis of sex or age. For this purpose a "second room" of some sort is a godsend.

Consequently, the combination of camping trailer and extra tent was exactly perfect for us as well as a solution to our budget limitations. Our Coleman 580 trailer sleeps two each in both of the fold-out wings and can sleep two more children in the bunk made by utilizing the drop-down table and side cushions. However, we discovered it works better

if we use the trailer for a maximum of five, sometimes only four—with the others using and sleeping in the wall tent.

The match-ups vary. Sometimes, the three oldest girls use the tent and the rest of us the trailer. Sometimes I'll take the tent with the two boys, the oldest and youngest of the group. At all times, we have at least two "dressing" rooms for changing. And we can convert this to four if necessary by using the privacy curtains for the trailer wings.

Now, even when I take only part of the family where the trailer can't go, or on canoe trips, we bring two smaller, Thermos pop tents—one for the boys and one for the girls.

Lately, we've begun taking one of these pop tents, in addition to the wall tent, on all-family trips. It can be used as a place to store gear in case of rain, as another dressing room, or as a bedroom if one of the children wants to invite

Wall tent makes spacious "second bedroom" for large families. Or, it can be used alone for three or four, as on this Baxter State Park campsite.

a new-found camping friend to stay overnight at our site. How many camping rigs have you seen that include a "guest" room?

There's one more major piece of our camping equipment that doesn't involve either road transportation or shelter. That's our canoe. Because we almost always camp next to water, like to fish and enjoy exploring the shores of lakes, we require some form of water transport. Since we tow a camping trailer, this additional piece of equipment has to be car-topped.

A canoe seemed like the most practical answer. But I also have need for a small fishing boat and a duck boat as well. And I didn't want to have to buy and store all three. Fortunately, I found the answer to all three needs in one craft—a 14-foot Sportspal canoe. The Sportspal is made of lightweight aluminum, is lined with flotation foam inside, and has foam sponsons on the outside. It is 44 inches across the middle and is flat-bottomed without a keel.

Canoe purists may not cotton to a Sportspal. It doesn't paddle as well as a standard canoe with keel, and its thin hull is not suitable for white-water use. But we usually employ a small outboard anyway, reserving the paddles for emergency use. With its flotation features and overall stability, the Sportspal reduces the chances of tipping with small children aboard. And it can carry over 800 lbs. safely. As a result, I can use it as a duck boat that will hold two hunters, a dog and decoys. I can also use it as a fresh-water fishing boat for two—it is stable enough to permit casting from a standing position. And, with my back-cast, I need to keep the fly rod as high above the water as possible.

The combination of equipment we've put together has already served us extremely well. I suspect we'll stick with it for a long time. Anyone with a large family and a need for a certain amount of economy couldn't go wrong with the same or a similar set-up.

However, I realize that not everyone will have a crew as large as ours, or be interested in the same style of camping.

Sharing the work load is a valuable lesson of family camping. Here, Dick vacuums out the trailer after a trip.

Number one son, Dick II, sleepily prepares breakfast at rough camp site on Maine's Allagash wilderness waterway. Two-man poptent in background also serves as "guest room" on family trips.

For many, a motor home, van conversion, pick-up camper or large trailer may be a better choice.

Nevertheless, I'd make a few strong recommendations to any camping family with three or more children:

No matter what type of camping shelter you use, bring along a tent as an extra room.

With children under six years of age, concentrate on camping at a single location. Save the touring until they get a little older. Also, with small children, try to limit your travel to no more than six hours a day.

Camp where there is a source of interesting activity for young children. If nothing else, water and a place to swim or splash around will keep all the kids busy and happy throughout the day.

For teen-agers, consider one of the latest "destination" or "resort" campgrounds that have special activities for this easily-bored age group.

Finally, bring your own source of entertainment in the form of books and games for road travel and rainy days. Better still, remember to take lightweight rain gear for all. There's no reason why the family need stay imprisoned under canvas because of a little precipitation.

IMPORTANT CHECK LIST
HOW TO SAFETY CHECK YOUR REC VEHICLE

by JOHN EBELING

LET'S START UP FRONT. Chances are, when it is raining, you cannot see to the rear or sides of your motor home. This creates a hazardous driving condition and, if this is true in the case of your motor home, try to correct it. It is probably caused by the aerodynamics of your motor home's front end. Turbulence at the front of your motor home and around your rear-view mirrors may be such that it throws water against the window making it difficult to see to the rear view mirror. Also, turbulence probably causes similar beads of water and road dirt to collect on the mirror.

Try waxing the mirror and also the outside of the window. This should cause the water that is collected there to form large beads that are somewhat less of a problem. If this doesn't work, you will have to try a new mirror and possibly a new location for the mirror. When you find a solution, write a how-to-do-it letter to the manufacturer and send a copy of the letter to: National Highway Traffic Safety Administration (N.H.T.S.A.), Department of Transportation, Washington, D.C.

On some older model motor homes there was a poor windshield wiper system. This system had a tendency to become inoperative. If you have such a motor home, you know that it needs windshield wipers. They do not always break at a convenient time. They may break when you have to keep driving and without windshield wipers you become a hazard, endangering your life and the lives of others. Your windshield wipers should be reliable and not prone to frequent breakdown. Write the N.H.T.S.A. describing the problem and they may issue a factory recall on equipment of this design. If they do not feel that the manufacturer should correct the windshield wiper system, keep your correspondence to and from the agency and have the wiper system fixed at your own expense. When it is fixed, notify the N.H.T.S.A. that you corrected the situation, how it was done and what it cost and that you feel you should be reimbursed.

On some motor homes, the nose of the body protrudes beyond the front bumper. This generally will not be a problem in the event an automobile backs into your motor home, but you will undoubtedly be around other recreation vehicles and they are high enough to damage your front end. Therefore, install some bumper extensions.

Seats and Seat Belts

Check your seat belts. If they are simply screwed into the wooden floor, they may pull out just when they are needed. They are supposed to withstand over 3,000 pounds of static pressure. I have known of seat belts that pulled out during a sudden stop when the passenger's weight could not have exceeded 150 lbs. If they are not bolted into a metal plate, that preferably is on the under side of your floor, they probably are not adequately anchored. If this is true, notify the N.H.T.S.A. They will probably see to it that the manufacturer of your motor home installs adequate seat belt anchor points.

If the pedestals of the seats in your driving compartment seem flimsy, notify the N.H.T.S.A. and ask their advice. I have known of pedestals that have collapsed while people were driving. This generally doesn't happen on the broad flat straight-away. It happens when turning, negotiating sharp curves and on rough roads. If you have any doubts about the stability of your driving seat, do something to correct it *before* your trip.

If the defrosters of your front driving windows are inadequate, get them fixed. One way might be with a small 12-volt accessory fan that will blow air with sufficient force to do an adequate job of defrosting or defogging.

Does your engine cover allow gases and fumes to leak into the motor home? Fumes can asphyxiate you and, also, there is always the danger of explosion. Many early model motor homes had inadequate mechanisms for securing the engine covers. Another hazard of these covers was diversion of the drivers attention when they popped off while the vehicle was being driven. If you have such a motor home, notify the N.H.T.S.A. of this driving hazard and, in the meantime, devise a better hold-down method. I have used a heavy rock in emergency but cannot recommend it, as a rock becomes another projectile in the event of an accident. Another method is to take an elastic shock cord and stretch it across the engine cover and fasten it to the floor on each side. This will help catch the engine cover should it release.

Mechanical Hazards

Check out your transmission cable and make sure that it does not run near sources of extreme heat, such as the exhaust manifold. If it does run near a source of great heat, here is what can happen. You are in the mountains and climbing a steep grade. Your speed is down and less air is provided to cool the engine area. The extreme heat fuses or melts your transmission cable together and you no longer shift. If you were in drive, you will not be able to downshift as you negotiate the down grade. On a steep down grade, your brakes may not take the heavy use that will be required of them. (This is especially true of motor homes with drum brakes instead of disk brakes.) If you have ever had this problem, notify the N.H.T.S.A. immediately. If you discover your transmission cable near a source of great heat or near a pully or belt which could cut it, notify the N.H.T.S.A. Ask them what to do.

Fuel Hazards

While you are checking out sources of heat, follow your exhaust pipe and see if it runs near your gas tank or tanks. If it does, you may recall having smelled gas while driving after a fill-up. Perhaps you noticed gas running out around the fill cap after you have filled and driven back to the campground and perhaps you undid the fill cap and it surged out. This has been due to the fact that the exhaust pipe has heated the gaoline in your gas tank, causing it to expand and create pressure. This is not an ingenious system designed to aid your fuel pump. I have driven many such motor homes and generally burned gas off both tanks, so that there was room for the gas to expand without creating pressure and causing the gasoline smell inside the motor home. If you can, get the station attendant to understand that he should *not* fill the gas tanks completely, thus allowing for expansion. This is especially true if you are going to stop shortly after your gas fill. It just isn't a good idea to have gasoline escaping out of your gas fill caps when someone may be around with a cigarette or charcoal fire. I am not aware of fires or explosions resulting from this situation, but the hazard certainly is there.

Fire and Explosion

While we're talking about fire hazards, do not leave pilot lights on while filling with gasoline. Fires and explosions in a gas station are real holocausts. These have happened.

Another opportunity for fires and explosions occurs with your motor home in the event of an accident. An LP gas supply line to an appliance breaks and fills the interior with gas, making it a veritable bomb. If your motor home doesn't have it, and it probably doesn't, you can get a device that shuts off the LP gas at the tank when there is a major break or rupture in the gas line. If you do not have this, do not drive with LP appliances in operation. Before you drive, shut off the LP gas at the tank. This may save your life and the lives of others in the event of an accident.

While we are talking about LP gas, you should get an LP gas senser and mount it in your motor home. In the event you have a leak, it will sound an alarm. This provides just one more system to safeguard your life and the lives of your loved ones.

Another LP gas safety tip is not to enter your vehicle after it has been sitting unoccupied, particularly after a trip carrying anything which could spark an explosion. Enter and be alert for the smell of LP gas. Gas appliances and connections are subjected to stresses in travel not experienced when permanently stationary. Connections can develop leaks and precautions with LP gas require little effort, so take them.

Anchor Equipment and Appliances

It is unlikely that your heavy appliances are anchored well enough to stay put in the event of an accident. Check them out and do your best to anchor them in such a way that they will not break loose in a collision. The water tank or tanks may be fairly easily secured. If you have two tanks, fasten them together so that you don't have a round tank to roll around. Then, with cable, see if it's possible to go through the floor and anchor to the frame. You may choose to travel with them empty. When it comes to anchoring your refrigerator and stove, you probably have a real problem. I'll not make any suggestions how to anchor them here. However, when these heavy appliances break loose in an accident, take my word that they add considerably to the mayhem.

There's probably little you can do with your dinette table, other than travel with it folded against the wall so that it doesn't become a projectile in the event of an accident.

Manufacturers are not required to give weight limitations for the overhead cabinets—therefore, do not keep heavy items in the overhead cabinets. Try to determine how strong they are and how likely they are to rip off with their load, in the event of an accident. I have seen cabinets over the galley area completely loaded with canned goods. The more weight, the more inertia force that can tear the cabinets loose and allow the heavy objects to become projectiles.

You probably got one small jack with your motor home. To safely change a tire, I would recommend two good jacks. Perhaps you can sell your jack back to the dealer if it is not adequate. One thing is certain, do not drive with a flat tire.

You may have dual rear wheels, but a flat tire flexes and generates tremendous heat. They have been known to burst into flames and to cause devastating fires.

If you have a motor home built on a 104-inch wheel base and it is 17 or 18 feet long by 9 or 10 feet high, you will probably have a tiger by the tail when driving in a strong wind. About all you can do is drive slow, or not drive at all while the wind is blowing hard. I feel that this wheelbase, with a motor home that is perhaps 10 feet high and 17 or 18 feet long, is a hazard on the highways. If you have driven such a motor home and experienced severe buffeting and control problems, I recommend you write the National Highway Traffic Safety Administration and inform them of the type of motor home and type of chassis.

Don't Overload

Determine whether or not your chassis is overloaded. Motor homes have been built that left the factory exceeding the Gross Vehicle Weight. Unload your motor home completely, water and all, and drive it to a truck scale. This may be at a grain elevator or highway weigh station. Weigh the motor home and, if it exceeds the GVW, notify the N.H.T.S.A. Be especially sure to notify them if the motor home has any handling characteristics that make it difficult to drive.

For example, some motor homes have been loaded with far too much weight on one side. It is a good idea to weigh the four different wheel points, if possible. In this way, you can determine the balance of wheel loads. Overloading can cause driving problems and also shorten the life of your motor home. No decision has been made yet regarding the manufacturers responsibility for overloading and its detrimental effects. More information is needed and you can get this information to the proper people.

Have members of your family or guests been cracking their heads on some protruding object? At times to cram the most into limited living space, designers engineer automatic accidents. At other times, the reason is the maximization of sales and profits. To limit pain and suffering and avoid lawsuits, try to rectify, or at least pad these objects. For example, overhead cabinet doors may not hold securely if they are the type that lift up to the ceiling. These are still preferable to overhead doors that swing out into the living area. You can remount such doors with hinges at the top and with adequate catches. It may save someone's skull when they raise their heads.

Round off sharp corners and remove handles and other hardware that can cut or catch and tear flesh. Some overhead ovens have handles similar to steer horns that are at eye level. If you fall against them, serious injury is almost certain.

Pulling a Trailer

With their tremendous overhang and load factor, some motor homes should never pull a trailer. If you plan to pull a trailer check that hitch. It should be solid with no play. Some factory trailer hitches do wag. I once saw a light trailer wear out the bolt of a hitchball and break loose. The so-called safety chains held for just two jerks and then the 700-pound trailer passed the braking motor home. Get a heavy chain for a safety chain, as it will have to withstand sudden severe stress. Small safety chains are inadequate. Further, some safety chain attachment loops are inadequate.

Check everything out and see that your motor home is as safe as you can make it. Let the manufacturer and National Highway Traffic Safety Administration know about design and manufacture defects that affect highway safety. When you go on a holiday with your family, an unnecessary accident should not be even a remote possibility.

CAMPING IN MANITOBA

LEISURE WHEELS

From provincial parks such as Grand Beach on the eastern shore of Lake Winnipeg, there are many activities to be enjoyed in Manitoba, like a fishing trip on the lake for ardent anglers or a twilight boat ride with friends.

by IRVIN KROEKER

MANITOBA camping runs the gamut from wilderness living to exploration out of campsites on the fringes of cities. In a province with more than 100,000 lakes, many of them in the northland but still accessible by car, others man-made for the urbanite's convenience, the opportunities for outdoor living are endless, no matter which way you look at it. If you and your group are loners requiring solitude for your enjoyment, you can set up camp in places where your only contact with civilization is the park ranger. If, on the other hand, you are the gregarious sort with a yen for an even mixture of sophisticated entertainment at night and ham and eggs fried over an open fire next morning, you can establish headquarters just outside Winnipeg, Manitoba's capital city.

The Manitoba Government operates a provincial park system in which close to 5,000 public campsites are maintained. Another 5,000 privately owned sites are located throughout the province.

The total area of Manitoba covers 251,000 square miles, a vast rectangularly shaped region stretching from the 49th parallel, the northern border of Minnesota and North Dakota 800 miles north to the 60th parallel where the North-

west Territories begin. The width of the province at its southern base is 300 miles, but beginning at the 53rd parallel, it widens to meet Hudson Bay, its northern shoreline resembling Alfred Hitchcock's profile as viewed from 1,000 miles above the earth's surface. The southern portion of the province is interlaced with a network of roads based on 19th century surveys when the prairies were neatly divided into mile-square sections, and it is in the south that most of the campsites can be found, many of them near towns, others halfway between, still others beside the lakes that dot the countryside, especially the Interlake region between Lake Winnipeg on the east and Lakes Manitoba and Winnipegosis on the west.

Travel north past the 53rd parallel, and the farmland disappears giving way to mile after mile of forest, hilly ranges and more lakes. It's north of 53 where you begin feeling the vastness and richness of God's country, far away from the madding crowd.

Drive up Manitoba Highway 10 toward The Pas or Flin Flon and Thompson then stop the car and listen. The silence hits you like a thunderbolt—no traffic, no planes overhead and no whine of industrial machinery, just solitude. Listen

For campers who prefer the northland and the solitude it offers, there is comfort in the knowledge that even though the nearest town is miles away, the park ranger is constantly nearby.

longer. Linger awhile and the silence gives way to the cacaphony of the forest, the cry of a loon from the shore of a lake you didn't know was there beyond the trees or maybe the mating call of a bull moose. Closer by, you hear the twitterings and chatterings of a thousand songbirds in the birches and the poplars. You may even see a black bear wander across the road in the distance, although this animal is a shy forest creature and stays hidden as much as he can. Don't rush away. Stay long enough to experience that feeling of northern loneliness. Maybe dusk is setting in. Listen to the frogs croaking in the marsh on the other side of the road, a raucous symphony of discordant sounds from a multitude of hoarse throats, yet in harmony with the world of wildlife, a microcosm of the universe.

But don't let the northland fool you. It can be as vicious as it is beautiful. Anyone who ventures into the wilderness must carry with him the right attitude and the right equipment. Take proper precautions to meet the wilderness on its own terms and you'll be safer than dodging traffic in your home town.

You're in for a delightful vacation when you start thinking Manitoba. Questions at the international border will be minimal unless you look suspicious and you may take all the equipment you need. Firearms must be declared and sidearms are not allowed anywhere in Canada.

Once you're in Manitoba, stop at a tourist information center to pick up literature about the province and maps of the areas you plan to visit. The one book you should make a point of getting is the *Manitoba Vacation Handbook*, which lists all campgrounds in the province, gives a brief history of each and every town or geographically unique area, and contains a complete list of phone numbers and contacts for all types of facilities and emergencies. It gives detailed descriptions of topography and terrain in all Manitoba's parks. It tells you, for example, that Duck Mountain Park is in the heart of the province's finest spruce forest country and that Mt. Baldy, Manitoba's highest point, is in the Duck Mountain range.

There are other parks far away from the cities. Asessippi Park, built in 1970 as a centennial project to commemorate the 1870 union of Manitoba with the Dominion of Canada provides year-round entertainment for outdoor enthusiasts —swimming, hiking, canoeing, skiing, fishing and of course, camping in well maintained sites.

There's the Turtle Mountain range with all conveniences located at the International Peace Garden on the Canada-United States border between Manitoba's community Boissevain and Bottineau, North Dakota.

Riding Mountain National Park, rated as one of Canada's best, has literally everything the outdoor vacationer could hope for. In Wasagaming, hub of activities in the park, you can camp in some of Canada's most modern grounds or

Family Camping in Manitoba's vast vacation country, is made easier and more pleasant with convenient government campsites located in all parts of the province. Uncrowded camping spots may still be found here where forests and streams are unspoiled.

Campsites can be found in many locations, some of them in picturesque settings on the shorelines of Manitoba's 100,000 lakes.

For campers who like an even mixture of sophisticated entertainment at night and breakfast cooked over an open fire next morning, Birds Hill Provincial Park just 15 miles north of Winnipeg on Manitoba Highway 59 offers the best in camping facilities.

venture out into the hills where facilities are more primitive.

In central Manitoba, there are numerous well-developed parks around Winnipeg. Grand Beach Provincial Park on the eastern shore of Lake Winnipeg is popular for sun worshippers and Birds Hill Provincial Park, only 15 miles north of Winnipeg on Manitoba Highway 59, offers horseback riding in addition to all other facilities campers need. Spruce Woods Provincial Park near Carberry is near a geologically unique area where sand dunes rise high above the treetops of the surrounding forest.

In eastern Manitoba, Whiteshell Provincial Park is one of the most highly developed vacation areas in the province offering a series of well planned nature trails and wildlife sanctuaries. Facilities range from modern motor hotels to camping areas beside lakes within the park.

The northland offers several provincial parks—Grass River with its rugged terrain which challenges every outdoorsman, be he a hunter, an angler or a canoeist. Not far away is Clearwater Park with its crystal clear blue lakes, a cameraman and fisherman's paradise.

Wildlife abounds throughout the province. If you plan to stay in the southern half, you will see an abundance of waterfowl—mallards and pintails, teal and wood ducks, Canada geese and canvasbacks. Go into the Interlake Region and you may find white-tailed deer, moose, black bear and farther north, woodland caribou. Upland fowl also range throughout the province—Hungarian partridge, ring-necked pheasant, prairie chicken, snipe and coots.

Fishing in Manitoba is tops with northern pike and lake trout the most popular species. You can catch some real lunkers in Manitoba's northern lakes. Last year at the annual Trout Festival in Flin Flon, the winning pike weighed 26 pounds and the biggest trout tipped the scales at 34. If catching fish like that isn't angling at its best, nothing will ever be.

For those interested in history, Manitoba offers a wealth of places to see—from completely restored Lower Fort Garry near Selkirk, where Scottish settlers established roots, to cairns throughout the province commemorating the arrival of pioneers from almost every European country.

The camping season in Manitoba runs from May through September and fees are set to fit family budgets. Daily entry into provincial parks is $1 or $5 for the season. Camping fees vary, ranging from $1.50 per day to $15 per week, depending on the type of campsite you choose. The parks and campsites are well marked along Manitoba's highways with triangular green and white signs. The *Manitoba Vacation Handbook,* available by writing to the Tourist Branch, 408 Norquay Building, Winnipeg, Manitoba, lists all facilities in each location.

Campers are a varied lot, some wanting to get away from it all, others preferring sites near urban centers close to entertainment, but their common denominator is that they are independent and budget conscious, wanting to do things for themselves. Whatever your perspective, there are places to suit your needs in Manitoba where the people are friendly and the facilities are great, where wildlife abounds and the air you breathe is fresh and invigorating.

PLANNING THAT CAMPING FISHING TRIP

The camper planning to fish in the
Southeast or Midwest should carry
the proper tackle for bass and
panfish—in other words light
spinning or casting gear.

by DICK KOTIS

SO YOU'RE going to take the kids and mommy on a first camping trip into new fishing country. That decision on what fishing tackle and allied equipment to take can become a headache.

Here are some suggestions which may help. To make it simple let's presume there will be two youngsters and two adults. Whether you will camp in a motorhome, trailer, truck camper, lodge, cabin, or tent, the basic fishing equipment will remain pretty much the same.

There are many different kinds of fishing available in the U.S. The type you will find will be pretty well determined by the part of the U.S. into which your camping travels take you.

The following three U.S. geographical divisions, the types of fish available and the equipment necessary to catch them

should enable your family to have fishing fun and eat fresh-caught fish at least once a day.

The U.S. Midwest, Southeast and Southwest

This area is primarily bluegill, crappie, bass and catfish country. Here natural lakes, reservoirs, rivers and ponds offer either free fishing or fee fishing and most campgrounds have access to fishing water. Fishing licenses are required on all public waters except salt water in most states. Better check on licenses locally.

For this area the family foursome should probably take two medium spin-casting rods and reels, one medium spinning rod and reel, one bait-casting rod and reel and at least one take-down type bamboo or fiberglass still-fishing pole equipped with line, bobber, sinker, and hook. Eight-

A three- or four-piece pack flyrod is the ticket for a backpacker to tote anywhere.

The boat camper will certainly encounter a variety of angling opportunities and should routinely carry along a variety of tackle and lures.

to 10-pound test monofilament line is adequate for all of the above equipment. If all else should fail, cane-pole still fishing with crickets, worms, grasshoppers or minnows should put meat in the frying pan. It is also an excellent outfit for young beginner fishermen.

Fishing from a boat in this area is most productive although shore fishing can also be a lot of fun especially if the kids are young and inclined to become restless.

A fish stringer or even better, a portable icebox will keep your catch fresh for the frying pan. A good sharp filleting knife and some sort of light cutting board back at camp will make fish cleaning much easier.

Probably here, as in any type of fishing, the best way to stock up on productive artificial lures and or natural live bait is to inquire at the nearest bait shop or tackle store as to what and where the fish are hitting best. I have found many fishing hotspots by acting on a tip from near-the-scene tackle store operators.

If the family transportation can handle a car-top boat and light motor—great. If not, rental boats and motors are usually available at most of the larger lakes in this area.

Mountain Country—West and Northeast

These areas are best known for trout fishing in both river and high country lakes.

My choice of fishing tackle for a family of four would consist of two light spinning outfits, one spin-casting rig and one flyrod.

For lures, a selection of small spinners and spoons and a casting bubble from which is hung a trailing fly or live bait will all work nicely on the spinning and spin-casting outfits. A selection of flies recommended by the area bait shop should take all the trout the gang can eat on the flyrod. Light monofilament lines in the four- to six-pound class are best for trout.

Other must items, if serious fishing is on the program, would be armpit waders or hip boots.

Remember that if all of the delectable flavor of any species of fish is to be enjoyed, the fish must be handled carefully.

Trout should not be strung on a stringer and permitted to die slowly. They should be tapped on the head with a stick or knife, then the entrails removed along with the gills. Wipe the inside of the trout with dry grass or leaves and pop the cleaned fish into a portable ice chest. Do not place the fish directly on the ice cubes or block. Place them in a plastic bag and close the bag to keep out moisture. Keep them cold and your evening fish fry or broil will be a thing to remember.

The plastic bags and small portable ice chest combination make the best method of keeping any fish fresh whether caught in fresh or salt water.

If the trout don't seem to like your artificial lures try digging a few worms or catching grasshoppers, small crayfish, or hellgrammites. Drift these natural trout baits through a deep hole and brace yourself. A small sinker and single hook hung a few feet under a casting bobber will make the spinning and spin-casting outfits deadly trout takers when one of the above natural baits is pinned on the small hook.

Of course a sharp, thin-bladed knife and cutting board are just as essential for mountain fishing as when fishing for warm water species.

Coastal Salt Water

These areas probably afford more varieties and more fish than any other U.S. waters. There are many ways to

America's seacoasts are especially good places both for fishing and camping. Why not take advantage of the splendid combination?

fish salt water such as bottom fishing from fishing piers and bridges, small boat fishing in bays and inlets, and deep sea fishing from charter boats.

For tackle: two medium spinning rigs, one bait casting outfit, and one bridge or boat rod with level wind star-drag salt water reel should keep your family of four happy. A supply of suitable hooks and sinkers for live or cut bait can be picked up at that on-the-scene tackle shop. If you plan to go deep sea fishing the heavy tackle necessary is usually furnished. Fishing piers also have appropriate tackle for rent at reasonable prices.

Other necessary equipment for family tidal water fishing would be the usual filleting knife and cutting board. No stringers should be used to keep fish in the water since a shark or other big predator might gobble your fish along with the stringer. He might even decide to inhale the helpless fish while you are adding another fish to the stringer. This can get pretty exciting or even dangerous.

If your campsite is near one of the hundreds of good pay-play fishing piers located up and down both U.S. coasts you and the family can watch the successful fishermen and copy their methods and baits. Prices on the piers are reasonable. Hundreds of bridges along both coasts afford good fishing for free.

Casting artificial lures at salt water trout, mackerel, bluefish, flounder, bonefish, tarpon, redfish, snook and many other species from your cartop or rental boat in the protected waters of tidal rivers, inland waterways and lagoons can be the most exciting fishing anywhere. These salt water species are savage fighters and usually are eager strikers at

the right lure. Most of them are excellent in the pan.

Surf fishing coastal waters is a specialized sport and special tackle is necessary in order to get your lure or bait far enough to reach the feeding fish. Surf tackle can usually be rented; however, the kids and mommy might need a few days of practice with the heavy rigs.

If you plan to charter an offshore fishing trip the boat's captain will furnish the tackle and show everyone what to do.

A few tips to help you take fish anywhere are: unless you can see what the fish are feeding on, open the first fish you catch and examine the stomach contents. Try to match the natural food on which they are feeding with either natural baits or artificials.

Use sharp hooks and the lightest line which will handle the size fish you are after. A small hook-sharpening stone is very valuable.

Long-nose pliers are a big help in removing hooks especially from toothed fish or catfish. In salt water treat every fish as if they had a mouthful of sharp teeth — most of them do.

No matter where you fish, a landing net is good insurance against losing that big one.

Buy the best tackle you can afford and take reasonable care of it. Reels should be wiped off and oiled each evening. Cut off a few feet of monofilament line at least once a day to prevent a good fish getting away because of frayed or chafed line. This will eventually happen to this section of your line.

May your next camping-fishing trip be a memorable one.

CARAVANING IN CECIL RHODES COUNTRY

by CLIVE WILSON
Editor, *Rhodesian Caravaner*

EDITOR'S NOTE: *More and more nowadays American campers are looking for camping opportunities beyond our own borders and in fact far overseas. There are both problems and rewards for making such a trip. The cost is one important item. So is time. The language barrier is another in some places. But high adventure is usually reward enough.*

Recently we have visited one distant land—Rhodesia, in southern Africa—which is made to order for the globe girdling camper. Here a visitor can rent all of the camping gear (tent, trailer, or camper coach) he needs on arrival—and then drive out into an exciting new world. He can in fact make a wildlife viewing safari to the greatest of all game parks and reserves on excellent paved highways, in security, and without worries about a strange language.

Only one thing is different than at home: any kind of camping vehicle is called a caravan and camping is called caravaning. For more detailed information, maps and rates, write to the Rhodesia National Tourist Board, 535 Fifth Ave., New York, N.Y. 10017.

A GROWING NUMBER of visitors to Rhodesia are opting out of the "jet-age" holiday rush, applying the sound principle that traveling itself is as enjoyable as arriving at a destination.

They are caravaners, who believe with the poet that: "What is this life if, full of care, we have no time to stand and stare." In Rhodesia, particularly, it is not difficult to appreciate the enthusiasm for their particular style of holiday.

Journeying at a relaxed, leisurely pace, they can truly appreciate the beauty that borders most of Rhodesia's roads: the msasa trees in their spring livery, their glossy leaves glowing with reds, browns, olives and varying greens; wide vistas of open plains clothed with tawny grass; and high kopjes of tumbled stones, coloured by bright lichens or the tones of the afternoon sun.

Rhodesia is an ideal country for the caravaner. The climate is temperate, there are none of the strong winds that plague the coastal traveler, and the hills are conspicuous by

Caravaners in Rhodesia can settle in for an enjoyable time at places such as this, the Mare Caravan Park in Inyanga.

their absence, except, of course, in the lovely Eastern Mountains. Even here the wide tarred roads linking the various centres are well constructed and sensibly cambered. Christmas Pass, the gateway to Umtali, is perhaps the steepest pass in the country, and is an impressive double highway, with wide curves, enabling the towing car to maintain a good pulling speed.

Near the top of the pass, on its eastern side, is the Umtali municipal caravan park, with wide views over the town and the surrounding mountains. Here one can unhitch and explore the nearby Vumba Mountains, with their beautiful garden national park. From Umtali a fine scenic highway also leads to the Rhodes-Inyanga National Park.

Despite the high standard of the road system in Rhodesia, caravaners normally, do not wish to travel too far each day. In Rhodesia this is certainly not necessary, for the places of major tourist appeal—the Victoria Falls, Wankie National Park, the Matopos, the Zimbabwe Ruins, Kariba, Salisbury, and the Eastern Highlands—can all be visited in turn without driving over 350 km a day.

And it is not always necessary to travel so far, for there are many smaller national parks and other places of interest in between the most famous attractions.

Wherever one travels the journey is a pleasant one, for Rhodesia's roads are notably free from heavy traffic. A thoughtful Ministry of Roads has also provided signposted lay-bys along main routes, usually under the shade of large trees, where the traveler can pull off the road. Stone tables, benches and braaivleis grates have been erected, and they are ideal spots for an *al fresco* lunch or a short stop for a cool drink.

In Rhodesia the visitor will find a vigorous Rhodesian Caravan Association and local regions of the Caravan Club of Southern Africa. Rallies are held regularly, and the visitor will always be assured of a warm welcome should he wish to join in.

The expansion of caravaning in Rhodesia has been made possible by the country's extensive network of well-engineered tarred roads between tourist centres and cities, and by the numerous caravan parks that have been established.

The steady growth of parks, conveniently spaced along tourist routes, and in almost all national parks, has enhanced the reputation of Rhodesia as a holiday destination for caravaners in central and southern Africa. All the parks have good basic amenities, while some, Bulawayo notably, are positively luxurious.

Situated in the heart of a city park and adjacent to a magnificent swimming pool, Bulawayo's park is one of Southern Africa's finest.

In the mountainous Rhodes-Inyanga National Park the parks are within walking distance of a natural swimming pool, trout streams, a hotel with historical associations with Cecil Rhodes, and an interesting nine-hole golf course.

For caravaners intent on seeing big game that Rhodesia

This is the delightful area of the Kyle Dam impoundment. Nearby is the famous Great Zimbabwe Ruins and Rhodesia's oldest town, Fort Victoria.

Animals That May Be Seen

Vervet Monkey

Waterbuck

In the Rhodesian Parks...

Black Rhino

Lioness'

Baboon

Crocodile

Cheetah

African elephant

Victoria Falls is world-famous and one of the most popular destinations for travelers. Should one tire of the sights of the falls and the wild animals in the area, one may just enjoy the pleasures of the caravan park.

In the Eastern Highlands of Rhodesia is the caravan and camping park of Kyle View Chalets on the shores of Kyle Lake. The Great Zimbabwe Ruins are only 6½ miles away.

Twenty miles from Salisbury, the capital of Rhodesia, lies lake McIlwaine National Park and a caravan park with all modern amenities for the comfort of its visitors. Boats may be hired and there is a fenced game park as well.

possesses, there are three parks in the Wankie National Park alone, each close to a licensed restaurant and general shop. There are also other caravan parks in national parks where there are wild animals present in large numbers, where the visitor is within earshot of the strange cries and sounds of the African night.

At the Victoria Falls, by contrast, all sounds at night are stilled by the constant roaring of the 1,700-meter wide Falls, a short distance from the luxury park.

Kariba, the premier location for exciting angling for the striped tiger-fish, can be reached from Salisbury quickly and conveniently. The journey of 370 kilometers is on full-width, tarred roads.

For the South African caravaner the main entry point is Beitbridge, although a coastal road is now open from Lourenço Marques to Beira in Mozambique, which provides an alternative route, entering Rhodesia at Umtali.

Traffic from Zambia normally enters Rhodesia at Chirundu or Victoria Falls. An interesting alternative route is via Kariba, for it affords the caravaner an opportunity to drive his combination across the 129-meter-high dam wall itself.

From Mozambique one can enter at Nyamapanda from the north, or Umtali from the central part of the country.

Whether bound for the bright lights of the cities, or the beauties of the scenery and the excitement of wild life in the wide-open spaces, the caravaner in Rhodesia is well catered for. Along the route, petrol stations are conveniently situated, and should a mechanical mishap occur, he is never far from help. The Automobile Association is represented in all centres, and their services are available to members from outside Rhodesia.

The first wagon in the train plunges and splashes across Buffalo Creek for an exciting start.

COVERED WAGON CAMPING IN AMERICA'S WEST

by JENNY REID

"ALRIGHT, ROLL!" called the huge wagonmaster.

Slowly and heavily the powerfully muscled team of horses strained forward in their harness. Each drooping strap and rein inched toward the horizontal and finally the first of the great canvas-covered Conestoga wagons moved forward. The second wagon lumbered after the first and at last all the train was on the move. Following the wagons in a loose band were riders on horse back. Some were children; a few were late teenagers with hair about Bill Cody-length and interspersed with the rest were those whose manner and shape bespoke a turn-of-the-century birth date. The entire procession wound along a thin cattle trail and disappeared from view into the spectacular beauty of the Teton Mountains in Wyoming.

A scene from America's past? No, although it does comprise much of the spirit of adventure of that time plus the actual appearance of wagon trains which carried our pioneers westward. This is, in fact, probably the newest way to enjoy the West. Its appeal is so wide-spread that it's bound to be one of the most popular ways for the tourist to camp.

There are many outfitters in Wyoming and one of the best is L.D. Frome of Afton in what is known as Star Valley. L.D. is a veteran in the pack-tripping and trail-riding business and in the past has catered to hunters and fishermen and their families. Frome is also a fairly keen student of American history who spends his spare time exploring the trails used by the first settlers to cross the continent. Recently he combined his two interests—outfitting and history, and Wagons West emerged: covered wagon tours of the West away from the highways, hot-dog stands and neon-studded vulgarities.

The tours were an immediate success which will surprise no one. Most visitors come with the hope of having a physical and even a spiritual meeting with the looming peaks of the Rockies, the masses of wildflowers which make the meadows blotchy with color and perhaps a tentative meeting with a grazing moose in the high country. But it was the fortunate few who could escape the crowded pavements for the wilderness experience. Those with young well-muscled backs and legs can back-pack and those with well-muscled wallets can afford a pack-trip, but until now

Wagons wind slowly upward followed by a loose band on horseback.

most of the rest of the travelers had to forgo what they really came for. Wagons West has changed all that and opened the wilderness to all, regardless of age and including many who must make do with a less than an extravagant budget.

During the winter of '71-'72 while many feet of snow lay on the ground the wagons were built in a barn in Afton, Wyoming according to plans nearly a century old —exactly as the original Conestoga wagons were assembled in Pennsylvania for the first pioneers. The staves for the familiar rounded roof were of hickory and bent by hand. Canvas was cut and carefully fitted to be smooth along the sides and to gather together at the ends. The only modern additions to the structures were steel leaf-springs on the underside and rubber-tired wheels instead of the old wooden type. Both these changes would add to passenger comfort even over rough trails and also permit the wagons to be towed in tandem behind a motorized vehicle when necessary.

Re-creating the wagons was not Frome's main problem as he had anticipated. It was, instead, in securing the proper harness tacking and horse collars! Frome spent many more hours in antique shops and dusty cob-webbed barns than he had intended and even then there was more scouting to be done to find men capable of handling a team of draft horses. Fortunately Frome's knowledge of his Star Valley and its inhabitants yielded several qualified teamsters who are as colorful as their profession.

Undoubtedly the most liked and admired is one Dean Humphreys—a man over six feet four inches in height with huge gnarled hands, a weather-folded face and western boots almost as big as the wagon he drives. Humphreys is the father of nine and in the absence of his own brood on the trail, herds, supervises, socializes, instructs and chastises all—wranglers, adult dudes and partly-growns with a paternal mixture of affection and sternness. I never saw Dean walk away from the camp group alone. Someone always followed—often one of my own kids anxious to learn the mysteries of hobbling, saddling or shoeing—or maybe just to be with him.

A trip by covered wagon is a happy experience as we discovered this July. The mood of adventure which the

At day's end the wagons begin to form the traditional circle. This evening's campsite is Lilly Lake.

pioneers must have felt was there but gone were the uncertainties and dangers which they all faced. The settlers were seeking new lands and a fresh environment and so were we.

My nine year old daughter, Liddy and her brother Charlie, older by three years and my husband and I began our trip with a dozen others in Turpin Meadow. This is along Buffalo Fork of the Snake River not far from Grand Teton National Park. In the summer the Buffalo is generally only a moist path over a wide bed of large glacier-rounded rocks, but this day it was swollen from snows rapidly melting in the high country. The wagons crunched over the cobbled bottom and the horses' shoes struck the rocks without mercy. Those who chose to ride in the wagon were bounced from side to side and those who chose a saddle horse instead splashed excitedly across the mini-torrent on still-strange mounts. It was a grand and exciting beginning.

From there it was a slow, steady climb upward through cool lodgepole pine forests here and there interrupted by open alpine meadows where one variety of wildflowers dominated the terrain and then gradually and imperceptibly gave

Dean Humpherys, the best liked and most admired wagon-master of them all.

Humpherys and author's son, Charlie, discuss the day's events and the mysteries of horseflesh.

Younger members of the group help unsaddle the horses.

Breakfast is a banquet cooked chuck-wagon style.

Hands and guests pitch in with dinner preparations.

way to another. The thin air seemed to carry none of the sun's warmth into the shadows of the towering evergreens so it was always with pleasure we broke into the sunlit areas. Great displays of yellow arrowleaf balsam roots were replaced by the purple of the larkspur and they in turn bowed to the red spikes of Indian paintbrush, the state flower of Wyoming. From certain vantage points the snow-covered tips of the Tetons broke over the tops of the rolling hills in their hazy majesty.

From time to time, as the original occupants of the covered wagons often did, the passengers climbed down from the wagons or the saddle horses to stretch their legs and would hike alongside. It was apparent from the beginning that the younger members of our party preferred the four-footed means of transportation, while their parents selected the four-wheeled variety. Our group included as its youngest a tiny 4-year-old female horseback fanatic named Angie who was traveling with her grandparents, and an unofficial guess is that our oldest was a retired botany professor traveling with a group of four maiden ladies from Louisville. The rest of us ranged between and there seems no way to measure what ages or interests were best served.

Flower-lovers identified nearly 50 varieties with the help of the resident botanist; bird-watchers compiled a lengthy list including a yellow-bellied sapsucker, two species of chickadees, white-crowned sparrows and all were enchanted by a mother coot shepherding her chick into the safety of yellow pond lillies. Her baby was covered with black down and looked as though it had spilled paprika over its head, so red was its halo.

All hands will probably treasure the memory of the evenings on the trail above all others. In the old days the wagons formed a circle in the interests of safety. Today our wagons come to a halt in a ring because it's traditional and maybe too because it seems so fitting to build a campfire in the center. Horses are unhitched, hobbled and fed for the night and the wagons unloaded so preparations for dinner can begin. Guests may help if they want—and the kids invariably do. The horses—both the riding string and the team horses—receive preference over kitchen chores by the younger members especially since these tasks are performed under the personal care of the wagonmaster.

Dinner is cooked chuck wagon style either over an open wood fire or in immense cast-iron Dutch ovens. Frequently everyone benefits when a guest offers to prepare her speciality over the fire—the cooks gladly accept all offered

This wagon, at the edge of Lilly Lake, could be a bedroom for the night. Or the stars could be the ceiling.

help. Breakfast assumes banquet proportions with the aroma of thick-cut bacon and strong coffee drifting through the trees more effective than any bugle call ever was. If there is a drawback to this kind of camping it must be noted with the difficulty toward the end of the trip one has in buckling the belt. It is almost impossible to remember that gluttony is one of the seven deadly sins.

After dinner one of the horse wranglers, or cooks—or anyone at all—produces a guitar. Then the soft cowboy music telling of lost sweethearts and hard times spreads over us all until the long summer day is finally lost to complete darkness. Now and then during the growing dusk a child is carried to bed already asleep in circling arms. One twilight as we camped beside Lilly Lake a deer appeared at its weedy edge to drink. The doe gazed at us around the fire and we watched her as she bent to the water then very slowly melted into the thicket behind.

We had several choices of where we could sleep: in the wagons on long foam-rubber covered benches, in a small tent, or just zipped into a warm bag under the stars. We chose the open air; but slumber comes easily anywhere. The last sounds we heard were of coyotes calling in the distance, the dying crackles of the fire and I half remember my husband saying "the sky is full of shooting stars tonight." Such nights with the cool breeze soft on your cheeks are not soon forgotten.

Not all wagon trips are in the Rockies. While the snows are still piled high in Wyoming and Yellowstone Park still sleeps, spring is breaking on the Utah deserts and winter's small moisture in the soil is coaxing the cactus to bloom. It is here from early April until mid-May that the wagons wind through the beautiful color country—the Escalante area and the lovely area around Lake Powell.

From there, with the West's migrating birds, the wagons

Wagonmaster Humpherys and youngsters ride through sagebrush and wild flower-covered country in northwest Wyoming.

wander northward to spend late spring on the prairies of central Wyoming, mostly to follow in the ruts of the historic Mormon and Oregon trails and the Lander cut-off trail. Beginning in mid-June, the wagons will explore springtime in the lower Rockies. Summer is the time for the Tetons area where we joined, or in the magnificent Wind River country. From April to September the trips coincide with

After dinner all hands gather 'round the campfire to hear tales of unrequited love or hard times in the West sung to the soft music of a guitar.

the best scenery and weather. After the western hunting season it's back to Utah in November and December for further exploration of the canyon country.

Each of the trips is quite flexible allowing passengers to join or leave almost daily. A trip can be of any duration—a few days to a few weeks. The costs are about $30/day per adult and $20/day for children. Reductions are possible for groups or long stays. For more information you can contact L.D. Frome at: Afton, Wyoming 83010.

So, along with country music, ankle-length dresses and hair long enough for the wind to blow, covered wagons are finding favor with modern folk. It just may be almost everyone's best way to camp and discover our wild West—a heritage which belongs to all of us.

A FIRST AID

Far away from home, as here on this Atlantic beach, every camping vehicle should contain a first aid kit. . . .

A CAMP SITE is inherently no more dangerous, perhaps even less so, than your home or back yard. Indeed, it should be safer because among the talents which every good camper should have is a better-than-average knowledge of emergency medical care. The most important piece of first aid equipment is the information packed in the gray matter that lies between your ears. First aid is perhaps not a good term because it does not necessarily indicate that the *first aid* given is the correct aid. A good rule of thumb is to do nothing unless you are sure that what you do is correct.

The camper first aid kit is designed for the immediate care of the usual hazards of outdoor activity, recognizing the fact that the major difference between camp and home is the length of time it might take to reach a doctor's office or hospital emergency room.

There are only two true life-threatening emergencies:

(1) cessation of breathing, and (2) massive bleeding. Responses to these should be immediate and nearly automatic. Literally, seconds count. This is where training comes in. The Heart Saver Program of your local Heart Association has a relatively short training program which gives the basis of mouth-to-mouth resuscitation, helpful for any breathing or circulation emergency. Programs for basic first aid can be obtained from your local Red Cross. Look into both; the knowledge can well be life-saving! And now to the first aid kit itself:

For Minor Injuries

Cotton balls
Liquid soap
70% alcohol
Pre-moistened foil-sealed towelettes.

These items are placed first on the list and lumped together to emphasize the importance of strict cleanli-

KIT FOR YOUR CAMPER

by C. JOSEPH CROSS, M.D.

. . . And campers should now how to use it. In places like this, take precaution against sunburn.

ness in any first aid situation, be it an abrasion, cut, burn, or deep laceration. Clean wounds heal quickly, while dirty wounds end up with a multitude of complications. Soap and water continue to be the most effective cleansing agent, preferably gently and softly applied with cotton balls. Alcohol is the only disinfectant which need be carried—in a tight plastic bottle—and must be used with a good deal of caution. The foil-sealed towelettes are useful for cleaning the area around the wound but should not be used in the wound itself.

Band-Aids, assorted sizes
Sterile gauze squares, assorted sizes
Gauze roller bandages, 1" and 2" rolls
Adhesive tape, ½" and 1" rolls

Band-Aids are by far the most practical dressing for minor cuts and scrapes and are best packed in the container in which they were purchased. Sterile gauze squares are the basis of most dressings, to be placed over the cleansed wound and held in place by roller bandages. They are provided in various sizes; 2"x2", 3"x3" and 4"x4", and are individually packed in sterile packets. The 1" and 2" bandage rolls are adequate for any first aid emergency. Remember to carefully rewrap the rest of the roll after use. Adhesive tape comes in a variety of forms. Waterproof tape is best, and the usual metal container is more bother than it is worth. Simple rolls, well protected in small plastic bags, serve best.

For Major Injuries

Compression bandages, 2", 3" and large.
"Butterfly" bandages
Elastic ACE bandage

In deep cuts, the bright red spurting of arterial bleeding and the duller red flow of venous blood are both stopped the same way — pressure over the wound hard enough and long enough to stop the bleeding. Pre-packed sterile compression bandages are the preferred method, but in an emergency, a clean handkerchief, shirt-tail, T-shirt or any other absorbent cloth will do, pressed firmly over the injury by the palm of the hand. If possible, the involved part should be elevated. Again, the principle of cleanliness should be followed as strictly as possible.

Suturing should be left to the physician; it is not a part of emergency medical care. However, in certain circumstances the wound edges may be approximated and held together by "butterfly" bandages, also pre-packed and sterile. In general, these do little more than hold dirt in the wound and are usually unnecessary.

Sprains and strains may result from many camp site activities and can usually be treated on the spot. The initial application of cold, either from immersing the site in a bucket of ice water or covering it with cold cloths, will prevent immediate swelling. An elastic ACE bandage wrapped in a figure-of-eight twist from the ball of the foot to a couple of inches above the ankle will provide more stability, and a crutch—or at least a cane—can be improvised from surrounding timber.

Triangular bandages
Splints

For the more serious injuries of dislocations or fractures, fortunately rare occurrences, there are a few points to remember. Under no circumstances should an attempt be made to reduce a fracture or dislocation at the site unless skilled orthopedic help is at hand. Immobilization of the part is mandatory, and if there is any doubt as to the presence of a fracture, "splint 'em where they lie," and quickly transport to the nearest medical facility. Avoid any unnecessary movement of the part, and use infinite gentleness and care in handling. Finger splints can be devised from tongue blades. It is possible, but perhaps impractial, to carry the larger inflatable splints which can be obtained from medical supply houses.

The use of the triangular bandage for immobilization of the upper extremity is important for the initial treatment of many conditions, including fractures, dislocations, severe sprains, infections and burns. A triangular bandage can be purchased at the drug store or home made by cutting a 40 inch square section of unbleached muslin or sheeting, and folding it on the bias. In applying it, remember that the apex should point beyond the elbow on the injured side. One end of the bandage should extend over the shoulder on the uninjured side. The arm is rested on the bandage bent at slightly more than a right angle and the lower end of the sling is brought over the shoulder of the involved side and tied behind the neck. Bring the apex forward around the elbow and fasten with a safety pin or strip of tape. Remember the sling tends to sag and will need occasional retying.

Equipment

Bandage scissors
Thermometer
Pencil flashlight
Safety pins, assorted sizes
Needles
Tweezers
Snake bite kit
Mole skin for blisters
Chemical ice pack

The purpose of most of the above items is self-evident and needs no further explanation. A fine sterilized needle is much more effective for removing splinters than tweezers, as the latter have a tendency to leave residual material behind.

Snake Bite Kit

A few words might be said regarding the snake bite kit. This is an important, perhaps life-saving, small unit for anyone who is planning a camping trip in an area where exposure to poisonous snakes is a possibility, and this covers a surprisingly large number of states.

Familiarize yourself with the contents so that there will be little wasted time should the occasion arise.

Remember:

(1) Be sure the snake is really poisonous, and be sure the fangs have actually penetrated the skin. Don't panic and don't allow the victim to panic. Kill the snake if possible to permit accurate identification.

(2) Apply a constricting band—I purposely avoid the term tourniquet—two to three inches above the bite. Keep it above the swelling. The band should be loose enough so that a finger can be easily inserted beneath it.

(3) The fang marks and the surrounding area should be sterilized and the sterile scalpel blade contained in the kit used to make two short longitudinal incisions deep enough to go through the skin and underlying tissues, but not involving underlying muscles, tendons or nerves.

(4) Gently suction, using the suction cup in the kit, or using the mouth (although there is a good chance of introducing infection by this method), or even by gently squeezing the area between the fingers.

(5) Get the victim to a doctor or hospital emergency room as quickly as possible, always avoiding undue exertion. Antivenom is the ultimate treatment of choice.

The Medical Kit

A medical kit is a very personal thing, and any special medical requirements should be reviewed with your personal physician. There are, however, a number of problems which are not serious enough to require prompt skilled medical attention which might ruin a day during your always too short vacation. For many years, I have prepared a small travel kit for my patients which has proven highly successful. Since some of these items are dispensed by prescription only, it will be necessary to check with your doctor for your proper dosage schedules. Because of reasons of individual allergies or personal preferences, he may desire to make some changes. I have attempted to keep it relatively compact, to use only tablets or capsules (fluid medications invariably leak into a sticky mess), and to anticipate most of the minor camping or travel medical disabilities.

For Pain

Aspirin—This venerable standby of the home medical kit is the same for the camp kit. Aspirin remains one of the most effective pain relievers ever discovered and is used for many reasons, from the sore muscles caused by unaccustomed exertion to the dull aches caused by infection or colds. If children are along, carry both the adult 5-grain size and the children's size.

Codeine—For the more severe pains which are not responsive to aspirin, a stronger medication may be necessary, as for a broken bone on the way to the hospital or an unusually painful sprain. Only a few need be included, as any discomfort requiring very many of these tablets should be promptly attended by a physician.

Stronger narcotics and injectable pain medications have no place in the first aid kit.

For Diarrhea

Lomotil—Changes in water, changes in diet (and quality of cooking), excitement and many other factors can and do often produce an unstable intestinal tract with the very annoying symptom of diarrhea. Lomotil is a tiny but potent tablet that in doses of 2, four times a day, will stop all but the highly infectious diarrheas.

The odds are stacked heavily against even seeing a poisonous snake anywhere in America. But especially when camping in the Southwest, carry along a snake bite kit and know how to use it.

For Nausea and Vomiting

Compazine—The stirred-up intestinal tract may decide to activate the other end of the body, and episodes of nausea and vomiting can yield some very uncomfortable hours. Compazine, again in a tablet form, is an effective anti-nausea agent and has an additional calming effect.

For Heartburn and Indigestion

Gelusil—The same factors which may promote nausea and diarrhea may cause a deep burning sensation in the pit of the stomach. Gelusil is an effective antacid (there are numerous others) which will often bring prompt relief.

Donnatal—Some of the discomfort in these cases is due to spasm of the smooth muscles of the intestinal tract. Again, there are many different types of antispasmodics, but my preference is Donnatal.

For Constipation

Milk of Magnesia Tablets—A simple over-the-counter remedy which will handle most problems of this nature.

Dulcolax—When a stronger laxative is required, this prescription item is practically guaranteed to do the job.

For Colds and Infections

Ornade—A case of the sniffles or congested head can dull an otherwise bright day, and a decongestant such as Ornade will often speed recovery.

Tetracycline—For more serious infections, such as a sore throat, acute sinus infections, earache or bronchitis, it is handy to have an effective antibiotic along. Obviously, any condition which does not promptly respond should be checked by a physician.

For Insomnia

Seconal—Inability to sleep is usually the least of the problems after a day in camp, but strange nighttime sounds, exciting days and strange beds may cause restless nights. A fast acting sleeping pill such as the one carried by the astronauts may smooth out the evening's rest.

For the Skin

One of the most vulnerable areas of the anatomy for anyone who ventures away from civilization is the skin. Unused to ultraviolet rays, strange plants, small mites and other irritants, it is likely to burn, itch, break out in a variety of rashes or even blister with very little provocation. Most of these occurrences are minor, and the discomfort can be readily overcome by a few medications.

A Mild Anesthetic Ointment—This is helpful for mild burns, both from sun, fire or hot utensils, for the discomfort of insect bites or stings and for uncomfortable abrasions. The usual ingredient is one of the ". . . . caine" drugs (local anesthetics) and your druggist can pick one for you from the many that line his shelves.

A Triple Antibiotic Ointment—Occasionally an abrasion or small cut can become secondarily infected, and an ointment containing an antibiotic may be helpful. The triple antibiotics can be dispensed without a prescription, but your physician may have some favorites of his own. Remember, there is a hazard in developing an allergic reaction and all antibiotics must be used with a great deal of caution.

A Sunburn Cream—This is included for obvious reasons and everyone probably has his own preferences. For anyone who is unusually sensitive to sunlight, a sun screen lotion or ointment should be carried.

A Cortisone Spray—A handy pre-packed aerosol medication which is effective for nettle stings or any skin problem which produces intense itching. This is a prescription item which must be approved by your doctor.

CAMP SAVVY ON THE SONORA COAST

by JIM TALLON

Within one-hundred yards of our camp, Jim Tallon and Swede Larsen show off an evening's catch of sea trout and an eight-pound red snapper.

THIS IS JUST an educated guess, but I'll bet that the wind was blowing between 40 and 50 knots. Amid its banshee howl and the booming of the surf, two figures looking like contenders for Rod Serling's "Night Gallery" rocked back and forth in the black Mexican night, apparently in some strange rite. A faint light glowing on the ground between them added eeriness to the scene. Boris Karloff and Lon Chaney? No. Just Frank Johnson and Jim Tallon pounding tent pegs into the ground by the yellow light of a tiny, two-cell backpacker's flashlight. With the pegs now deep, I crawled inside the flapping, old-style umbrella tent and raised the center-pole. It was like opening a sail. Tent-pegs on the up-wind side popped out faster than corks during Prohibition. The tent nearly blew upside down and I clawed like a cat to find the door and get out; Frank hung onto a corner. It started to rain and the whole picture took on the appearance of a Mack Sennett slapstick comedy.

At this point, a sensible person might have stuffed the tent back into his vehicle and driven into town to rent a nice, dry, windless room in a hotel or motel. But town was 65 miles away, 45 of them over primitive desert roads. Too, I hadn't been accused of being sensible for awhile.

As an alternative, Frank and I and our wives could have huddled for the night in the small confines of our pick-up-truck camper shell which really slept only two. Instead, Frank and I tied the tent to the bumper of the pick-up to

keep it from blowing into the nearby estuary, crawled into the camper shell long enough to toast the wild night with a straight shot of dark, Mexican rum, chuckled at the situation in general, then went back out into the wind and rain, moved the tent to a new site and drove the pegs into the ground with a renewed vigor. But this time, *before* we raised the center-pole, we stacked heavy gear such as ice-boxes, dufflebags, and grub boxes along the outer perimeters of the inside of the tent. When the pole went up, the tent contorted like a ghost with a belly-ache, but stayed put. Vicki and I moved in it; we felt it the polite thing to do. Frank and Diane Johnson were our guests and unused to sleeping in a quiet tent let alone one that twisted in misery. Up until about two in the morning, before the storm seriously attacked our canvas quarters with its pluvian lances and opened up a hole in the roof the size of a lead pencil, I didn't envy the Johnsons. Cold water streamed in my face. But we solved that minor emergency by pushing a two-inch-long piece of ⅜-inch cotton rope through the hole. The next time I awakened, the sun had split grey clouds on the eastern horizon with a bright orange smile. The sky overhead, and from the direction of the prevailing winds, to the southwest, was clear.

We were camped at Lobos, Sonora, on a sand-packed finger of lava that juts out into the Gulf of California. For the past 10 years we have been camping on this particular stretch of Mexican coastline and we are conditioned to meet its demands. For us, camping is a means to an end, and the end in this case is fishing. Some of the finest fish-

◀ Mexican gillnetters patrol the Sonora coast for surf species.

Frank Johnson with sharks caught at Lobos on the Sonora coast. Lemon sharks this size are potentially dangerous to man.

ing in the world can be had on the coast of Sonora, but without the ability to deal with a primitive environment, the whole outdoor experience may flop. The single, most important element in successful camping and fishing along the remote Sonoran coast is being self-sufficient.

The Sonora coast remains one of the last Edens for the outdoorsman who likes his camping and fishing on the pristine side. The part I'm referring to lies between the mouth of the Colorado River on the north and Guaymas, a city of 35,000, on the south. The two are separated by over 400 miles of mostly golden sand beaches. In the upper section lies the little city of Puerto Penasco with a

population of about 10,000. Guaymas, including San Carlos Bay and Puerto Penasco, including the gringo fishing village of Cholla Bay are the only "high-density" population centers on the Sonoran coast. Puerto Penasco, Guaymas, Cholla Bay and San Carlos Bay: we love them. Some of our best times ever were had fishing and socializing with the folks of these cities. But we like our socializing split with a healthy balance of unpeopled situations and that desire usually puts us in the seascapes around the tiny fishing villages of Puerto de Lobos and Libertad, a length of shoreline about 50 miles long. I'll venture to say that the population of Lobos is about 30 and Libertad gets an estimate of 50. There are no hotels, motels, restaurants, grocery stores, tackle shops, hospitals or mechanics. But we "survive" without them and try to exercise enough caution that we don't need medical aid. However we do have to dip into our first aid kit to administer to minor cuts and bruises.

Camping on the Sonora coast is hinged directly to the fresh water supply. You'll need it for drinking and cooking of course, and maybe to soak a handkerchief to put on your head during a hot day; and perhaps some for your radiator, since putting salt water in it would finish it. And for rinsing off yourself and pots and pans. I say "rinsing" because we extend our water supply by washing pots and pans in saltwater then rinsing them in fresh water. We use those new plastic-coated paper plates than can be burned. No dishwashing. We bathe in salt water too, then wipe ourselves off with a rag or sponge soaked in fresh water. It is never poured on. We bring the supply from Arizona; Mexican water—unless bottled, rarely agrees with the gringo constitution. The Lobo villagers must haul their fresh water from Caborca, 65 miles inland. I'm not sure where the Libertadians get theirs but certainly not on the coast. We supplement our water supply with drinks such as beer, "naturally-flavored" fruit drinks, and some soda pop. I dislike carbonated drinks, but we stock a few for friends and my wife. Whatever milk we take along usually goes into cooking.

The Sonora coast is back to back with a desert that has changed little in the past five centuries. In summers you will find temperatures well in excess of 115° while crossing it. On our first mid-summer trip about seven years ago, it was our ample water supply that I credit for helping us to cross that desert. Of course we used some on the inside, but most of it went on the outside. At that time I still owned the pick-up with the shell camper and had made the mistake of not ordering refrigeration when I bought it. In Phoenix, which gets nearly as hot as the Sonora desert, the rule is you order refrigeration first, then have them build a vehicle around it. On that trip everytime we started to melt, we would saturate our shirts and hats with water. This helped to cool us by evaporation. That run brought about the absolute rule that we would never cross the Sonora desert alone. With a second vehicle along you are relatively assured of escape from the blistering heat should your vehicle break down.

After fresh water, I personally feel the next most important item on a trip to Lobos or Libertad is frozen fresh water—ice. Boy, nothing perks me up after a hot and hard day of fishing better than a drink with ice tinkling in it. If we've hung up our rods for the day, that usually means a cocktail, something simple like rum and coke with a lime twist. Some novice campers and fishermen I have teamed up with over the years will open the icebox, *then* start looking for a glass to put ice in. And sometimes the ladies (names on request) will take one item out of the box and leave the lid up until they return for a second item . . . five minutes later. Ice goes in a hurry given this kind of treatment. So, on summer trips to the Sonora coast, I like to supervise the iceboxes to stretch this precious commodity to the end of our stay, and hopefully have enough to ice down the fish for the average nine-hour drive home. The procedure is basically this: (1) everyone gathers at the icebox with his glass; (2) the icebox is quickly opened and ice chipped for the drinks; (3) the icebox is slammed shut; (4) apologize to Harry for slamming it on his fingers. Just kidding a little here, but when it is necessary to get into the icebox, keep it open but a few seconds.

According to past experience it takes about 75 pounds of ice to last four people for five summer days on the Sonora coast. That's block ice mind you; only the inex-

Enroute to Lobos. One of the better stretches of road. The road to Libertad is basically the same.

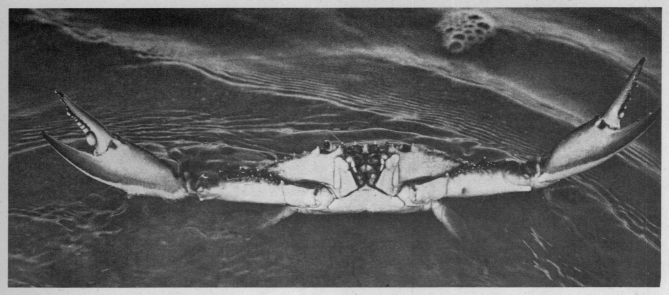

This sand crab latched onto a shark bait and rode it to shore. Now it stands ready to fight all comers, yet it is only about four inches across the back.

perienced camper buys crushed or cube ice for more than an overnight trip. To increase the life expectancy of our ice, we pre-cool or freeze all items intended to go into the box with the ice. Frozen foods are packed around the ice so that the lack of airspace between results in longer life for both.

Seventy-five pounds of ice means two 56-quart ice boxes to hold it. The first box gets a 25-pound block, and the remaining space is jammed with cold supplies. The second box gets two 25-pound blocks, or a 50-pound block if we can find it, and it is stocked with cold stuffs that will not be used until the last day (or days) of the trip. Then they get wrapped in a couple of blankets, or even better, a sleeping bag for additional insulation. Under good conditions, using this trick, I have found as much as 40 of the 50 pounds of ice remaining after six days! However, with this much ice in them, the two boxes will not hold enough cold foods *and* drinks to last four people for five days; additional drinks are kept as cool as possible then put in the number one box when melting ice allows more space. Too,

we generally eat a restaurant meal or two enroute to and from the coast. On longer stays we may take a third box.

The selection of foods and coordinating them to our ice supply is a job now handled by my wife. She does it better than I ever did, but I must constantly interrupt guests complimenting her on this virtue to explain that it was the skilled training she received during our eight years of marriage that lead to it. Anyway, we prefer cuts of meats to ground meats; they stay fresh longer and invariably taste a heck of a lot better. Too, we far prefer frozen or fresh vegetables to the canned or dry varieties, and in essence, our store of the the latter is for emergency use. On occasions we may make a meal out of the "convenience" freeze-dried foods that you can find in any modern supermarket, i. e. skillet dinners. We rarely bake or roast on a camp trip, but Vicki will whip up bisquits from scratch at a moment's notice and I'm not about to complain. I am a salad nut, and we generally have fresh salads on every trip. Vicki prepares all the food except steaks and chops (and frequently fish); that's my bailiwick and I charcoal them on

Brown pelicans are regular residents of the Sonora coast. These shown here rest on a reef north of Guaymas.

a hibachi. I like poking at broiling meats and listening to the surf, seabirds, and tinkling ice. And I've lot of company here.

All this is designed to keep our insides happy, including the spirit. Keeping the outside the same is largely a matter of common sense. Protect yourself from the sun. Wear long sleeves, long pants and a hat. Suntan lotion helps to save the skin too *underneath* your shirt, because the sun's rays will still burn you through lightweight, porous material. Finally, getting a good night's sleep is no less important. All of our campers have had four-inch foam pads or mattresses, and we use the same pillows we use at home. Frankly I sleep better in our camper than I do at home.

Thus far the palaver here has been slanted directly at *how* to camp the Sonoran coast, not *why*. But let me say that it takes far more knowhow to camp in comfort at Liberatad or Lobos than it does to catch fish here. If you have a small boat and the seas are calm, you can run to nearby reefs and tangle with such bottom-dwellers as pintos, cabrillas, sardinaros (all saltwater basses), and dozens of species that even experts may have trouble identifying. A shiny lure, feather jig, or small piece of bait will get you an instant hook up if you're in the right place. If not, just move over a dozen feet and try again. Fish in the 200-pound class are known to swim within 200 yards of Punta Tepoca, the point at Lobos.

With the exception of a couple of diehards in our group, we prefer surf fishing. What is better than fishing from a litter-free, unpeopled stretch of golden sand? However, surf fishing may be interrupted by dry spells. The bait is moving, the game species are moving, your lure is moving and you are moving. When the four of these come together, and very frequently does, WHAMO!, you're really in business.

No one knows how big the fish get in the Sea of Cortez. This 205-pound black sea bass was caught southwest of Puerto Penasco. One-hundred pounders frequent the reefs off Libertad and Lobos.

Jim Tallon with a pair of yellowfin corvina, one nine pounds and the other 11 pounds. This is a hardpulling surf species that gives excellent sport.

At these times you can expect to hook into yellowfin corvina, white sea bass, corbinas, seatrout, bigjaw leatherjackets, an occasional sardinaro, and numerous other surf species. Be prepared for that rare individual fish that may weigh 50-pounds, even though you may not hook him this trip. A serious surf-man on a five-day trip can expect to land a number of surf-fish in the eight-to 15-pound bracket, and always enough to feed everyone on his home block. We return most of our fish, keeping just a few for the skillet or hibachi.

Over the years I've worked out the "perfect" surf tackle for me, and that is an eight-foot, fast-tip, saltwater spin-rod, a medium-size saltwater, open-face spin-reel, and 17-pound test monofiliment. This gives me good distance and I can use it all day without being beat down. The 17-pound test, which may seem a bit heavy to some fishermen, is often frayed down to about one-pound test before I land some fish. My favorite terminal tackle is a one- or one and one-half ounce Eppinger Seadevle in chrome or chrome and blue, with a "Reckless Redhead" streamer tied 18 inches behind the lure. The Seadevle gives excellent distance and can be "swum" over reefs that would gobble up certain other chrome wobblers. The "Reckless Redhead" is my own concoction, tied with a green back, a white belly, a mylar body, and a red head. Any large similar saltwater pattern will probably work fine.

Camping on the Sonora coast and fishing the Gulf of California gets chalked up as our most rewarding outdoor experiences. It gives us an opportunity to re-assert our ability to cope with a rather harsh environment. It puts us back in touch with Nature. It is recreation personified. We always bring home a few fish and maybe have friends over to help us eat them, and recall our fun of catching them. But the biggest reward of all is spiritual.

A Rig for All Seashores

by FRANK WOOLNER

FIRST REQUIREMENT: a motor vehicle designed as a completely mobile home-on-wheels far from paved roads, versatile enough to challenge rough lumber tracks into remote hunting grounds or conquer the sandy wastes of an American seacoast. Specifics: this machine must be spacious enough to sleep at least four adults in comfort, it must be equipped with modern cooking facilities, a refrigerator—and certainly a self-contained toilet. There must be adequate duffel space to ensure self-sufficiency away out in the blue for days on end.

An impossible dream? Only for those who haven't investigated optional equipment and imaginative conversion to fit a need. It is unfortunately true that a majority of America's "camper" vehicles stray off the hardtop at their owners' peril. It doesn't have to be that way, and a mechanized army of eastern salt water anglers offer proof.

On any summer or fall day, from Maine to Cape Hatteras and beyond, home-on-wheels trucks bump out over the dunes, often dragging sizeable trailered boats. Collectively, and it has unfortunately become a generic term, these rigs are called "beach buggies." Actually, they are very far removed from the original small sand vehicle and they are quite as versatile on the hunting grounds as on the sea rim. Such capable machines are the result of ingenious specialization to fill a need, yet most of the modifications add efficiency for use on any ground. The average family camping enthusiast, particularly folk who *really* want to get away from ultra-civilization, should be interested.

Big buggies for salt water angling evolved. Sometime in the early 50's, a few thoughtful types decided that a combination of adequate power, clearance, and proper flotation tires could make almost any motor vehicle a sand traveler. Pilots of ancient Model-A Fords and military Jeeps scoffed at the suggestion, but their eyebrows raised when walk-in trucks not only appeared on the dunes, but seemed to rumble along as unconcernedly as medium tanks. In short order the pick-up truck with coach-camper unit added became quite as popular. For the first time, an entire family could fish together and camp together—comfortably.

Evolution has been pretty rapid, and there is now an assortment of smaller live-ins that function, even though quarters are cramped. These range from the bus-like Volkswagon and Chevy vans, up through carry-all suburbans that can be rigged to take a couple of fishermen, although never so elaborately and spaciously as the true big rig.

Choice of a basic truck for conversion still boils down to walk-in or coach-camper. Each offers debits and credits. New, the coach-camper combination is somewhat less expensive than a factory-built walk-in mobile home, and the owner can always trade his pick-up prime mover for a later model, while keeping the camper unit. This rig, however, is far less spacious than the walk-in—which is probably the finest camp on wheels yet devised.

Don't jump to conclusions. Most of the brand new mobile homes sold to knights of the open road are designed for the highway and not for the boondocks. Many of them feature dual rear wheels: these fail on a soft sand beach and they are not very efficient at anything other than load-carrying on pavement. Nobody seems to have experimented with four-wheel-drive and lots of clearance, plus proper flotation tires for a given discipline. Nobody

but mechanized anglers, that is.

Let's qualify a statement. You *can* get along with two-wheel-drive, and lots of adventurers do. They manage even on soft beach *if* weight is properly distributed, *if* there's plenty of clearance, and *if* the tires are large enough and soft enough. Four-wheel-drive is better and the 4x4 pickup is readily available. All-wheel-drive walk-ins are as scarce as Rhodes scholars in ward politics.

Because mobile home manufacturers haven't the foggiest notion about requirements on a soft beach, and seem psychotically opposed to optional equipment, most of the sea rovers who embrace mechanization buy used bread trucks, and then customize. This type offers lots of usable space and there is a sense of togetherness missing in the coach-camper with its separate cab and box slung aft. Picture-windows, fitted with shatterproof glass, can be installed—and it's a nice feeling to awaken at dawn, climb out of a comfortable bunk and scan the sea.

Since prices are away up there and few walk-ins come equipped with all-wheel-drive, most of the big "bread trucks" now traveling soft beaches are two-wheel-drive. Some are fitted with Positraction, and many feature four-speed transmissions. Their primary secret of success is proper distribution of weight, plus big, mushy tires. For best results, you get most of the weight aft and then mount flotation tires with ordinary road tread. Shoes can be four-ply in a very light machine, say a Volkswagon bus or a carryall, but camper and walk-in weight invariably dictates six- or even eight-ply. They'll be 950x15 at minimum, larger where necessary. Special sand tires are readily available: they're excellent, but far from efficient on paved roads when traveling to or from beaches. The squiggly tread design doesn't adequately grip a road surface, especially when that surface is wet.

Most of the specialists who use motor vehicles on soft sand prefer four-wheel-drive, so a lot of them choose pickups with this option, plus the coach-camper unit. The thing to remember is this—a 4x4 doesn't insure smooth sailing. Innocent citizens entertain the curious notion that if it's four-wheel-drive it will go anywhere. It won't. You can get bogged down in anything from a military Jeep on up to a mechanical dinosaur *unless the tires are of proper size and are properly deflated.*

Take, for example, a Jeep or a Blazer, two very nimble little vehicles. I use the latter, and it is equipped with L78-950x15 high-walled nylon four-ply tires. Sure, I can grind along and make some progress on soft sand with road pressures, but I would be beating the guts out of power plant, clutch and cooling system. I might even get bogged down in soft sand with a rising tide threatening to take the whole expensive little toy out to sea.

It is *always* necessary to deflate in soft sand, and pressures will depend on the consistency of that sand. Drivers may operate at highways levels on Daytona Beach, Florida, but don't try it at Race Point, Provincetown or at Cape Hatteras.

Whatever the vehicle, there will be a tire size that is right for the work. Then, make no mistake, it will be necessary to operate at low air pressure. One never *digs* in sugar—one *tracks* like a tank. Therefore the shoe must mush out. There will be standard pressure for a given area and vehicle weight: even then, there will be nuances, for sand will be harder after a few days of steady rain, and softer after a period of hot sunlight.

It is absolutely impossible to list precise pressures, because there are all sorts of little nasties in the equation—

Pick-up and coach-camper unit (facing page), probably most popular to date. This is a 4x4 with 1100x15 tires.

Coach-camper is favored by a majority of coastal anglers. Boats in the 16-foot range bracket are easy to tow.

like the weight of a given vehicle (which can be changed by the addition of passengers), like the weather and the consistency of sand at a given point. If this sounds rather vague and non-scientific, take heart. Deflate until you track easily. Its as simple as that, and often a couple of pounds of pressure makes all of the difference.

Beginners are always afraid to deflate: they conjure up all sorts of horrible things, like tires disintegrating. As a matter of fact, you're safe so long as the shoe exhibits no crease. When that happens, problems certainly arise—things to do with ruptured fabric and rolled rims. At low beach speeds, heat is no ogre, yet the tire that must be

deflated to crease-level is a poor choice for the vehicle on which it is used. A hand pump is better than nothing, but most beach drivers install air compressors to ensure inflation immediately after leaving the beach.

Always carry an accurate tire pressure gauge, or better —two of them in the event that one is misplaced. If 14 pounds seems adequate, make it an even 14 on front and rear wheels. Sometimes there is a necessity, because of weight distribution, to carry less air in front tires than in rear, but note that matching shoes must be balanced, else the harder tire will dig and impede progress.

Logically, one would think that broad, low profile tires

A big 4x4 rig custom-built for Joe Pol of Woonsocket, Rhode Island.

Rebuilt walk-in trucks are popular, and lots of them feature "bustles" extended aft. Most of the vintage machines, carefully rebuilt by enthusiasts, are two-wheel-drive. Properly balanced, and fitted with flotation tires, they are surprisingly nimble.

would be best on sand. They are not—again due to that necessity to "track." Favor high-walled, limber types that will balloon out and provide the rolligon effect when soft. Also, stick with standard road treads, never knobs or snow tires. While it is true that a "baldie" is best on sand, there's always a necessity to travel the highways from beach to beach. Smooth shoes are illegal in many states: they are also dangerous, particularly on a rain-swept pavement.

Clearance and flotation apply as well on a boat trailer. You can drag a surprisingly big boat if the trailer's wheels and tires are adequate. Where standard 9 to 12 inch running gear guarantees a bog-down, customized 14 or 15 inch wheels and deflated shoes in the 800 to 900 size range track beautifully. Often such wheels have to be custom made, with flanges reversed: any capable local welder can do the job, and it is worth noting that clearance has its benefits on rough lake approaches in the hinterlands.

A beach buggy is designed to be self-sufficient. In other words, you are not going to plug in electricity or water, or any other aid. You'll be out in the blue and either fully operative—or in trouble. Enthusiasts experience no difficulty because they have planned each working unit.

Propane gas powers interior lighting, cooking ranges and refrigerators. Generally, there'll be one 20-gallon tank in service and another in reserve, both racked outside, usually on an extended rear bumper. Power to fuel lights and other creature comforts is taken from the machine's battery only in an emergency. Needless to say, any off-highway buggy boasts a heavy-duty battery which is kept well charged.

Fresh water tanks are either gravity-fed or operate under air pressure—and the latter is favored. Either way, the tank must be big enough to provide lots of aqua-pura over a period of days. Ten gallon capacity is an absolute minimum: 20 is better, and 30 is pretty sure. If there are ladies in the party, figure on greater volume: they use this stuff like it is never-ending. Naturally, if a shower bath is built into a compartment, usage will be tremendous. Problems arise when fastidious girls and teen-aged members of the family forget that fresh water is just as scarce on an ocean beach as it is in Death Valley. Water discipline is necessary, and tanks must be topped off on every trip to the fringes of civilization.

Practically all of the big beach buggies are fitted with

Author Frank Woolner and Jack Townsend with one night's catch of bluefish and striped bass. Four-wheel-drive Wagoneer is used as a "chase car," and as a prime mover for a trailered 16-foot Boston Whaler.

CB radio; indeed it is not unusual for a fishing family to boast three sets. One will be installed at a mobile head-quarters, another in a small 4x4 "chase car," and a third in a trailered surf boat. Perhaps less specialized family campers do not need this aid, but it is comforting to know that CB ensures contact with other roving adventurers, or possibly with the Coast Guard in an emergency.

Transistor radios are almost universal, if only to catch the latest news and weather reports, and there is a trend toward portable TV sets. Somehow it still seems incongruous to spot a coach-camper away out on wild dunes—with a TV antenna sprouting amidships!

Regardless of creature comforts, aids to navigation and all the rest, any vehicle used off the hardtop must carry certain tools. There are no service stations out there; in fact there may not even be a driftwood plank on which to set a jack in the event of need. So, you carry a stout hard-wood plank! That's a minor item, yet sometimes it is a lifesaver.

A functional jack is necessary—not one of those Mickey Mouse affairs that so often is included with a car or truck right out of the showroom. A shovel can be mighty essential and should always be included. Pack a tow chain or a heavy tow rope. Power winches mounted up front are good sense, but are rarely needed on the beach. Check in such valuables as a working fire extinguisher, a basic tool kit, a hand flashlight, and—don't forget those tire gauges.

For back country comfort, all windows and doors of a coach-camper or walk-in should be screened. If there's a breeze on the coast, daytime plagues are unlikely, but sleep may be rendered impossible on a humid summer night when gnats and mosquitoes come charging out of brackish estuaries. It's easy to defeat them with screens and, possibly, with a puff of mist from an aerosol bug bomb before retiring. Beaches, compared to inland lakesites and early hunting grounds, are surprisingly free of bothersome insects—yet there are days and nights of torment when the green-heads attack like waves of miniature stukas, no-see-ums appear in clouds, and mosquitoes exult in a lack of wind.

Obviously, and whenever possible, it is wise for a prospective beach camper to ask the advice of an experienced dune driver. Over-sand operation is a technique in itself, and the beginner's troubles usually stem from a reluctance to deflate tires. There is a further unfortunate tendency to apply power in an effort to "gun out" of a bog-down. It just doesn't work: indeed, any spinning of wheels guarantees that you'll go down like a demented elevator.

First off, if there is a track—stay in it. Such tracks, at the height of a vacation season, are always there and are reasonably hard-packed. All beach drivers "follow the track" until it's time to cramp out of that aboriginal road and park. Of course you can make a new "road," but it's wise to remember that this will be hard on engine, clutch and cooling system. Keep out of dune grass and upland cover. Traction may be feasible, but local authorities and conservationists rightly take a dim view of destruction.

In a bog-down, accepted practice is "to make a track." You do this, not by using the gun, but by a slow process of moving forward a few feet, and then reversing. Gradually, this packs soft sand and you've make a track. If all else fails, if you've been impetuous, there will be a necessity to use shovel and jack. An ordinarily lazy character can get very industrious when the tide is rising.

While dad goes fishing, his family enjoys life on an ocean beach.

The big-rig anglers catch a lot of fish. Jack and Kay Townsend of Shrewsbury, Massachusetts with a haul of striped bass from Cape Cod. The Townsends are famous New England surf casters.

First-timers should be very cautious about running below the high tide mark. A bit of trouble there can escalate into nightmare proportions and even disaster as the merciless sea advances. Moreover, with a heavy vehicle, there is a tendency to side-slip on a slope that runs down to the shingle. Mean high tide always is marked by a definite line of grass, trash and assorted flotsam. Travel well above this line, and always choose a higher elevation for overnight parking.

Mechanized surfmen in most cases are helpful: they'll offer accurate advice about tidal phases and tracks that lead to magnificent vistas. Usually, if there's trouble, whiskery fishermen will pitch in to help with the necessary jacking, shoveling and shoring-up to get a vehicle back on hard sand. This is a defense mechanism because, out in the blue, strangers observe the Golden Rule. Tomorrow, *they* may need help.

Many of the great ocean beaches are now administered by rangers of the U.S. National Seashore. There, permits will be necessary for any overnight stay, and you'll probably be required to have a self-contained vehicle. At Cape Hatteras, North Carolina, there are public campgrounds close to the shore. Cape Cod allows vehicular camping by permit for short periods, in designated areas. Controls are increasing with each passing year, but there are many areas still wild and beautiful where a family can enjoy mechanized camping far from telephones, juke boxes, pizza palaces and traffic. Moreover, the fishing is likely to be good and the sea will be clean.

A pick-up truck and coach-camper unit properly rigged with flotation tires will be equally good on highway or beach. The walk-in is never so versatile in traveling, because it is admittedly big and bulky: on site it is a joy, truly a home on wheels. Those used as living quarters by surf casters are intricately rigged to provide every comfort plus efficiency in operation. Either vehicle can be converted, very swiftly, to serve as an upland or big game hunting headquarters. One simply replaces flotation tires with knobs, carefully maintaining the clearance so necessary in any off-road area.

With a machine so rigged that it can venture out into wild country, as well as move over modern road nets, the camper enjoys a new measure of versatility. There's nothing wrong with plugging in electric lights and attaching a water line in a trailer park or commercial "backwoods" campground, yet it's pretty nice to be independent.

I rather like to drive far out on an open ocean beach in July, out where my only companions are gulls and terns, out where the only contact with near-civilization is another beach buggy or a jet plane tracing contrails across the top of the world.

It's just as pleasant in the fall, in a grouse covert reached by a farm track that would be off-limits to any low-slung standard motor vehicle, or spending the night before a deer season's opening day well up on some lofty ridge reached via a muddy lumberman's tote road.

The big rigs can be versatile. Salt water anglers developed the camp-on-wheels beach buggy to fill a need. They won't mind if you copy salient features in customizing a vehicle that is entirely suited to inland fishing, hunting— or just true family camping far from neon lights and super-highways.

CHOW TIME

REPRINTED FROM KOA HANDBOOK

AVAILABILITY OF QUICK, easy-to-prepare foods has contributed significantly to changing the image of camping —measurably adding to its enjoyment. No longer must activities revolve around a timetable dictated by meal preparation. Whether time is spent actively—sightseeing, hiking, fishing or recreation—or just passively relaxing, there's more time to indulge personal preferences.

Still, many a camper craves the spoon lickin' good, sitdown, family-style meal that often comes on leisurely weekends at home. Take the aproned gent I met in a primitive campground last summer. He was basting a 21 lb. turkey rotating on a battery-powered spit over an open campfire. "Heck," he explained, "we eat better when we're camping, than at home."

Turkey in July may not be every camper's dish, but it proves a point: good eating in the campground doesn't have to be a compromise. Plus, it provides a perfect opportunity for dad to demonstrate his culinary talents. Let him experiment. Outdoor appetites are robust—and often forgiving.

In compiling the following recipes, food companies were invited to share with us their favorite dishes. All have been kitchen tested. Some are simple; others more along the gourmet line.

Whatever your preference we invite you to enjoy them with us, and, perhaps, become familiar with new brands which may become a staple item in your cupboard at home.
The Editors

CAMPERS' SCRAMBLE

1 can (10¾ oz.) Campbell's Cream of Celery, Chicken, or Mushroom Soup
8 eggs, slightly beaten
Dash Pepper
2 tablespoons butter or margarine

In bowl, stir soup until smooth; gradually blend in eggs and pepper. In 10-inch skillet, melt butter; pour in egg mixture. Cook over low heat; do not stir. As mixture begins to set around edges, gently lift cooked portions until eggs are completely set, but still moist (about 8 minutes). Makes 4 servings.

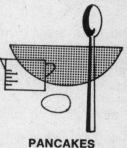

PANCAKES

2 cups Bisquick
½ cup dry milk
1 cup water
1 egg
Margarine
Syrup or jam

Mix Bisquick, dry milk, water and egg; beat with rotary beater or spoon until smooth. Bake on hot, lightly greased griddle, turning when bubbles appear. Serve with margarine and syrup or jam. Makes about 18 four-inch pancakes.

Blueberry Pancakes: Add 2 tablespoons sugar to pancake batter; fold in 1 cup fresh or drained canned blueberries.

Cheese Pancakes: Add 1 cup shredded sharp cheese to pancake batter. Serve with creamed meat or vegetables.

Corn Pancakes: Stir 1 cup drained whole-kernel corn into pancake batter. Serve with honey.

Ham Pancakes: Add 1 cup chopped cooked ham or Canadian bacon to pancake batter.

NOTE: for syrup, use packaged instant syrup; or heat 1½ cups brown sugar (packed) with ½ cup water until sugar is dissolved.

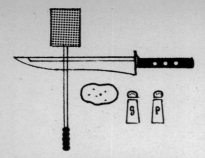

COUNTRY FRIED POTATOES

5 medium size potatoes
¼ cup Mazola Corn Oil
1 teaspoon salt
⅛ teaspoon pepper

Wash peeled potatoes and cut into thin slices. Dry thoroughly with towel. Heat corn oil in large skillet over medium heat. Add potatoes and fry, turning once, about 20 minutes or until browned on both sides. Season with salt and pepper. Makes 4 servings.

PATHFINDER TURKEY & DUMPLINGS

2 cans (19 oz. each) Campbell's Chunky Turkey Soup
1 cup biscuit mix
⅓ cup milk

In saucepan, empty soup; bring to boil. Meanwhile, combine biscuit mix and milk with fork. Drop 5 to 6 spoonfuls in boiling soup. Cook uncovered over low heat 10 minutes. Cover; cook 10 minutes more. Makes 4 servings.

ISLAND TREATS SANDWICHES

½ cup Skippy Peanut Butter
⅓ cup drained crushed pineapple
2 bananas, sliced
8 slices bread or toast

Mix peanut butter and pineapple. Spread on 4 slices of bread, top with banana slices. Top with remaining bread. Makes 4 sandwiches.

Note: Chopped apple may be used instead of pineapple.

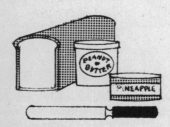

RUSSIAN TEA

1¼ cups (or one 9-Oz. jar) Orange Flavor Tang Instant Breakfast Drink*
½ cup sugar
⅓ cup instant tea**
½ teaspoon cinnamon
¼ teaspoon ground cloves
Dash salt
Boiling water
Ice cubes (optional)

*Or use 2 cans (4⅝ oz. each) Start Instant Breakfast Drink Orange Flavor
**Or use Lemon-flavored unsweetened instant tea or lemon-flavored instant tea with sugar.

To Prepare Russian Tea Mix, combine instant breakfast drink, sugar, instant tea, spices, and salt. Store in tightly covered jar. Makes 2 cups mix.

For each serving hot Russian Tea, place 1 well-rounded teaspoon of mix in a cup. Add boiling water; stir until dissolved. Serve immediately.

For each serving of iced Russian Tea, dissolve 2 well-rounded teaspoons of mix with ¾ cup boiling water. Pour over ice cubes in tall glass.

For 1 quart of hot Russian Tea, combine ⅓ cup of the mix with 1 quart boiling water in a heatproof pitcher or serving bowl. Serve with lemon wedges, if desired.

CREAMY PEANUT BUTTER SOUP

3 cups milk
¾ cup Skippy Creamy Peanut Butter
Dash cayenne, chili powder, Worcestershire sauce or Tabasco sauce

Gradually stir milk into peanut butter in 2-quart saucepan. Cook over low heat until heated. Sprinkle with cayenne, chili powder, Worcestershire sauce or Tabasco sauce. Makes 4 servings.

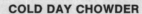

COLD DAY CHOWDER

4 frankfurters, cut in 1-inch pieces
2 tablespoons butter or margarine
1 can (19 oz.) Campbell's Chunky Vegetable Soup

In saucepan, brown frankfurters in butter. Add soup. Heat, stir now and then. Makes about 3 cups.

HOT SWISS'N HAM SANDWICHES

4 split hamburger buns
4 slices cooked ham
4 slices Swiss cheese
1 tablespoon chopped onion
1 tablespoon soft butter or margarine
1 teaspoon prepared mustard
Chipos® snack

Separate buns; arrange cut sides up in broiler pan. Place ham slices on bottom halves of buns and cheese slices on top halves, covering buns completely. Mix onion, butter and mustard; spread over cheese slices. Set oven control at broil and/or 550°. Broil buns about 5 inches away from heat 3 to 5 minutes or until bubbly and light brown. Put top and bottom half of each bun together. Serve immediately with snack. 4 servings.

®Reg. T.M. of General Mills, Inc.

CAMPER'S RICE

1⅓ cup Minute Rice
2 tablespoons Grapefruit Flavor Tang Instant Breakfast Drink
½ teaspoon salt
1 tablespoon butter
1½ cups water

Measure one 18-inch square sheet of heavy duty aluminum foil. Place on top of medium bowl; press down to form pouch. Combine rice, instant breakfast drink, salt, and butter in pouch. Fold foil to seal tightly and remove pouch from bowl. When ready to cook, add water and close pouch tightly. Bring to a boil on grill over hot coals. Move to side of grill and let stand at least 5 minutes. Open foil and fluff rice with a fork before serving. Makes about 2⅔ cups or 4 servings.

ORANGY COLE SLAW

4 cups finely shredded cabbage
1 cup shredded carrots
2 tablespoons Orange Flavor Tang Instant Breakfast Drink
1 tablespoon water
½ teaspoon celery seed
½ teaspoon salt
Dash of pepper
¼ cup salad oil

Combine cabbage and carrots in bowl; set aside. Combine instant breakfast drink, water, celery seed, salt, and pepper in cruet or small jar with tightly fitting cover. Shake until dissolved. Add salad oil and shake again. Pour over cabbage mixture; toss well. Makes about 4 cups or 6 to 8 servings.

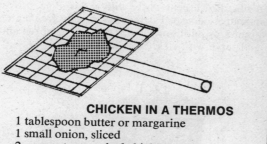

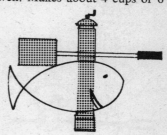

CHICKEN IN A THERMOS

1 tablespoon butter or margarine
1 small onion, sliced
2 cups cut-up cooked chicken
1 can (1 lb.) peeled tomatoes
1 envelope (1¼ oz.) Lipton Beef Flavor Mushroom Mix
1 cup water

In large skillet, melt butter and cook onion until golden. Add chicken, tomatoes, beef flavor mushroom mix, and water. Cook, stirring occasionally, until heated through. Makes about 6 servings. Place in Thermos for a hot meal while fishing or boating.

FISH KENTUCKY

⅓ cup flour
⅓ cup corn meal
1 teaspoon salt
⅛ teaspoon pepper
1 pound fish fillets or cleaned small whole fish
½ cup milk
⅓ cup (about) Mazola Corn Oil

Mix together flour, corn meal, salt and pepper, Dip fish into milk; then roll in flour mixture. In skillet heat 2 to 3 tablespoons corn oil over medium heat. Add fish and fry, turning to brown both sides, 5 to 10 minutes or until easily flaked with fork. Add more corn oil as needed. Drain on absorbent paper. Makes about 4 servings.

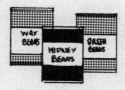

CALICO BEAN SALAD

1 can (16 oz) wax beans, drained
1 can (16 oz) whole green beans, drained
1 can (15¼ oz) red kidney beans, drained
1 small onion, sliced
¼ cup chopped pimento
¾ cup Karo Light Corn Syrup
⅔ cup red wine vinegar
⅓ cup Mazola Corn Oil
1 teaspoon salt
½ teaspoon dill weed

Toss together first 5 ingredients. Mix together remaining ingredients and pour over bean mixture. Toss lightly. Refrigerate overnight. Drain before serving. Makes 8 (¾ cup) servings.

VEGETABLE STROGANOFF DINNER

Prepare Betty Crocker® Hamburger Helper® Potato Stroganoff Dinner as directed on package except—ten minutes before end of cooking, stir in 1 can (16 oz.) mixed vegetables, drained.

®Reg. T.M. of General Mills, Inc.

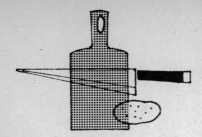

HOT DOG POTATO SALAD

1 cup Hellmann's/Best Foods Real Mayonnaise
¼ cup vinegar
2 tablespoons prepared mustard
1 tablespoon salt
½ teaspoon paprika
2 quarts (about 4 pounds) diced cooked potatoes
1 pound cooked frankfurters, cut into ¾ inch diagonal slices
½ cup chopped celery
½ cup coarsely shredded carrot
½ cup finely chopped green pepper
¼ cup chopped onion
2 tablespoons chopped pimiento

Mix together mayonnaise, vinegar, mustard, salt and paprika. Toss potatoes, frankfurters, celery, carrot, green pepper, onion and pimiento with mayonnaise mixture until well mixed. Chill until ready to serve. Makes about 3 quarts or 12 servings.

STUFFED FISH ROSÉ

½ cup Wish-Bone Italian Rosé Dressing
1 cup soft bread crumbs
½ cup diced celery
1 can (3 oz.) sliced mushrooms, drained
1 sea bass, flounder, or trout (about 1½ to 2 pounds dressed weight) pocketed for stuffing
Heavy duty foil

In medium bowl, combine ¼ cup Wish-Bone Italian Rosé Dressing, bread crumbs, celery, and mushrooms. Sprinkle pocket of fish with salt. Fill with stuffing mixture; close opening by tying fish with string. Place fish on foil, baste with remaining dressing; wrap loosely, sealing edges airtight with double fold. Grill, turning occasionally, 30 to 40 minutes. Makes about 4 servings.

NO-BAKE STUFFED PEPPERS

6 medium green peppers
1 pound ground beef
¼ cup chopped onion
2 tablespoons butter
2¼ cups water
½ cup Open Pit Barbecue Sauce, any flavor
1½ teaspoons salt
1½ cups Minute Rice
1 cup cubed process American cheese

Remove stem ends and seeds from peppers. Cook in boiling water 10 minutes. Meanwhile, brown beef and onion in butter in deep skillet. Add 1½ cups of the water, ¼ cup of the barbecue sauce, the salt, and rice. Bring to a boil. Then cover

and simmer 5 minutes. Add cheese. Drain cooked peppers. Fill with rice mixture. Place upright in skillet. Pour remaining water and barbecue sauce around peppers. Cover and simmer 5 minutes. Serve sauce with peppers. Makes 6 servings.

SIERRA RANCH RIBS

4 pounds country style spareribs
Dash salt and pepper
2 cans (8 oz. each) tomato sauce
½ cup Karo Dark Corn Syrup
¼ cup Worcestershire sauce
1 cup chopped onion
1 teaspoon salt
1 teaspoon monosodium glutamate
1 teaspoon dry mustard
½ teaspoon chili powder
¼ teaspoon pepper

Trim and cut ribs into serving size pieces. Sprinkle with salt and pepper. Place in large saucepan. Add water to cover. Bring to boil over high heat, reduce heat and simmer covered 1 to 1½ hours or until ribs are fork tender. Meanwhile, combine remaining ingredients in 2-quart saucepan. Bring to boil over medium heat. Reduce heat and simmer 10 minutes. Drain ribs. Brush generously with sauce. Place ribs 6 inches from source of heat, basting and turning frequently, about 15 minutes or until browned. If desired, heat remaining sauce and serve with ribs. Makes 4 servings.

SPORTSMEN'S SKILLET SUPPER

½ pound ground beef
1 envelope Lipton Onion Cup-a-Soup
1 envelope Lipton Tomato Cup-a-Soup
¾ cup water
¼ cup sweet pickle relish

In medium skillet, brown meat; stir in Lipton Onion Cup-a-Soup, Lipton Tomato Cup-a-Soup, water, and relish. Heat, stirring occasionally, until bubbling. Makes about 2 servings.

CHICKEN BARBECUE

3 pounds frying chicken pieces
3 tablespoons Orange Flavor Tang Instant Breakfast Drink

1 teaspoon salt
Dash of pepper
Dash of ground celery seed
½ teaspoon Worcestershire sauce
½ teaspoon prepared mustard
¼ cup sherry wine*
¼ cup salad oil
*Or use ¼ cup chicken broth

Cook chicken slowly over hot coals for 20 minutes, turning occasionally. Combine instant breakfast drink, salt, pepper, celery seed, Worcestershire sauce, and mustard. Blend in water and sherry. Add oil and mix well. Brush on chicken. Continue cooking, turning, and basting chicken with sauce, about 20 to 25 minutes or until chicken is tender. Makes 6 servings.

HAWAIIAN POTATO PIE

1½ pounds ground beef chuck
1 medium onion, chopped (about ½ cup)
⅓ cup chopped green pepper
1 teaspoon salt
1 can (13¼ oz.) crushed pineapple, drained (reserve syrup)
¼ cup soy sauce
2 tablespoons cornstarch
1 can (3 oz.) sliced mushrooms, drained
Potato Buds® Instant Puffs (enough for 8 servings)
Paprika

Heat oven to 350°. In large skillet, cook and stir ground chuck, onion, green pepper and salt until meat is brown; drain. Add enough water to reserved pineapple syrup to measure 1 cup. Blend soy sauce and cornstarch into liquid; gradually stir into meat mixture. Cook, stirring constantly, prepare potatoes as directed on package. Add pineapple and mushrooms to meat mixture; pour into lightly greased 1½ quart casserole. Top meat mixture with potatoes; sprinkle with paprika. Bake uncovered 30 minutes. 6 servings.
®Reg. T.M. of General Mills, Inc.

ORANGEY KEBABS

1 bouillon cube
1 cup boiling water
¼ cup Orange Flavor Tang Instant Breakfast Drink
¼ teaspoon thyme
⅛ teaspoon pepper
½ cup salad oil
2 pounds leg of lamb, cut into 1½-inch cubes
2 to 3 tomatoes, cut into wedges*
2 to 3 medium green peppers, cut into 1-inch pieces
2 to 3 medium onions, quartered**
*Or use 1 pint cherry tomatoes
**Or use 1 can (8 oz.) small white onions, drained

Dissolve bouillon cube in boiling water. Add instant breakfast drink, thyme, and pepper; stir to dissolve. Add salad oil; mix well. Pour over meat in shallow pan. Refrigerate at least 3 hours to marinate. Remove lamb from marinade, reserving marinade. Alternately arrange on skewers with vegetables. Boil over glowing coals; turn and baste frequently with reserved marinade for 20 to 30 minutes or until browned on both sides. Makes 8 kebabs or 8 servings.

Note: Vegetables may be parboiled before placing on skewers, if desired.

SKIPPY DATES

2 teaspoons instant coffee powder
2 teaspoons water
½ cup Skippy Peanut Butter
1 (10 oz.) carton pitted dates
Sugar

Mix coffee and water. Add to peanut butter and mix well. Stuff dates with peanut butter mixture; roll in sugar. Makes about 34 stuffed dates.

FROZEN CHOCO-CAKE

Slice one 11¼ oz. frozen Pound Cake lengthwise into 4 equal slices. Blend together 1 cup heavy cream, whipped, and two 1 oz. envelopes of Nestle's Hot Cocoa Mix. Spread mixture between layers and then frost sides and top of Pound Cake. Freeze until firm. Cut into ½″ slices. Makes about 12 slices.

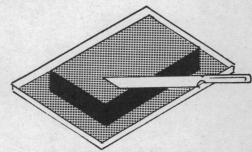

CHOCOLATE SPREAD

Blend together ¼ cup butter, softened, or one 3 oz. package of cream cheese, softened, and one 1 oz. envelope of Nestle's Hot Cocoa Mix. Spread on Plain Cookies. Makes ¼ cup of spread.

POPCORN

¼ cup Mazola Corn Oil
½ cup popcorn
Salt

Heat corn oil in large (4-quart) heavy skillet or kettle over medium heat about 3 minutes. Add popcorn; cover, leaving small air space at edge of cover. Shake frequently over medium heat until popping stops. Salt to taste. Makes 2 quarts.

Note: DO NOT DOUBLE RECIPE

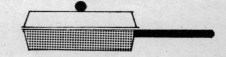

MAINE'S BAXTER STATE

PARK -- formula for the future of wilderness camping

by DICK DIETZ

Wilderness is a valuable and limited resource says the author, one that can be both used and preserved only by sensible limitations. A dedicated and tenacious "Down-Easter" may have shown us the way.

Background at Sandy Stream Pond is typical of Baxter Park beauty. Rock in center of pond is not rock at all, but a breakfasting bull moose.

Dick II utilizes our Baxter Park water hook-up—clear, cold water carried from Roaring Brook in a Coleman jug. Car-topped canoes are usual water craft on Baxter Park's interior lakes—outboard motors are prohibited.

WITH MY EYES CLOSED, I can still see the glittering plain of the remote lake. If leaves are Nature's garments, then lakes and streams must be her jewelry. Once, from my vantage in a game warden's plane, the lake resembled a single blue sapphire set in the emerald velvet of the surrounding forest. From the shoreline camp the rays of a mid-morning sun turn it into a shimmering sea of silver sequins. Just as clearly, I can hear the soft slap of wavelets against the rocks and the surf-like sound of wind sighing through the trees.

Then I open my eyes to the affront of four, landlord-beige office walls and become aware again of the muted, machine-gun rattle of a typewriter drifting through the door.

This is my favorite and most frequent daydream. Whenever things get a bit tight or I begin to chafe from an incipient case of office-cabin fever, I deliberately conjure up the desired image for a few seconds. It works wonders for me, I think, because the image is based on a wilderness spot that really exists, one I have visited in the past and

Hiker heads up trail toward Chimney Pond, one of Baxter State Park's walk-in campgrounds.

have every expectation of seeing again in the future.

Let's agree without getting into a social science discussion that, for many of us, today's hectic world can often be a bit wearing on the spirit. The solution, for those smart enough to seek one, is usually a change of pace, as a complete a break as possible from normal activities. To me, the ultimate break is a trek into the wilderness. An increasing number of Americans are discovering the same thing. The ecology boom has undoubtedly triggered much of this new awareness. And, with the advent of constantly more

sophisticated and comfort-laden camping equipment, plus the three to six-lane speedways probing like laser beams into the very heart of our remaining wilds, it becomes easier each year to reach such once-remote sanctuaries. The results in some of our most beautiful state and national parks have been catastrophic.

A lonely lake with a few cabins or primitive camp sites spread around its shores and only an occasional canoe rippling its waters, can retain a wilderness atmosphere. But develop the same lake with campgrounds, connect it to the world by hard-surfaced roads, lay in pads for the largest RV's, string in electricity, put motor boats on the waters, and you may still have a handsome vacation resort. But you no longer have wilderness or any semblance of it. The tragedy comes from the fact that in many parts of this country we are already running shy of unspoiled wilderness, and once a formerly primitive area is opened to development its wilderness aspects are destroyed forever.

Before you get the wrong impression, let me state quickly that I am in no way against all organized and developed campgrounds. We need these, and we need 'em in spades. In fact there are times when a well-organized campground with all sorts of conveniences, comforts and facilities is exactly what I want. I usually seek the best spot of this type I can find for all-family vacation trips.

On the other hand, we also need, and have to somehow preserve, the relatively undeveloped wilderness locations. Not only are we entitled to these, but we owe their preservation to future generations. By now we have ample and sometimes unfortunate examples that the two, development and wilderness, cannot coincide. But each has its rightful place.

Preserving and maintaining a legitimate wilderness setting, however, requires some definite restrictions and controls. There are many solutions put forth on just how this should be accomplished. I've had personal experience with one point of view that might well serve as a prototype for many. The subject is Baxter State Park located in the middle of northern Maine.

Throughout our history, Americans have been heirs of men of great foresight, courage and tenacity. Baxter State Park is such a legacy. Back in the early 1900's, a young man from Portland, familiar with the wild and still-unspoiled beauty of Maine's Katahdin Mountain area, became obsessed with the idea of preserving this section for the enjoyment of future generations. Percival Baxter devoted literally the rest of his life and all of his physical and financial resources to the project and accomplished his objective almost single-handed.

Beginning in 1916 as a State Legislature representative, and continuing through a four-year term as governor from 1921 to 1925, he pushed incessantly to have the area set aside as a state park. Unsuccessful, but undaunted, he finally determined to bring it about himself.

In 1930, Baxter purchased a 5960-acre section that included most of Mt. Katahdin and deeded it to the state with the proviso that it "be forever kept by the state in trust for the people of Maine" and further that it "forever be left in its natural wild state and forever kept as a sanctuary for wild beasts and birds."

The Maine Legislature accepted his gift in 1931, named it "Baxter State Park" and renamed the top of Katahdin "Baxter Peak" in his honor. He continued to purchase additional lands, deeding these always to the state and protecting as much as possible the original concept of a wilderness area. By the time Percival Baxter died in 1969, the park had grown to over 200,000 acres. But his concern didn't end there. Baxter's will left a substantial amount of money to the state, the income from which is to provide for continued administration and upkeep of the park in accordance with his concept of a wilderness retreat.

Few individuals have left the people of their state, or visitors to that state, a legacy as magnificent as Percival Baxter's. Today, the park is administered by the Baxter State Park Authority, composed of the State Attorney General and the Commissioners of Forestry and Inland Fisheries and Game.

Preserving Percival Baxter's dream has proven to require a delicate balance between maintenance of the park's natural state and use of it by the public. The task has not been, is not now, and probably never will be, an easy one.

After three separate visits to the park during the past two years, I've reached the firm conclusion that the state has been about 90 per cent successful in adhering to Percival Baxter's original intent. The park is not a true wilderness in the complete sense of the term. No area can be, once man has entered it permanently.

The basic operating concept of the Baxter State Park Authority seems to be this: limit the size and number of those specific locations that must, of necessity, be something less than true wilderness. These are the designated campgrounds. Limit the number of people present in these areas at any given time so that their use of the remaining parts of the park is not so heavy as to damage its natural and unspoiled atmosphere. Here you can see where the delicate balance must be maintained as a judgment factor by the Baxter State Park Authority.

The balance is maintained as much by leaving some things undone as by doing other things under specific restrictions and regulations.

One of the things left undone was the construction of high speed, primary roads to and through the park. If we have learned anything about preserving an area's natural and unaltered beauty, it is that wilderness tends to endure in reverse proportion to its relative accessibility. While a number of super highways now link Maine to points south and east, Baxter Park is not reached conveniently. Its location alone, in the northern half of our most northerly state, creates a distance barrier. The south gate to Baxter is over 600 miles from my southern New England home in Connecticut. Consequently, I am not inclined to attempt to run up there on the spur of the moment or on weekends.

Then, from Millinocket, the termination point of reasonably good roads, the nearest campground, Abol, is 23 miles in over mostly narrow, rough, dirt roads. All roads within the park are similar and the maximum speed permitted is 20 mph. Two of the most remote and beautiful campgrounds, Russel Pond and Chimney Pond, can be reached only by backpacking over trails. And the hiker must carry in all the food he'll need for his stay.

In fact, all campers must bring their total food supplies into the park—none is available there. Neither is gasoline, so campers are advised to "tank up" before entering.

Campground facilities include tent spaces, lean-tos and some bunkhouses. Those not planning to use either a bunkhouse or lean-to generally bring in a tent or tent trailer. No single vehicle over 7 feet in height or width or over 20 feet long is permitted in the park for camping purposes. Combination units (vehicle with trailer) can't exceed 40 feet in length. In addition, self-contained conveniences, such as sinks and toilet units in small trailers, may not be operated within the park.

Another sensible practice at Baxter Park, and one I would heartily recommend for most state and national parks, is a reservation system. Reservations for any specific campground must be made in advance by writing to the reservations clerk at Millinocket and enclosing the correct fee. Charges are assessed on a per person per night basis and amount to $1.50 for bunkhouse space, 75¢ for lean-tos and 50¢ for tent spaces. Total length of stay by reservation is one week, although campers may stay longer if space is available when their week is up. One further restriction limits reservations to residents of Maine only between January 1 and March 31. After March 31 they will be accepted from all applicants. As a non-resident, I believe this restriction for a state park is totally fair, and it has my complete support.

No motorcycles, trail bikes or all-terrain vehicles may be operated within the park. Outboard motors are allowed only on the perimeter lakes of Matagamon and Webster.

I'm sure by now you are beginning to see the picture. Baxter State Park is not for everyone. And that, in a nutshell, is why it remains a wilderness area. But for the special breed of camper who seeks the unique experience that rewards one's presence in such an area and is willing to accept the limitations on 20th century comfort that go with it, Baxter Park is a paradise.

The park now has eight, well-separated campgrounds, each one with its own rewarding characteristics. It also contains over a hundred miles of well-marked trails leading to many remote and exceptionally beautiful locations.

One morning two years ago, I remember taking three of my children on a short little hike to Sandy Stream Pond from Roaring Brook campground. We wound up spending a fascinating two hours watching two, four and, finally, five moose leisurely munching their breakfast out in the middle of the pond. Last September, my son and I stopped off at South Branch campground on the way back from an Allagash canoe trip. We thought we had absorbed our fill of wilderness beauty in the Allagash, but we were stunned by our first sight of Lower South Branch Pond. Set in a bowl of surrounding mountains, it is one of the most beautiful lakes we have ever seen. The many trails to the upper reaches of the park and to Russel Pond and Chimney Pond campgrounds are also memorable in their quiet grandeur and sense of detachment from the rest of the world.

Wildlife is abundantly present throughout the park. Deer, moose, black bear and beaver are readily found and observed. You may also chance across more rare species such as pine marten, fisher, mink and weasel. Eastern brook trout are present and catchable (depending on your skill) in all of the park's clear, cold waters.

Reigning over the park visually from all points is the majestic presence of Mt. Katahdin, the highest point in Maine at 5267 feet above sea level and the legendary home of the Indian Gods.

Not all of us are fortunate enough to know the secret and rewards of the wilderness. Sometimes I think the world might be a little better if more of us did. Nevertheless, we have an obligation to preserve the opportunity for others yet unborn.

The people of Maine can take well-deserved pride in the existence of Baxter State Park. There still remain other parks, parts of parks and areas not yet parks that cry out for some sort of protection as wilderness retreats. We have at least one good lesson on how to accomplish this. Perhaps there are others. Wherever they are, let's not ignore them.

Morning tooth-brushing chore by author on Roaring Brook. Parts of streams are set aside for dish-washing; others for bathing or drinking water.

Jack McKey and Kit Hunn paddling on the Alapaha River in South Georgia.

Canoe Camping in Southern Georgia

by MAX HUNN

ROUNDING A BEND in the placid, dark colored Alapaha river, we spotted a big alligator easing himself into the water, wanting no part of our silent and unexpected intrusion into his wilderness domain.

Quickly paddling to the opposite shore—no use taking any chances the 10-foot 'gator would get too friendly—we continued half paddling, half floating along the little known, meandering river in South Carolina.

A cathedral-like hush hung over the stream as we moved along. Towering trees, both cypress and tupelo, rising from the foot of the steep banks, arched overhead, blotting out the frenetic 20th century.

The Alapaha is almost as primitive today, as it was centuries ago, fortunately having escaped the bulldozers and draglines of the U.S. Corps of Engineers. Yet, oddly, only a few miles away, 20th century motorists were wasting gasoline with their lead-footed driving. Fortunately, the strident sounds of the brassy civilization couldn't reach us.

Sighting the alligator during the first hours of our canoe-camping trip on the Alapaha river was an appropriate introduction to our three-day float on one of the few remaining primitive rivers in Georgia. In the wilds you expect to see 'gators, and we did, although not in great numbers.

The wilderness quiet, broken infrequently by the squawks of startled birds, engulfed us within minutes after we left our launching site east of Lakeland, a small, south-central Georgia town, off the beaten tourist track. Immediately we felt as if we were the first to explore the river, although obviously we weren't.

Indians had been here centuries before the first white man, and even the first whites arrived some four centuries ago, probably when Hernando De Soto blundered through this territory in search of gold for the King of Spain. We weren't seeking gold, but an equally precious commodity—peace, quiet and elbow room far from the throngs of the greatly overcrowded 20th century.

In recent years, the yearning of city-bound Americans to get away from the concrete canyons, to find elbow room, peace and quiet has been felt in South Georgia where the establishment of a series of canoe camping trails now provides the getaway keys.

Once canoemen were rarities on the primitive, little damaged streams in the southern part of the Peach State, but now things are changing. Canoeing is a family fun sport, and as canoe trails have been developed and publicized, the sport has grown.

Today, there are canoe trails on such rivers as the Alapaha, the Withlacoochee, the Suwannee, the Satilla and even in the Okefenokee Swamp. Canoeing and canoe camping have come to the land of peanuts, cotton and corn.

It's not difficult to plan a canoe trip in South Georgia because free brochures provide information as to the length of the trails, location of camp sites, and warnings of river hazards. Information on the Alapaha, Withlacoochee and Suwannee river trails can be obtained from the Coastal Plains Area Tourism Council, P.O. Box 1223, Valdosta, Ga., 31601. For details on the Satilla trail write the Slash Pines Area Planning and Development Commission, P.O. Box 1276, Waycross, Ga. 31501. Information on the trails in the Okefenokee Swamp National Wildlife Refuge can be obtained from the Refuge Manager, Okefenokee Wildlife Refuge, P.O. Box 117, Waycross, Ga., 31501.

Naturally, advance planning is necessary if your canoe trip is to be more than a single day. Most canoeists sample as much of each trail as possible in the time they have available. Some travel in groups, others alone, but all find the escape to the wilderness fascinating. Although paddling and floating is the most popular means of following a canoe trail, some use small, outboard motors either utilizing the square end, work canoes or having a special mount installed on the conventional double end type. Of course, it's a lot easier to use mechanical instead of muscle power, but it also destroys some of the feeling of being in the wilderness.

Campsites have been designated along the trails, and most of them have litter barrels, which makes trash disposal easy. However, if no litter barrels are present, or you elect to camp on sandbars (as we did twice on our three-day Alapaha trip), then make certain you carry your trash out with you. These are primitive, yet unspoiled rivers. Don't be the first to leave the inevitable trash marks of the 20th century on them.

If you elect to camp on sandbars, and there are many along all of the rivers, their availability depending upon the height of the river, remember this: many of the streams rise and fall rapidly, and a sudden downpour at their headwaters can cause them to rise within hours. Obviously, don't camp on a sandbar with a river rising.

Naturally, you travel as light as possible, for although you can stow a lot of gear in a canoe, there are limits. Freeze dried foods are very handy (and very tasty, we found), reducing the bulk as well as weight of your provisions. Too, you don't have to be a master chef to whip up a good meal. It's advisable to carry your own drinking water, and water purification tablets as well, just in case you run out. On some streams, such as the Alapaha, you are never more than a mile or so from a safe, fresh water source at any of the highway bridges. However, on others it's a mighty long hike to fresh water.

Most canoeists use small tents—mountain, pup or pop types—although some sleep in the open, or perhaps under tarps. Sleeping in the open is o.k., *if* it doesn't rain. Then it can be a soggy mess. Most of the time, sleeping bags—the lightweight models—are quite comfortable, unless you elect to do your canoeing in the late fall or very early spring. Then you will want heavier sleeping bags.

The rivers are not in the white water classification, but you can get in trouble. The amount of trouble the rapids and falls can cause depends upon the height of the river. At high water, you ride over most of the hazards. However, on low water, some of the rapids are dangerous. The Suwannee River trail, the stretch from the Georgia state line to White Springs in Florida, has a number of bad rapids and falls which require portages. Inexperienced canoeists have attempted to run these rapids and have met disaster. On the Withlacoochee trail, too, there are several places where portaging is wise, unless you want to live dangerously and are an expert canoeman. Even then don't forget your life jackets.

On the Alapaha, Rock Falls can be tricky, although they are no problem for an expert. But even experts, sometimes make mistakes, as our guide, Jack McKey told us on our three-day trip. Ruefully, he related how he made one miscalculation on the rapids while scouting the trail, and spilled.

"My bedding was a mess, although I saved my gear," he explained. "It just proves you've got to be alert all the time while canoeing."

John Lampp, another member of our foursome exploring the Alapaha, and I, too, almost got in trouble near Cow Creek. After Kit and Jack ran the very shallow and short

Camping on a sand bar on the Alapaha. The river is almost as primitive today as it was centuries ago.

Rest stop during a canoe float trip on the Alapaha River.

rapids successfully, John and I began our run. We miscalculated the current at the only short turn, suddenly found ourselves bouncing off the willows, and after teetering precariously for a few seconds escaped turning over. It was close. Don't take any chances with any rapids when canoeing; even experts can make mistakes. These canoes at the bottom of the falls above White Springs on the Suwannee river are evidence of this.

The oldest of the South Georgia canoe trails (established in 1969) is on the Alapaha river, which covers 83 miles between the little town of Willacoochee and the end at the U.S. 94 highway bridge just west of the little town of Staten-

Heading up the Withlacoochee River in a motor powered canoe in southern Georgia.

Jack McKey runs the Rock Falls rapids with no problems this time. No wet bedrolls for us, thank goodness.

ville. A few miles farther south near the Georgia-Florida state line, the river disappears into a sink hole, then reappears farther south and eventually joins the Suwannee river.

The Withlacoochee trail is 56 miles from its starting point at the Georgia Highway 94 bridge crossing the river north-west of Valdosta to its terminus at the Suwannee River State Park in Florida. Twenty-four miles of the trail are in Georgia, and 32 in Florida, but there's little difference in terrain. You can extend this trip by canoeing down the Suwannee river to the Gulf of Mexico in Florida. Gung-ho canoeists are doing this, but it takes at least a week.

The Withlacoochee River canoe trail, 56 miles long, runs into Florida from South Georgia.

The Suwannee river trail is the longest in the two states. You begin this canoe-camping trip by crossing the Okefenokee Swamp Wildlife Refuge following the marked trails in the Swamp, then portage the Sill on the southwestern edge of the Swamp, and pick up the river canoe trail there. Again you can paddle and float to the Gulf of Mexico. This is a long, long trail, about 250 miles, depending upon your exact routing. You've got to be gung-ho for paddling, and allow plenty of time to make the trip. Fortunately, you can re-provision once in Florida.

There are a variety of marked canoe trails in the Okefenokee Swamp, beginning at Kingfisher Landing, off U.S. 1 and 23 highways between Waycross and Folkston; at Davis Landing, another entrance between Waycross and Folkston, also off U.S. 1; and at the Suwannee Canal Recreation Area, reached via Georgia Highway 23 from Folkston. Stephen Foster State Park on Jones Island in the southwestern part of the Swamp near Fargo is the terminus for all trails. Naturally, it also can be the starting point for canoe trips, although if you start from there, you will be paddling against the current. The Okefenokee is not a stagnant swamp, but actually is a watershed, draining roughly from northeast to southwest. There is enough of a current when the swamp water is high to make canoeing hard work when

you start from the south side.

Basically the Okefenokee is a wildlife refuge, and to protect the area's wilderness quality, strict rules have been established. Only one party—consisting of a maximum of 10 canoes and 20 people—is permitted on each trail daily. You are responsible for keeping the trails free from trash, and for bringing out your own or other's litter.

Before beginning the wilderness paddling, a permit is required, which can be obtained from the manager of the

Canoe trail in the Okefenokee Swamp in Georgia is restricted to one canoe party—10 canoes and 20 people—per day.

Okefenokee Wildlife Refuge, P.O. Box 117, Waycross, Ga., 31501. In applying for a permit, you should advise the date of your trip, choice of trails, number of canoes in your party, person in charge, and addresses of all party members. The permits are free.

Overnight camping is permitted only at designated stops. In order to make certain these are reached by dark, no canoe party can depart after 10 A.M. There's a lack of firm land at the overnight sites, thus you must be prepared to sleep in your canoes, or in jungle hammocks.

Open fires are permitted only at specified overnight stops. Gasoline, bottle gas or alcohol stoves are recommended. Portable toilets with plastic bags are required and such wastes must be disposed of at designated areas at the canoe trail exits. You can spend only one night at each rest stop, and you must remain there between sunset and sunrise. But then who'd want to paddle around that swamp in the dark?

The Satilla river trail is the longest canoe route entirely within south Georgia. Beginning northeast of Waycross, this trail follows the snake-like Satilla for 149 miles to its terminus at Woodbine on U.S. 17. Although the trail officially ends at Woodbine, it is possible to canoe down to the Atlantic mouth of the river. However, this gets to be big water, and requires careful canoe handling, particularly when boats kicking big wakes are encountered. There are 20 designated campsites along the 149-mile trail. You need not paddle the entire length, however, for you can launch from near the highway bridges which cross the river, and divide the trail into convenient segments ranging from 24 to 41 miles in length.

Whether you want to canoe camp on a beautiful, primitive river or in the equally beautiful and primitive Okefenokee Swamp, South Georgia provides the necessary opportunities. Canoe camping has come to South Georgia to stay.

The Rage Is BACKPACKING

...BUT ARE YOU *READY* FOR IT?

by CHARLES J. FARMER

FUNNY HOW things get started. There was a time when loading 30 or 40 pounds on your back and hiking 10 miles was strictly involuntary . . . Army all the way. Torture, some of the boys called it. Pure hell. Sore feet and skinned shoulders. How in the world could anybody in his or her right mind call that fun? But backpacking is the thing . . . why?

Backpacking is liberation. Despite the work involved—and it is work—the finest reward derived from packing a complete, comfortable camp on your back is FREEDOM. Freedom from pistons, gears, mufflers, gasoline, oil, concrete, carburetors, fan belts, radios, stereos and television. That's freedom. Escape might be a better word. Backpacking is an escape from the jack hammers, disc jockeys, Avon ladies and Fuller Brush men.

The backpacker, whether the escape be for a day, a week or a month, is saying goodbye to air conditioning, padded vinyl seats, drive-in movies, imitation oak paneled offices, executive directives and executive orders. All the necessities of life . . . or are they?

Enter the silent, padless, motorless, unhurried world of the backpacker. Different isn't it. The birds and animals are there . . . and the mosquitoes too. And there are fish in the streams and lakes. And you like catching them . . . for awhile.

Then your mind is filled with cold beers in the refrigerator. Monday night baseball. A soft bed with clean, white sheets. Shaving. Orderliness. The 10 O'Clock news and . . . food that is real—solid, fresh and not freeze-dried to the point that it looks like petrified wood.

Are you really a backpacker? Do you crave wild flowers? Would you trade a bottle of chilled mountain wine and a candle lit restaurant for the chance to see pink fairy-slippers living wild in the bog?

Does the glimpse of a western tanager send you screaming for a pair of binoculars or a telephoto lens?

And the velvet-antlered bull elk . . . is your trip into the woods a success if you spot one up close?

The sage, the bogs, tiny trickling streams, alpine meadows, jagged rocks, serpentine trails, fragrant smells, sweat, leg power, fatigue, relief—the elements of backpacking. The tiny things that make up the whole. If you want those experiences; if your body needs a test and you want to be free, then maybe . . . just maybe you are ready for backpacking.

The Sales Pitch

Possibly the worst thing that has happened to the sport of backpacking is over-commercialization. Cigarette companies, cosmetic companies and backpack equipment manufacturers have painted a rosy picture. So rosy in fact, that advertisements and commercials have persuaded persons that are too old, too fat, too young, too out-of-shape and too uninformed about the outdoors—to take up backpacking. It is a sad trick.

The ultra-neat, unblemished, long-haired smiling beauty of a girl with her "25 pound" (foam filled) pack standing arm-in-arm with her super cool, clean shaven he-man of an outdoorsman with the big cigarette just ain't so. Unreal. Backpacking is sweating, a bit on the smelly side and a little dirty too. But most of all, it is work . . . and there is no way to get around that.

So Who Can Backpack?

Anyone can. But only those persons, regardless of age, who are in top physical condition will enjoy it. And, it

The rewards of backpacking are many, but they don't come without effort.

My wife, Kathy and our beagle, Radar in our nylon fly tent. Kathy's boots are heavy duty, Vibram-soled climbing type.

takes more than a two or three week fitness program to qualify a packer for a week in the hills. To be a good backpacker, one who thoroughly enjoys the art of packing and camping, a man, woman or child should be considered a sincere outdoors-type person—thoroughly versed in outdoor knowledge from practical experience in the field. Book or magazine worms, who want to try backpacking because they read it is the ultimate outdoor experience, will most likely end up tired, sore and disappointed.

Legs, Lungs and Love

More specifically, you can rate your ability as a backpacker, before you even set foot in the hills, by following a simple, three-word code . . . Legs, Lungs and Love (not necessarily in the order of importance).

Does the old football injury still give you trouble? Bad legs? Are your ankles notoriously weak? Here is the point. If your legs or ankles tend to bother you under normal walking, running, or standing situations, you can rest assured that when you add 20 to 40 pounds of pack to your frame, the weakness or pain will be intensified.

Good legs just don't apply to athletes, women and chickens. You have to have them for backpacking. If you do not, and there is no way of strengthening them, choose another sport like ping-pong.

Good lung power can be developed provided you have good lungs to start with. Exercise, of course, is the best way to increase lung capacity. A backpacker without good lung power may never stop gasping for air. Since much backpacking is done in the mountains and higher elevations, strain on the lungs is increased by altitude. Combine this with climbing and the weight of the pack and lung strength becomes critical. Gasping for air may not kill you (unless your heart is weak) but it can make you a mighty uncomfortable packer.

If your lungs are good, start with easy trips and work up to heavy, long climbs. Anyone can get out of breath. Pacing is important. Conditioning good lungs is as important as conditioning good legs.

How much do you *love* the outdoors? If you love it a lot, and your physical condition is good, your potential as a backpacker is good. With love, comes desire. And the desire to be free and mobile in the wilderness is why you put the pack on in the first place. Fortunately, there are no second or third bests in the love department.

Rate your love for the outdoors . . . the total experience. This can include hiking for hiking's sake, rock climbing, fishing, camping for camping's sake, hunting, bird watching, wildlife photography, woodsmanship and just plain nature loving. If you love everything mentioned above,

An array of backpack gear—fly tent and standard mountain tent, plus packs, wind shirts and cook gear.

your chance to succeed as a backpacker is good, because backpacking gives you the opportunity for the total experience. No other mode of back woods travel can do this.

A backpacker who does not take a keen interest in one or more of the above outdoor categories, also lessens his chances for being a good backpacker.

For example, I have participated in many backpack trips where the primary motive for packing was reaching a good fishing lake or stream. Nothing wrong with that. But some of my partners on the trip could see no other values in the hike except reaching our destination—as quickly as possible—and catching fish. If the fishing was slow, or poor, the trip was a failure. They were overlooking the total, outdoor experience . . . the best reward backpacking has to offer.

If, in your opinion, your love for the outdoors is average or fair, forget about backpacking. Chances are you will not see its worth. The hard work will not be justified. And you'll return to civilization disappointed.

The Mind of a Backpacker

There is, in the mind of a packer, a flicker of Spartanism. "Hard work, self-discipline, personal sacrifice and making-do with what is on hand, make up the backpacker's mind," a friend of mine once told me.

"I'm not a Spartan," I replied, "and I like backpacking."

"But," he said, "you have a degree, although it may be ever so slight, of Spartan attitude in you. Why would anyone hike 14 miles, with a 40 pound pack—just to catch a fish or two?" he asked.

"Maybe so," I nodded. "Maybe I'm a Spartan and didn't know it." And I thought about that many times afterwards. Backpacking tests the mind, body and very spirit of a person. I know. There have been times, along the trail, when I wondered whether the hike, with a heavy pack, was worth the effort.

But there has never been a time, after a pack experience, whether the fishing or hunting was good or not, that I did not feel satisfied and somewhat proud. "My body and mind did it again," I sometimes say to myself. "I beat the trail . . . I whipped the mountain and I lived with nature. I can do it."

I have heard many people say, "Why would anybody want to climb to the top of the Grand Teton?" A climber would answer, "Because it is there." I would say, "I don't know why." Yet deep down I do know why.

And, I agree, backpackers have a little Spartan blood in them.

So . . . your mind and body qualify and now you think about gear . . .

I have read articles on backpack gear that have made me so tired I'm worn out before the trip begins. Why do some persons take something basically very simple and make it complicated? It seems that anything worth its salt has to be complicated these days. There must be some kind of tricky formula for success.

Backpacking has caught on in a society of complexities because the equipment involved and the techniques for enjoyment, are simple. Simple.

If there be one general guideline to follow in the selection and purchase of backpack gear, it is to buy the best. Bargain pack gear is non-existent, despite advertising claims. Cheap gear is a myth. Second best won't do the job. And good backpack equipment is expensive.

Hiking Boots:—The foundation to enjoyable and com-

Here is popular Kelty pack.

Coleman pack features heavy duty
nylon sack and aluminum frame.

Gerry sacks with compartments for various pieces of equipment.

Closer look at some pack gear—note Vibram soled boots and packs. Sack near right corner of backpack contains dehydrated food.

fortable backpacking is found in the selection of boots. And rather than talk about a variety of boots, I will discuss the boots that have proven best for me. They cost between $30 and $40 and are built like bricks. But they are comfortable. They feature smooth leather construction and genuine Vibram soles. Rough-out cowhide or leather, in any way, shape or form does not compare to smooth leather finishes for water repellency and abrasion resistence. This is the straight scoop. Try not to be talked into them because the rough-out finish outnumbers the smooth finish boots in shoe shops—two to one. They are not as good.

Buy the boots in person. Try them on with one or two pairs of heavy wool socks. Despite the climate, one or two pairs of heavy wool socks are great protection against blisters when the boots are fitted properly.

There are many fine, good quality brands of mail-order

boots. Ordering them by mail is a gamble. And the price is too high to gamble. Choose a reputable shoe store or climbing supply outlet. You won't regret spending the extra money. The boots are good for all sorts of outdoor activities. And once you get used to the heaviness (to protect your feet against rock abrasions) you will love them. Wear them as much as you can before field trips. Break them in with the socks you will be wearing on your hikes.

Pack Frame and Sack:—Gerry, Kelty, Camp Trails, Eddie Bauer and Coleman are good names in the frame and sack department. Unlike good hiking shoes, most of which are made in Italy and often manufactured under a variety of different names, American made frames and packs are standard. They can be purchased in most sporting goods stores.

Aluminum frames and heavy nylon sacks are superior

to steel or wooden frames and canvas sacks. And that is usually where the price difference comes in.

Good frames come in sizes: small, medium and large according to your height. When they are fitted to your build, they are more comfortable to carry. Sacks or bags can also be purchased in sizes depending on how much you want to carry and the number of compartments you want. If you are undecided on whether to buy a large sack or a small one, choose the bigger model. Packs never seem to have enough room. You can grow into a larger sack.

Good frames cost from $20 to $30. And a good sack falls into the same price bracket. So you can expect to pay from $40 to $50 for frame and pack.

elsewhere in this issue—Ed.)

The Extras:—With good shoes, backpack and sleeping bag, you have, in your possession, the essentials—the nucleus of the gear. Of course, you might consider a nylon mountain tent as essential. Or a nylon tarp or fly may handily serve the purpose.

In areas where firewood is scarce or where wood fires are prohibited (such as many of our national parks and monuments), a lightweight pack stove can be considered an essential.

Cooking gear, flashlight, utensils, maps, compass, clothing and food round out the extras. The selection of these items depends on individual tastes. Dehydrated or freeze-

Hikers show Eddie Bauer frames and packs.

Sleeping Bag and Pad—There is a tendency to skimp here. And it's the worst place to do it. Expect to pay from $60 to $110 for a name brand down or Dacron sleeping bag. I prefer down, the prime, northern white variety because it is warm and compacts easily into a stuff bag.

Gerry, Eddie Bauer, Coleman, Alpine Designs, Recreational Equipment, Outdoor Leadership Supply and Powderhorn are reputable brand names.

Bags, too, are sold in small, medium and large sizes so they fit the sleeper better. No wasted space. Bag manufacturers call them cold spots. Choose the best insulation for your climate and needs. Then pick a bag that is thick and has good loft qualities. Dead air space, and good insulation is the secret of a warm, comfortable sleeping bag. A foam pad, with nylon shell, smooths out the bumps and its weight is minimal. (See: A Good Night's Sleep,

dried foods prevail on the menus. Some foods are tasty, others bland. Their main purpose for being is nutrition and light weight. They are expensive, but convenient.

The art involved in backpacking is being able to pack everything you need for comfort and enjoyment into your pack. And, at the same time, keep the contents of the pack light enough so you do not feel like a weary, bone-tired pack animal.

Some persons require more food than others. And some packers need more clothes. There is no set formula. And the only way to find out what you really need is to experiment.

If you are completely honest with yourself, you can answer the question whether or not you are ready for backpacking. If you are undecided, but your thoughts turn to the hills and you want to be free and mobile, try it. The feeling is a good one.

COOKING UTENSIL BAG: Makes finding cooking outfit easy and quick. Nest of pans, plates and coffee pot fit snugly inside bag with pads and cutlery in outside patch pocket. Made of army twill remnants, purchased at a surplus store. For bottom of bag, cut circle of cloth a little larger than your plates. Notch the circle about ¼-inch deep at ½-inch intervals. Sew to it the body of the bag, which should be about 5 inches higher than the height of its contents. A draw string—heavy enough to serve as a handle, too—closes the top.

10 HOME-MADE GIMMICKS

CAMPING isn't all that manufactured that it precludes ingenuity on the part of the camper. There's still plenty of room to come up with home-made gimmicks that will add convenience to your family's life on the road. For example, here are ten helpful ideas picked up from campers who had designed and were using them.

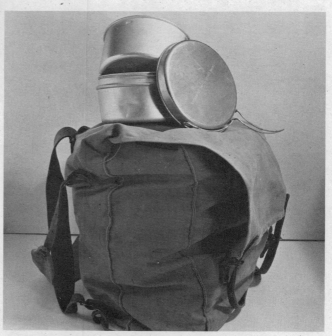

BEAR ALARM: If you can't hang your grub sack in a tree, place it at a distance from your tent, but pile pans on top of it when you retire. If a bear grabs it, the pans will tumble off, a burglar alarm that will frighten the bear and wake you. Another gimmick: string pans across your tent floor. If bruin tries to enter, he will rattle them.

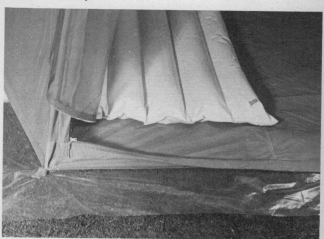

BUILDER'S PLASTIC FLOOR: Buy a piece of plastic wide enough to lay beneath your tent floor to keep out ground moisture and dampness. Easier to handle and more compact than a tarp. Place so sides of tent rest on the plastic—keeps edges of tent dry.

CAMP LANTERN STANDARD: Bend a steel reinforcing rod, weld a hook to the end, and stick standard in ground anywhere. Enables you to erect light away from your table for illumination without attracting bugs to the table.

FOR CAMPERS
by HANK and VERA BRADSHAW

TENT ANCHORS: Weld shaped piece of bar to another bar to form a hook. Slip tent ropes over the hook for increased hooking surface. The metal slide will grip the rope better than wood.

RUBBER MALLET: A rubber mallet prevents battering of end of tent stakes. Also drives tent stakes quietly if you pitch camp late at night. Will not awaken your neighbors.

TOASTER: Punch a large number of small nail holes in a coffee can. Then cross two wires from a coat hanger over the mouth of the can, sticking ends through four holes punctured by nails. Bend wires down to hold them in place. Sit the can upright on your portable stove and lay bread to be toasted on the wires.

HANDY AIR MATTRESS PUMP: Rubber, bellows action. Employ with hands or foot. Beats blowing up with mouth all hollow. Fast. Light. Especially beneficial on horseback or canoe trips. Metal nozzle in end of hose permits use with insertion-type valves. Remove nozzle when necessary for hose to fit over valve.

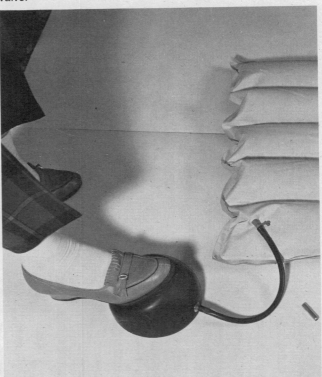

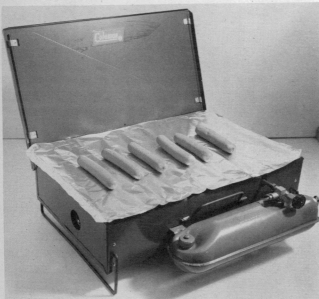

ALUMINUM FOIL USED AS SKILLET: To eliminate the delay of washing pans, especially at lunch time when you're on the road. Spread a sheet of aluminum foil across top of stove, lay food on it, light burners, and cook as with skillet.

ICE IN MILK CARTONS: For portable ice chest. Cartons serve as insulation to add life to ice. Also will keep loose water out of chest. No draining necessary. Get cartons refrozen nightly at filling stations or restaurants.

WHY NOT WINTER CAMPING?

The winter camper can work up a thirst as massive as any summer camper's. Here is an effective way to quench it.

by ED PARK

FOR MOST OF US, the camping season extends roughly from the time school is out in June until school begins again in September—with maybe a few odd weekends in spring or fall when we camp while fishing or hunting. The thought of camping during the winter months has probably not occurred to most of us—or if it did, was quickly dismissed as something only for Eskimos or some hairy-chested show-off who is trying to prove something.

Actually winter can be one of the most pleasant times of year for the camper. A person can easily become a winter camper if he develops an interest in that great white world, if he'll gain enough knowledge to keep himself and his companions out of trouble, and if he'll invest in a few needed items of equipment.

True, it can get cold out there in all that snow and ice, but that problem can be solved. So let's forget the cold for a moment and consider the advantages.

For one thing, there are no bugs. That in itself ought to interest anyone who has fought the swarms of mosquitoes and black flies that are too often encountered while camp-ing in warmer weather. On a recent canoe trip into northern Minnesota in June, our family was so badly bitten by flies that our boy had to see a doctor and all of us were tormented by the burning bites for many weeks. This sort of thing just doesn't happen in the winter.

Another point is the lack of crowds. And yes, I can just imagine some of you thinking—"Aha. No crowds. Other people know better!" But if you've tried to find a camping place in Yellowstone Park in August, or had to camp only inches away from noisy neighbors in some "aluminum city" called a private campground, you'll appreciate the tremen-dous solitude our woods offer in winter.

In my home state of Oregon, for instance, it is very difficult to find camping room in the summer. We're over-run with visitors from other states, many state parks require prior reservations and forest campgrounds are jammed. Often I've had to pull off on a lane to a farmer's field, park in an old gravel pit, or even stop in the back lot of an all-night service station—just because it was not possible to find a camping spot.

The camper on touring skis find countless subjects for photographs. This is the author, Ed Park.

But the white solitude of winter is another thing, a great thing. There are no facilities such as running water from a faucet or picnic tables, but then you don't have to wait in line for anything either. The only person you are apt to see are those in your own party. We often speak of solitude as an exclusive thing, but it is very real, and very important, to many of us.

And while your human neighbors might be few or non-existent, winter is an excellent time to see wildlife in many areas. Have you, along with millions of others, experienced the disappointment of driving hundreds of miles in the summer to see the highly-publicized wildlife of Yellowstone Park—and ended up seeing not even one big game animal? With thousands of cars patrolling the roads, and hundreds of tourists with cameras chasing them, it's no wonder these animals move back to the cool shelter of the forest. Yellowstone's wildlife is there, but you'll not see much of it in the heat of summer.

In winter, with few people to harass them, Yellowstone's wildlife is much easier to observe. In many areas, heavy snows force the animals down to lower elevations and many species are easy to see along major highways. Even a short snowshoe or ski trip will often let you see many magnificent animals. The beauty of a big bull elk, purposefully striding through two feet of new snow, with the low winter sun adding sparkle to everything is a scene that repays many chilly moments. Moose, biting off willow tips, gaze at the winter camper.

Winter camping is also worthwhile to many of us just to view the awesome beauty of snowy scenes. A small creek, winding through a meadow, is an ordinary summer scene, but add 12 feet of snow and that creek becomes a spectacular sight.

Common trees, bent and burdened with a layer of new snow, take on added interest. And of course a mountain, completely snow-covered, standing sharply against a cobalt-blue winter sky, is a sight to warm any soul. Such scenes—which we often admire on Christmas cards or calendars—are commonplace for the snow-country camper.

A final reason to discover winter camping could be called the satisfaction of being self-sufficient—the same reasons we go backpacking, mountaing climbing, river running, or cave exploring. It's a sense of accomplishment that comes from learning how to safely do something that has just a bit of implied danger to it. And since there is obviously some danger to being exposed to weather that can easily drop to

The winter camper on snowshoes brings a shovel which can be used to excavate a cozy snow cave for shelter.

below zero, the most important asset you can have is knowledge.

We sometimes read in the papers where a hiker, caught out overnight in chilly and damp weather, has died of "exposure." What the paper really means is that the person died of hypothermia—the loss of body heat.

Hypothermia is the number one killer of outdoor recreationists. It is caused by cold which is intensified by wetness, wind and exhaustion. It is something all outdoor-minded persons should be familiar with, for deaths from hypothermia can occur in weather most of us would consider quite warm. In fact, most hypothermia cases develop when it's 30 to 50 degrees—not in sub-freezing weather.

A typical case would be a hiker, overweight and in poor condition like most of us, who goes on a summer hike. It's 58 degrees and clear. He heads up a trail along a ridge, and eventually is several miles from his car. A sudden summer storm comes up, the temperature drops to the low 40s, it rains, the wind picks up. Our hiker, wearing cotton clothing, gets soaked and begins to chill.

He heads for home in a hurry and this increased activity keeps him warm for awhile. But he's out of shape, so exhaustion soon catches up with him and he pauses to rest.

He begins to shiver—the body's attempt to keep warm. The dampness and wind rapidly suck away his body heat. This cold quickly affects the brain, depriving it of full reasoning power and the hiker really isn't aware that he's in trouble. He does note he hasn't enough control of his hands to light a match for a warning fire. If he tried to speak, a listener would note his speech is slow, vague and slurred, as if he were drunk. He'll have memory lapses and a stumbling, lurching walk. If he doesn't reach outside help very soon, another "exposure" death will be recorded.

What could our hiker have done to prevent this situation?

1. First—stay dry. Wet clothes lose up to 90 percent of their insulation value. Therefore rain gear that will protect you from wind-driven rain, is an important investment. Underneath your rain gear, wear wool. Wool is the best material for outdoor clothing for it remains warm when it's wet. Cotton is the worst.

2. Get protection from the wind, as wind quickly carries heat away from damp skin or wet clothing by evaporation. We stand in a breeze to cool off when it's hot. That same breeze may kill you in a hypothermia situation.

3. Get external heat, such as a campfire. If you're caught in a storm and have any doubts about making it out alright,

With some modifications the autumnal hunter on foot becomes the winter trapper on snowshoes.

Snowscapes and the pattern of snowshoes
make a memorable photograph.

Winter snows drive big horn rams to lower elevations where they can be seen and admired by the winter camper.

make camp and get a fire going while you are still able to think straight and work efficiently.

4. Get internal heat with hot liquids, such as tea or soup. Food will also provide your body with calories to provide heat. Stay strictly away from all alcohol.

5. Avoid exhaustion. A good year-round program of jogging or other endurance exercise is something everyone should have, and especially those of us who enjoy outdoor living. If our hiker had been in top condition, he could have jogged back out along the trail and arrived in great shape. But a person in the usual poor condition should stop and find shelter before becoming too tired. Once the body becomes exhausted—runs out of fuel—hypothermia can occur quickly.

It's important that all members of a family or group learn the symptoms of hypothermia, because it is rare that a person can detect it in himself.

If you detect the symptoms in another—uncontrolled shivering, vague and slurred speech, fumbing hands, stumbling or lurching walk, memory lapses, apparent exhaustion —get busy and do something about it immediately. The victim will often deny he's in trouble, but believe the symptoms and not him. First, get him out of the wind and wet. Take off *all* wet clothes. If the victim is only mildly impaired, get him into dry clothes or a warm sleeping bag and next to a fire. Feed him warm drinks and food. If the victim becomes semi-conscious or worse (and this can come about quickly), try to keep him awake. Feed him warm liquids. Put him in a sleeping bag with another person (both completely stripped) for skin to skin contact is the most effective heating treatment.

Of course the best way to handle hypothermia is to avoid it by getting and staying in good shape, keeping warm and dry by using the proper clothing, and by keeping your activities within your personal limits.

One way to test your personal limit is to begin winter camping on a limited basis. It might seem silly to you, but I often suggest to beginning snow campers to camp near their car. Drive to a ski area, as an example, then camp a few

yards away. That way, if the night gets too rugged, you can give up and head for home.

Later on you will want to branch out and head for distant places by snowshoes, cross-country skies or snowmobile. I've probably taken more trips by snowshoes, if you count over all the years, but in recent years I've gone almost entirely to cross-country skis and now enjoy the pleasure of gliding over the snow with much less effort and much more speed than I ever knew with snowshoes.

And although I do use a snowmobile on occasion, I'm not too fond of the noise. Still, the machine gives you a margin of safety if a storm hits unexpectedly; it allows you to travel further, and also you can haul more equipment. If the snowmobile manufacturers will ever quiet the racket, they'll find their machines much more acceptable in the stillness of the winter woods.

The clothing you need will depend on your method of travel and the weather. When you ski or snowshoe you just naturally keep warmer from all the work. Sitting on a snowmobile at 40 miles per hour can be chilling. If you do travel on foot, take care not to overheat and sweat, for this moisture will chill you when you stop. Take off a layer of clothes before you begin to get damp from sweat.

Following the advice of the world's top cold weather experts, the Eskimos, wear several layers of light clothing rather than one thick layer. The trapped air between layers is great insulation and you'll keep warmer with less weight. Then, as the Eskimos do, take off layers as you work harder —putting them back on when you stop and begin to cool off.

As stated earlier, wool is the best material. For sitting around in the evening, or before you get going in the morning, down clothing is great. Down provides the greatest warmth for the weight, but again, it is no good when wet.

Cotton underwear is worse than nothing if it gets wet, so wear wool if you can. Have a wool stocking cap that covers ears and neck, wool gloves or mittens and wool sox. If all your clothing is wool, except for the outer waterproof layer, you'll be well dressed for winter.

That waterproof layer is important, for this is what will

keep you dry if it storms. If it is cold enough to snow—a dry snow—wool will shed it nicely. But for rain or wet snow you'll need something waterproof. Coated nylon is the best invented so far. Vinyls will do, but are not as tough. When wearing anything really waterproof, take extra care not to overheat. Open the neck and cuffs when you can for ventilation. A waterproof suit will hold in body heat and moisture and you can easily become soaked though doing very little work.

The cooking and eating gear you take is the same as you'd use for a summer backpacking trip, minus the metal plates. Find some light plastic plates for winter use, as metal is too cold. The small stoves, lightweight mess gear and lightweight foods you use in summer are fine for winter too.

You'd be wise to take some extra high-energy foods such as candy to aid if exhaustion hits or you have to sit out a storm for a day of two.

Backpacking tents can be used for winter camping with the modification of adding much longer tent pegs that will hold in the snow. Stomp down an area big enough for the tent and pitch it as if were in a summer meadow.

Usually—since I'm usually after photographs—I'll go camping only when its clear. Clear weather after a storm is

an ideal time. There's new snow on everything, few tracks cluttering up the landscape, and a cleanness that is refreshing. In such nice weather I often use no overhead shelter— or just a light nylon tarp. It's great to lie out in the winter woods, watching the stars overhead until I drift off to sleep.

For the ultimate in a winter shelter, dig a snow cave. I count a shovel as one of the more important pieces of gear for winter camping. If the snow is shallow, only a couple feet, I'll dig down to bare ground to make camp. If the snow is deep enough, a snow cave is fun. They can be big or small, depending on your ambition, and will provide a cozy "cabin" for the night. It's easiest if you tunnel into a big bank, then enlarge a room inside. Leave sleeping shelves along the side for your sleeping bags, use a candle for light, and settle down. Be sure to poke a good hole up through the roof with the shovel handle, then enlarge it, to allow ventilation.

One winter I took some Boy Scouts on a winter trip and we camped early so the boys would have time to dig good caves. Some only made simple, shelf-like caves into a bank —sufficient in non-stormy weather. The most elaborate was dug by four scouts and was large enough for ten of us to sit and talk. The ceiling was over six feet high and they had dug several candle shelves around the walls. It had a good,

The bison in his luxurious winter coat sweeps snow from the underlying grasses. He is unconcerned by the visitor.

Winter campers emerge from their snow cave for a warming drink. The equipment is almost identical to that used during the summer.

ventilation hole in the roof. All in all it was comfortable.

You'll want some sort of light tarp between you and the snow for, as in all other phases of winter camping, you want to keep dry. On top of that tarp you can put your air mattress—or one of the foam pads, such as Ensolite.

The foam pad will provide insulation as well as padding, so for warmth it is superior to an air mattress. Also, you won't find yourself on a deflated bag at about 2 A.M.

A good sleeping bag, capable of keeping you warm in the temperatures you'll be sleeping in, is the most important item for the camper, whether its summer or winter. Nothing else ever seems to go right if you don't get a good night's sleep. Down is again the best material for any bag you have to carry very far and it gives maximum warmth.

Of course there are other items you should take along, mainly for emergencies. Bring fire-starting gear such as matches in waterproof containers, candles, fire starters, etc.

These should be reserved for emergencies only. Carry sunglasses and sunscreen lotion if you burn easily, for the winter sun, reflected off the snow, can be brutal. Extra light nylon rope, plastic tape, wire and a pair of pliers will be useful in making repairs such as cleaning a spark plug or changing the drive of a snow machine. Take spare parts and a small tool bag along and don't forget to include a saw and axe for firewood, or for cutting poles for your tent or tarp shelter.

If you keep a list of all the gear you take, then review it later noting which items were used or not used—and also the things you wished you'd had along—you'll soon work up "the" list.

Finally, don't let the thought of camping in the snow scare you. It does take a little more equipment, a little more planning, and a lot more thought than summer camping, but there are very special rewards in venturing out into that sparkling white wilderness of winter.

Camping and Fishing the Seacoast

by MILT ROSKO

Here's Milt Rosko fighting a striped bass he hooked while fishing the Saco River in Maine. Almost all tidal rivers in Maine hold a number of stripers, and they may be taken on the same tackle and many of the same lures you might use for largemouths.

June Rosko takes some fresh fish steaks from the oven while they motored along the seacoast in a motorhome. Fresh caught fish just can't be beat when it's cooked just hours after being hauled from the water.

MY FIRST EXPERIENCE at seacoast camping goes back quite a number of years. I was in the Marine Corps, stationed at Camp Lejeune, North Carolina. With a pack on my back and a vintage two-man pup tent we moved out through the dense pines of the Carolina coastline, where quail flushed ahead of our long column and made me wish I had a scattergun instead of an M-1.

On reaching the coast, a beautiful picture unfolded, one that is still firmly implanted in my mind. There the broad expanse of the ocean tumbled on clean, white beaches, where for as far as the eye could see in either direction there was not a sign of civilization. The beautiful New River emptied into the ocean, with bars, rips and eddies that made me wish I had a fishing rod along.

We selected what appeared to be a nice, scenic spot to pitch the tents, scattered among the dunes and along the edge of the pines. It was then that we first realized seacoast camping was a bit different than inland. Tent pegs that had to be hammered but inches into the ground inland to hold securely, simply would not support a thing in the soft, moist sand—thus necessitating a bit of ingenuity and Marine Corps improvising in order to set the canvas. Through wise use of ropes and freshly cut saplings we finally made camp.

Where we'd been accustomed to swimming inland and enjoying the refreshing fresh water, we did the same in the ocean, and found it equally refreshing, but awfully itchy as the salt and hot sun were a combination that made you literally "itch" for a fresh water shower.

That night the fresh easterly winds of the late afternoon diminished and there was a gentle breeze from the west. This carried hordes of mosquitos from the back marshes to our campsite. These were mosquitoes the likes of which you never saw before. They left bites the size of a quarter!

On arising shortly after daybreak we found our food covered with colonies of ants, and then the gnats began to enjoy their breakfast, which was us!

Would you believe, that from such beginnings, I've come to enjoy seacoast camping immensely? Well, I have, as has the entire Rosko clan, including my wife, June, and our two teenagers, Linda and Bob. who began camping with us shortly after they were out of diapers.

Seacoast camping, and the fine fishing you can do while camping, takes on a whole new perspective today, simply because camping equipment and campers are more sophisticated than they were a score or more years ago.

I recall our early camping trips, when pickup campers were the rage. We made our first junkets to Cape Cod, and then on to Maine, fishing along the New England coast all the way. With that behind us, we moved south, enjoying the DelMarVa Peninsula, and then the Outer Banks, and finally south to Florida, where a whole new series of camping and fishing adventures awaited us along the shore.

Over the years, we've tried the whole thing, from tent campers, to huge motor homes, to backpacking over the dunes, to towing a trailer. All have been fun, and today the camping enthusiast desirous to enjoy himself along the seacoast has accommodations available that add to the fun—simply because there are more and better campgrounds and campsites than has been available previously. Indeed, when we began camping along the ocean over a decade ago I doubt if there were ten percent of the facilities that are available today. Indeed, on our first trips out you really had to rough it, even in a pickup!

Tent camping has grown especially popular along the beaches, especially among older teenagers and newly marrieds, including those with tiny tots. I suspect it's because with a small investment in some backpacking gear, a light-weight tent, sleeping bag and dried foods, several people can camp very economically and without much fuss. It's the

It's always nice to have a charcoal grill along with you while camping. Keeps the camper cool when you cook outside and nothing tastes better than grilled steaks, or fish fillets wrapped in foil.

trend among the young to, as they put it, "really camp" which is either under the stars or in a tent. Although, I have noted (particularly along the DelMarVa Peninsula and along the outer Banks) that lots of older folks enjoy pitching a tent, catching some fish for a fry, and living life wearing nothing but a bathing suit from the time the sun peaks over the horizon until they climb into their bag at night.

Speaking of catching some fish and having a fry, I can't help but recall the many wonderful fishing experiences we've enjoyed along the coast while camping.

Down in Maine there are literally hundreds of rivers meandering from inland to the sea coast. Because of this you simply cannot drive along the coast in a car, as the roads are well inland; you must move out along fingers of land, flanked on both sides by rivers, to reach the ocean. These rivers, and the open sea beyond, literally teem with fish during the summer months. In my experience I never fished a spot such as Maine, where even the newest new-

comer to fishing could experience such great success. Many of the fish are small, but by fresh water standards, to which many of our campers may be accustomed, they're quite large.

The same tackle you're accustomed to using in fresh water will serve you well along the seacoast. Your pet baitcasting outfit works out fine, as does a worm-action bass rod and spincast reel, or a bass-action spinning outfit.

Winter flounder virtually pave the muddy bottoms of most rivers, and by fishing with small pieces of sandworm or bloodworm, both of which are readily available, it's not unusual to catch a couple of dozen ¾- to 1-pound flatties in short order. Frequently while fishing for the flounders you'll catch small codfish and harbor pollock weighing about a pound, which are not only fun to catch, but excellent table fare.

Atlantic mackerel are extremely plentiful in all the coastal waters off Maine throughout the summer, and you'll

Striped bass are found in the surf from Maine south to the Outer Banks and provide great sport. They strike a wide variety of lures, including plugs, metal squids, bucktail jigs and rigged eels cast into the surf.

find they'll readily strike the small chromed and copper-plated Daredevils and Johnson Silver Minnows and other such lures you're accustomed to using for bass or trout inland.

I've also enjoyed superb striped bass fishing in Maine. Casco Cay has a huge population of stripers, and many may be caught casting from the rocky shoreline. The Saco River also holds an abundance of bass, as do many of the other river systems. Most are landed by boatmen using small outboards, but good light tackle sport may be enjoyed from the many readily accessible banks along most of the rivers.

Massachusetts has a beautiful coastline, and is steeped in colonial American history, which makes camping along it fun for the entire family. There are countless sights of interest such as Plymouth Rock, the Whaling Museum in New Bedford and even the city of Boston, although this is some distance from the sea. Should you elect to visit Province-town, on the tip of Cape Cod, you'll enjoy a ready access to the National Seashore area, with fine facilities. You'll also be visiting a spot where many say the Pilgrims *really* landed!

The fishing in all of the Bay State is great during summer. There are tautog around most every rock formation, and scup too. Weakfish, popularly called squeteague by natives, have made a strong comeback in recent years, and surf casters take an appreciable toll of bluefish and stripers. Indeed, still another fine camping and fishing hotspot is right on the banks of the Cape Cod Canal. I have often caught big striped bass and bluefish within a few minutes walk of our campsite beneath Borne Bridge crossing the big, man-made ditch joining Buzzards Bay with Cape Cod Bay. Digging quahogs for clam chowder is good sport too. No tomatoes please, for the traditional dish.

In little Rhode Island perhaps the nicest spot we've camped is at Charlestown Breachway. There we were within sight of the inlet and could avail ourselves of good fishing, fresh breezes and sunshine, and beautiful coastline. Depending on where one stops, Rhode Island has sand beaches or beautiful natural rock formations, the latter ideal casting platforms for striped bass, bluefish, tautog and a host of other species.

Along the Connecticut coastline, bordering the northern shore of Long Island Sound, there's not as much camping as along the Atlantic coastline. Hammonassett Beach is the most popular area. During the fall, the coastal rivers and estuaries which dot the Connecticut shore harbor an abundance of migrating waterfowl, and I've spoken with many bird watchers who annually camp along the coast just for the pleasure of observing the parade of ducks and geese heading south—often speeded by north winds.

For the camper with a yen for fine fishing there is beautiful Long Island, and its many fish-filled bays and inlets. Unfortunately there are limited campgrounds and public lands, but do try the south shore east of Shinnecock Inlet. Go all the way to Hither Hills and Montauk Point for beautiful seascapes and off-shore fishing. There are many spots where I've camped thanks to the courtesy of private individuals. This is especially true of rowboat livery owners along the south shore, who will usually permit you to park your rec vehicle off to the side, providing you hire their boat for your fishing.

I've experienced excellent summer flounder fishing during the spring and fall. There are also many fine catches of weakfish and porgies to be made from most of the bay waters. Along the surf the stripper and bluefish sport is excellent during the fall, although this calls for specialized gear most campers don't carry with them, including boots or waders, foul weather suits, and heavy, high surf casting tackle and big lures.

By all means bring the family dog along when you camp along the seacoast. Here "Trixie" watches attentively as the family enjoys dinner in a motorhome in Delaware.

New Jersey has a long seacoast, but unfortunately in the northern part of the state it's so built up that it's virtually impossible to camp along it. Throughout South Jersey, however, there are many fine campgrounds right on or near the ocean. Close at hand is fine fishing for summer and winter flounders, weakfish and small bluefish. Surf casters enjoy good sport with a variety of species, including kingfish, summer flounders, striped bass, bluefish and weakfish.

Moving south to the DelMarVa peninsula we find an area that has lots of campgrounds right along the coast, with fine beaches, and good fishing. Here too, in the fall there are huge flocks of waterfowl passing through, with rafts of geese and ducks settling down in the grain fields of the Eastern Shore to refuel for the next lap. In addition, the camper who mixes scattergun sport with his camping can enjoy fine dove and quail shooting.

Chincoteague Island and its nearby campgrounds is still another picturesque spot for campers to visit. Each year there is a roundup of the wild Chincoteague ponies, which proves exciting. There's an auction of the ponies followed by a gala parade. This area also has fine fishing, and in the fall I've had the finest railbird shooting one could ever ask for while being poled among the tidal marshes.

As the camper moves south along the North Carolina coast there are the beautiful Outer Banks, a long, narrow spit of sand comprising Hatteras and Ocracoke Islands and several long, thin slivers of sand extending south to Cape Lookout. I suspect that more campers have fallen in love with this area than any other because you can camp, fish and relax without the glitter and the metropolitan flavor associated with so many of the big-business-type campgrounds. There are several fishing piers on Hatteras Island from which the camper may try his luck, or try the surf. He'll be rewarded with summer flounders, whiting, spot, croakers, weakfish, seatrout, and even the prized king mackerel and cobia, plus a host of other species.

The scene here is Indian River, Delaware. The remains of the bridge spanning the river was left as a fishing pier. State operated campground in the background is a favorite of sea-coast campers; the ocean is just a short walk, with clean beaches and fine swimming.

There are many spots I've visited in North and South Carolina that I thought would be the ideal for the backpacker with a yen for solitude. For in many coastal areas of these two states there are literally dozens upon dozens of miles of open sand beaches with nothing but sand dunes, marsh grass and sea gulls to keep you company. I'd think that backpacking in to them, and just setting up would provide picturesque camping, especially using some of the old logging roads that crisscross the area. Many of these spots, it should be noted, are open to the public, but seldom used.

Georgia too, has a rather underdeveloped shoreline, and lots of camping opportunities, plus several fine campgrounds right on the coast. Florida, while a large state, has much of its coastal land extensively developed, hence there are few campgrounds in some areas, particularly along the Atlantic coast. But by perusing Woodall's *Trailering Parks and Campgrounds Directory,* which we've used religiously for years, we managed to select some fine sites. Of late,

especially during the winter, the many areas located in the Florida Keys have come to be very popular, as they're in a beautiful, semi-tropical setting, with fine boating, fishing and swimming opportunities readily available.

Florida's west coast is quite another thing from the east, with a whole new selection of species. The seatrout, cobia, snook, redfish, tarpon and a large number of small bottom feeders are to be found in most of the bays and rivers which empty into the Gulf of Mexico. In the main, the camping enthusiasts can enjoy fair sport off most of the beaches, both in the bays and along the Gulf. I've often waded wearing a pair of bathing trunks, using a one-handed spinning outfit and live shrimp as bait. I have landed a selection which included seatrout, Spanish mackerel, snook and jack crevalle, all great sport, and the first three fine on the charcoal grill.

Moving northward along the Gulf coastline you'll find scattered campgrounds all the way to Pensacola, and some

The Roskos landed this mixed catch of spot, summer flounder, whiting and seatrout while fishing the waters of Chesapeake Bay near Kiptopeke, Virginia. The entire DelMarVa peninsula is a beautiful place to camp.

fine fishing too, plus that ever-present sunshine, and good, warm water for swimming. Seashells, absent on the eastern coast, abound here to the delight of all.

Louisiana has at its southern terminus Grand Isle, a pretty island sitting practically in the Gulf of Mexico. It has numerous campgrounds, is steeped in pirate lore, has excellent fishing, plenty of open beaches and people whom we found most cordial to visitors.

Texas has a long coastline, and many fine beaches, mostly shallow, with an abundance of redfish and seatrout for the angler who just likes to wade and cast. Padre Island National Seashore is prime territory for the Lone Star camper. And if it's sunshine and salt air that you enjoy, this is a good spot to visit especially in early spring.

Camping along the seacoast, I've found, differs somewhat from what we've experienced inland. The scenery's different, as is the ocean compared to lakes. There's a constantly changing coastline, from the huge, rugged cliffs of Maine,

to the rocky shoreline of Rhode Island, to the flat, sandy beaches of the Outer Banks. In fresh water one finds essentially the same species throughout much of the country. Not so along the coast. Each region has a group of species all its own, and during a week's camping vacation it's not unusual to catch eight or ten different varieties of fish. There's a type of fishing well suited to the camper, because even the shore-based angler can run up a good score, and there's always a pier, bridge or bulkhead from which he can wet a line, too.

Yes, for something different, you might try seashore camping on your next vacation. Wrap some snowy white fish fillets in foil and put them on the charcoal grill, mix up a tossed salad and roast some fresh picked corn. Sitting along the dunes, listening to the waves crash on the beach, with gulls setting their wings as they wheel and turn and call overhead! It's a great way to enjoy a meal or a whole vacation—letting the tide carry your worries out to sea.

BIRD WATCHING WHILE CAMPING

by KARL H. MASLOWSKI

Redwing blackbird is a common species often seen around lakeshore camps.

I WAS A ten year old when I went on my first genuine camping trip. Now, 50 years later, the only incident still memorable from that experience in central Kentucky has to do with a sparrow hawk nest.

I found it in a woodpecker hole 10 feet off the ground in an old stub that stood forlornly in a big pasture. From a thicket at the edge of the field I watched as several times the parents flew to the hole with mice and grasshoppers in their talons and disappeared inside to the accompaniment of shrill comments from the hungry young. Aside from this memory I cannot recall even the names of my fellow campers, the quality of the food we ate, or even if we fished or went swimming!

I have been fortunate enough to sleep under some kind or another of camping rig on three continents and many islands and certain of my fondest recollections have to do with some kind of experience I have had with birds. By contrast, I must comment that some of my worst memories have to do with leaky roofs, poorly cooked meals, cranky companions, and balky lanterns and stoves. No doubt these resulted from poor planning and preparation. But to enjoy birds while on a camping trip, diligent pre-planning is usually not essential.

It is truly amazing how often campers will have birds as close neighbors. From the doorway of a tent or trailer I have literally had eyeball-to-eyeball or ear-to-mouth confrontations with such species as ptarmigan, pelicans, spotted sand-

◀ Author Maslowski has often found barn owls living in vicinity of campsites.

pipers, ruby-throated hummingbirds, screech owls, poorwills, evening grosbeaks, gray jays, and chipping sparrows. Some of these had nests close by, others came to scavenge table scraps, and some just happened to be passing by.

For example, while camped on the shores of Crooked Lake in Michigan years ago it was pure chance that we pitched our tent near an old snag whose hollow trunk harbored a family of bluebirds. Dish washing and other camp chores for a teenager were made endurable by the fact that I could easily observe the activity at that nest while engaged in distasteful work!

Admittedly, though, a bit of forethought will add immeasurably to the joys of birdwatching while camping. First, while you can "naked-eye" birdwatch, you can enjoy birds a lot more with a pair of 7x35 or 8x40 central focusing lightweight binoculars. There are myriads of good makes, mostly foreign, on the market which may be purchased for less than $50. Be sure your pair will focus down to at least 25 feet because oftentimes you will see birds at close range yet, even then, you will not be able to enjoy all the action and color except through the magnification of binocular lenses.

Then if you want to be able to identify the various birds (and in America north of the Rio Grande about 800 species have been recorded) one should have a good field guide. *A Guide to Field Identification: Birds of North America,* published by the Golden Press and selling for about $4 in soft cover and $6 in hard cover, is excellent. Be sure to read the short introductory chapters to derive full benefit from this volume. The two volumes of Roger Tory Peterson's *Field Guide to the Birds*—one for the east, one for the west—are equally good. They are published by Houghton-Mifflin Company. Both are profusely and superbly illustrated.

A walk in the woods near camp may reveal a scene like this—of a ruby throated hummingbird feeding young at nest.

When camping along southern seashores, watch for antics of brown pelicans. Always carry along a camera.

Should the camper be genuinely interested in birds a bit of research beforehand will enable him to be at the right spot at the right time to enjoy certain aspects of bird behavior to best advantage. Thus, to see the really enormous concentrations of wintering shorebirds along the San Diego coastal region, for example, he should plan his camping trip for a period between mid-December and mid-February. But if he should want to be on hand for the spring migration of whistling swans through the southwestern Lake Erie marshes he had better get his camping gear set up somewhere near Oak Harbor, Ohio, by mid-March. And if he wants to observe the nesting activity of mew gulls he had best arrange to have his tent pitched near a big island-dotted lake somewhere in the Yukon Territory or Alaska no later than July 4th.

Once a camper learns to recognize birds by shape, color, and action, his pleasure and sometimes peace of mind will increase if he can identify them by song. I have been camping with people who considered the wild bird symphony at daybreak on an early June morning as sheer bedlam and a worse sleep robber than a crew of rookie trash collectors. Had they been able to identify the solos of wood thrush, Kentucky warbler, cardinal, Carolina wren, and so forth, the serenade would have sounded more like a lullabye than a cacophony.

I well remember my seven year old twin sons' frightened "Wh-aaat's that, Daddy?" in response to a nearby scream which sounded as though a woman was in distress. We still lay awake in our tent on the Eastfork of the Little Miami River on an October night years ago after a successful day of bass fishing and squirrel hunting when the shriek was heard. I was able to reassure the boys that it was only a barn owl. I had learned the call the hard way as a boy when one almost frightened me out of 10 years growth by screaming as it left a barn-loft directly over my head one moonlit night. You may learn bird calls by listening to records. Some of the best are those of Dr. Donald Borror, released by Dover Press.

Poorwill is a bird easier to hear than see after dark.

The now rare eastern bluebird brings a moth to its nest hole in a dead tree trunk.

Sometimes birds have been the salvation of camping trips that were originally planned as fishing or hunting forays. Once on the Elkhorn down near Frankfort, Kentucky, I was able to show an avid angler—but neophyte birder—her first wook duck and pileated woodpecker after she had spent a fruitless day fishing that fine little limestone stream. She was more ecstatic than if she had caught a limit of 3-pound smallmouth bass.

On another occasion while elk hunting in the San Juan Wilderness Area in Colorado the only pleasant experiences from an otherwise disastrous trip were adventures with water-ouzels, golden eagles, and blue grouse.

It is trite, but it is also true, that life becomes more meaningful in direct relationship to increased knowledge. An increased awareness of the identity, color, and action of birds will make every camping trip far more pleasurable. You will enjoy them most, however, if you have a weather-tight roof and well prepared food—but that requires a lot of planning and preparation.

By contrast your bird-watching may be haphazard, but it will be filled with a series of constant but delightful surprises. Bobwhite may dust in the ashes of your campfire, a green heron may compete with you for minnows, a whip-poor-will may serenade you from one of your tent poles, or a Baltimore oriole may take loose threads from your airing sleeping bag for its nest. Herewith are the portraits of just a very few species you might meet on your next camping trip.

The sparrow hawk is a small, beautiful bird of prey which might be seen near a campground anywhere in America.

KENTUCKY

This beautiful scene is not the view from a private estate, but available to all. It's Cumberland Gap National Historical Park.

CAMPING

by PEGGY PETERS

IT SOMETIMES appears that Americans are subject to seizures. The desire to own something recently only dimly perceived or dreamed of becomes absolutely overwhelming.

Recall, if you can, the years following World War II. Each returning service man wanted to own his own home (remember Levittown?). Some years later television swept over our nation and the unbelievable became commonplace. A box containing a cross between a radio and a motion picture was installed in even the most modest of dwellings. Having two automobiles and sending all post-high school offspring to college seemed the desirable American Way. Now there is a new wave breaking in full force over all of us. Anyone who has visited our national parks or travelled our highways, or even ventured out to buy a loaf of bread could not have failed to notice the tremendous increase in the numbers of campers and motor homes of all sorts. It is estimated that there are five million recreational vehicles in use. The urge to leave our mechanized, computerized, sanitized lives for something more real is the motivation for so many to invest in this means of escape.

It has been widely reported that the common destinations for too many of us are Yellowstone, Yosemite and others of our national parks. During the peak of the season (and it's a long, flat peak) campsites are often filled by mid-day and sometimes are just unavailable to the hopeful camper at any time. It is also true that a large number of travellers come from the eastern metropolitan centers while a great number of the parks are in the West. The trip from home to the destination probably involves more time and certainly greater expense, to say nothing of using a lot more gasoline than we seem to be able to spare.

Given all this it is no miracle that Kentucky is an increasingly popular area for campers. It is closer to home for many, its beauty rivals that at more distant places and the state has more parks and shrines than most would believe. These public areas occupy nearly 39,000 acres and are scattered over the whole state. Happily they are open to everyone and many are open every day of the year and at absolutely no cost. Honestly.

Officialdom in Kentucky is unable to issue complete figures for camping within its boundaries. They do know that 563,000 people camped in the state parks in 1972, but how many camped in the other 200 Kentucky campgrounds is anybody's guess.

There are more than 20,000 campsites in the Bluegrass State, ranging in quality from the completely primitive to the deluxe places that provide probably more than you want. By far the great majority of the campgrounds (23 out of 27) provide service buildings with conveniences like well-lit wash basins and showers with abundant hot water, telephones, and they even sell grocery staples. The

Well known fisherman, Dick Kotis, who has fished most everywhere, at the Land Between the Lakes.

Campers can often visit famous Kentucky horse farms free of charge.

remaining four offer primitive camping for those who prefer to rough it. Altogether there are about 3,000 sites in the Kentucky state park system! Add to this over 17,000 more areas provided by municipal and county parks as well as national areas such as Daniel Boone National Forest, Cumberland Gap National Historical Park and others and there is little doubt that Kentucky offers the camper more than just mint juleps and fine horseflesh.

While there are increasing numbers of back-packers and older, retired persons taking advantage of our outdoor areas, the most popular type of camping remains that done by the entire family vacationing once a year. Those things which should be included in a family campground fall in two areas: conveniences so that familiar, tiresome chores are at a minimum for all (especially Mother) and lots to do (especially for the kids).

In this lots-to-do category include the world-famous Cave Area in Central Kentucky. There are chairlifts that whisk you up a hillside to see Western gun fights, scenic boat trips on the Green River, wildlife museums and spectacular cave tours and even a wax museum featuring more than 100 of our nation's great personalities.

Mammoth Cave is an exciting place to see and a good place to stay while seeing this and other great caverns in Barren River Lake State Resort Park. Take your choice from 101 campsites for tents or recreational vehicles.

For some of the finest fishing anywhere try Cumberland Lake. The state runs a resort park on the edge of this, one of the largest man-made lakes in the world. If fishing isn't for everyone in your group you're still in luck. Others can swim or bask in the sun and for a really different experience how about renting a houseboat? These are available and large enough for a good-sized family. Houseboats are also available in Kentucky's "Western Waterland," where three Kentucky state resort parks provide campgrounds near all water activities.

This Western Waterland is a heavily forested recreation area almost completely surrounded by two of the largest

Here visitors enjoy Mammoth Cave, a tourist attraction for over 150 years. The place to camp in this area is Barren River Lake State Resort Park.

Houseboating, either motoring along at a good pace, or anchored in a quiet cove of your own, will make an unforgettable Kentucky vacation for the family. The boats may be rented and include everything but the food.

man-made lakes in America. It is called, appropriately, the Land Between the Lakes, and is a 170,000 acre peninsula between Kentucky Lake and Lake Barkley. It offers just fishing, boating, hunting and hiking. All this in a beautiful setting which is all the more appealing because of its lack of commercialization. You can rent that houseboat here, but you will find no motels, restaurants, or resorts anywhere on the peninsula. And there are more than 300 miles of back-country drives and trails that provide visitors with

area is open all year and is popular with youth groups. Other groups may use indoor housing and dining facilities at Brandon Spring, a new, modern camp on Bards Lake. With all these lovely spots open to groups, it would almost seem a fine idea to form a club just to take advantage of them! A fishing club, for instance.

There are over 3,500 miles of shoreline along the two lakes and the fishing and boating opportunities are almost unlimited for visitors. Fishing for crappie, largemouth

Kentucky, not a large state, has more miles of running water than any other state except Alaska—14 times its size. 15,000 tons of fish are caught yearly by sportfishermen.

ample opportunity to find their own wooded retreat or lakeside fishing hole.

Camping, obviously, is the favored activity here and there are three family campgrounds — Hillman Ferry, Rushing Creek and Piney.

Hillman Ferry and Piney are open all year, but Rushing Creek is a different sort of place. It is not open during the winter, but from early spring through fall, camping clubs and other organized groups or associations may make reservations for its use.

Another reservable group camp is Camp Energy. This

bass, white bass, bluegill and catfish is among the best in the country and it's a year-round sport in the twin lakes area The spring crappie run in Kentucky Lake is still regarded as one of the biggest fishing attractions in mid-America. If you don't have your own boat, both the boat and the motor can be rented at any of the docks on the west shore of Kentucky Lake and the east shore of Lake Barkley. If you don't want to be bothered with a boat at all, just bank fish from any of the ideal spots along the deep coves of the two lakes.

Wildlife observations and bird watching are favorite

The Bluegrass State provides about 3,000 sites for campers—some with every facility, some with none. Here two families vacation together with neither bearing the full responsibility for all.

pastimes in the Land Between the Lakes. Visitors driving or hiking the heavily shaded back-country roads have opportunities to see a great variety of wildlife, from deer and native wild turkey to giant Canada geese and even the magnificent bald eagle.

Trail maps and other visitor information are available by writing Land Between the Lakes, TVA, Golden Pond, Ky. 42231.

Kincaid Lake State Park at Falmouth, in north-central Kentucky, is the largest recreational complex of all the state parks. There are 80 full service campsites, and numerous activity areas such as: handball, tennis, basketball and shuffleboard courts, a miniature golf course, a swimming beach, bathhouse, boat dock and launching ramp, to name a few.

In the topmost corner of Northeast Kentucky is Greenbo Lake State Resort Park, near Greenup, where there is a new central service building for campers. About 35 miles away is Carter Caves State Resort Park, Olive Hill—the building here is being enlarged. There are 71 new sites at Grayson Lake State Park and 50 at Buckhorn Lake State Resort in Eastern Kentucky.

All this expansion and new construction is underway to accommodate the annually-increasing number of visitors to the Bluegrass State. A recent survey undertaken by the parks department under the direction of Ewart W. Johnson, the commissioner, shows "over 100 per cent" occupancy (because they'll always try to find a place for you, even if all the regular spots are taken). Hopefully this program will keep the available spaces in greater supply than the number of campers needing them.

If you are the wilderness sort of camper you can forget about available spaces and tramp off into the eastern mountains of the state. Here one can uncover anew the beauty and solitude of still primeval land.

Wherever you or your family choose to go in the wonderful state of Kentucky you will find beauty, hospitality and variety. A comprehensive booklet: "Campgrounds in Kentucky," write Travel, Frankfort, Kentucky 40601, is available to interested campers.

TENNESSEE

Reelfoot Lake

Dale Hollow Lake

S. Holston Lake

Watauga Lake

Center Hill Lake

Great Smoky Mtns. Nat'l Park

Appalachian Trail

TOPS FOR TENT CAMPERS

by H. LEA LAWRENCE

TWO THINGS MAKE Tennessee terrific for tent campers—lakes and mountains—and while this may not immediately sound exceptional, a more detailed look at the implications will indicate the immense potential that exists.

For one thing, it doesn't mean "some" of each. The topography of the state is such that it forms a natural cross-section of about any kind of land type imaginable—mountains, valleys, plateaus, rolling hills and forested river bottoms—and across that 300-mile East-West expanse are sites to meet any tent camper's desires, whether it be drive-in, boat-in or walk-in. There are 221 camping areas of all sorts which can be utilized, ranging from the luxurious to the primitive, and many of these remain open on a year-'round basis.

Impressive perhaps, but it doesn't begin to illustrate the tent camping possibilities, because beyond the designated locations are countless places where fabulous vacations can be enjoyed in an environment which provides all of the elbow room anyone could ask for. Privacy is at a premium

in most states today, but an ambitious camper who has familiarized himself with the state by benefit of maps and other information sources will have no trouble finding all of the territory he could explore in several years' time.

Part of this is due to the availability of resources which have not been destroyed by man's influence; on the other hand, the human factor has been of inestimable value in creating and enhancing many things which provide for this abundance of outdoor recreation.

As an example, there are 17 major impoundments in the state which were built by the Tennessee Valley Authority and the U.S. Army Corps of Engineers which have a total of more than 15,000 shoreline miles. These shorelines are a mecca for campers, and particularly tent campers, since a large portion of this land is available for such purposes. Those who do not mind hauling water and pitching a tent on an undeveloped site can literally pick as they choose, for the most part.

The selection can be fun, and it can be done by car, roam-

A trio of campers set up camp on the Little Tennessee River in eastern Tennessee.

ing around on back roads which border the lakes. However, to find the best "away from it all" places, cruising the banks and in and out of the coves can be the best method. It is also the way to look over the islands which are present in almost all of the lakes, and which can offer sites of a very special kind. From an island camping spot, one has access to all of the water related activities, and being alone on your "own island" can make for an exciting and memorable trip.

Too, lake camping has benefits in some locales which are not immediately obvious. This applies particularly to those impoundments which lie in the mountainous portion of the state—the East—where one is virtually surrounded by scenically beautiful and recreationally rich country. At such locations you can get up in the morning and head out into wild, rugged territory and hike to your heart's content, or fish in one of the tumbling streams that cascade down from the high elevations. Lakes, streams and mountains are a hard combination to beat!

Watauga Lake, in the extreme northeastern section of Tennessee, is a good example of this kind of area. Practically all of the land around it is owned by the U.S. Forest Service, and there are campsites at lakeside. A segment of the famed Appalachian Trail parallels this impoundment, the length of which can be covered in a day's hike, and there are trails developed by the Forest Service that wind back through some magnificent terrain. Watauga has 13 species of game fish, and it is probably the most under-fished reservoir in the TVA system.

Watauga's sister impoundment, South Holston, lies only a few miles to the West, and it is almost a carbon copy in the way of recreational opportunities. Fall campers might take note of the fact that both of these lakes lie in excellent hunting country which is tops for deer, squirrels and ruffed grouse. Springtime offers some fine wild turkey hunting.

In the mid-state region, Dale Hollow and Center Hill Lakes stand out as superb camping locations. Both of these are splendid, scenically, and there is minimal shoreline development in the way of resorts and summer homes. Finding an ideal camping site is no trouble, and the fishing is great at both places. Too, both of the tailwaters of these lakes have especially good trout fishing for both rainbows and browns. The former North American brown trout record, a 26-pound-plus fish, was taken below Dale Hollow, and trout of the five-pound-and-up category are not uncommon. A Dale Hollow smallmouth, incidentally, holds the world record.

To the West, in the extreme upper corner of the state, is Reelfoot Lake, an earthquake-formed body of water that is unique in many ways. A nature lover's paradise, Reelfoot has a fantastic songbird, shore bird and waterfowl population, and it boasts the northernmost stand of bald cypress in the nation. The crappie fishing is so good that it has long been known as the "crappie fishing capital of the world," and it also has fine bluegill and largemouth bass fishing. Because of the swampy terrain, the use of the state-owned tent camping facility is recommended.

One delightful water-oriented tent camping plan which can provide all the excitement and variety anyone could

River camping can be a great change, and an exciting kind of trip.

hope for is what could best be described as a "modern day Huck Finn" trip, using the waterways as the routes of travel, and pitching camp along the way wherever you please. This kind of a trip can be as lengthy time-wise or distance-wise as preferred, since the TVA system is navigable from Fort Loudoun Lake in East Tennessee all the way through Kentucky Dam in Kentucky. In the process, the river runs through portions of Alabama and Mississippi, making it a four-state sweep. Along the way there are 17 state parks, as well as many docks and marinas where food and supplies can be obtained. Navigable lakes permit travel from Cordell Hull Lake in the mid-state area through Barkley Dam, which lies parallel to Kentucky Dam.

This kind of a trip can be made in any type of craft, all the way from canoes to cruisers, and it can be a truly educational voyage. Canoeists, in particular, discover the full feel of real adventure, as well as the luxury of picking camp sites where no tent has ever been pitched before. There is no hazardous water along these waterways, and the only danger is in the form of storms and big waves from the barge traffic.

Back to purely terrestrial Tennessee opportunities, the Great Smoky Mountains National Park always looms high in the minds of campers heading southward; however, there are implications relating to this favorite playground which should be considered.

The Smokies encompass over 800 square miles of mountain country, which is a lot of territory in anybody's book, so much, in fact, that it would appear to provide limitless camping potential. It just isn't true anymore. The Smokies are the nation's most-visited national park—over 5 million people last year—and the park has become sorely pressed to meet the needs of this vast influx of travelers. There are six campgrounds in the park, all of them of the primitive type, and the number of sites ordinarily totals 1004. Presently, though, and probably until 1975, one of these is closed due to road construction, which drops the total sites to 634. Match this figure with the number of visitors and further explanation is unnecessary.

Too, there are problems at the places other than the developed campgrounds, such as the Appalachian Trail, which has shelters along its 71-mile course through the Smokies Park. Traffic along this trail, as well as other backpacking trails, has become so heavy that restrictions on the number of people using them has become a must. Since no camping is permitted except at specifically listed places, finding a site can be a gamble with odds on the opposite side.

Further complicating the problem for tent campers is the lack of facilities or locations outside the park boundary. A number of trailer and RV campgrounds are available, but virtually no places can be found where just plain tenting is allowed.

The sensible alternative is to seek out areas within the Cherokee National Forest, the huge, 609,000 acre hunk of land that extends from the Virginia line to the North, to the Georgia line to the South, blanketing almost all of the eastern Tennessee mountain region except the Smokies Park. This is a part of the U.S. Forest Service's southern complex, and the agency has done an exceptional job in recreational development to date, with expansion of this program continuing on an accelerated scale.

What has been overlooked in the past by many persons looking to Tennessee for a camping vacation is the fact that the Cherokee National Forest is, in essence, the Smokies, also. It borders it on both ends, and the scenic and recreational opportunities are just as bountiful. The Tellico and North River area, for example, which lies near Tellico Plains, is spectacular country which offers a wealth of camp sites, hiking trails and top-flight trout fishing. In the fall, fine big game and small game hunting can be right at hand.

Tent campers can get a broad look at the Appalachians by hop-scotching around at the 25 developed campgrounds in the Cherokee Forest, and since undeveloped sites can be utilized with permission from the supervisor, the possibility of getting caught with a tent and nowhere to pitch it is practically nil. What's more, right across the mountains on the North Carolina side, the Forest Service's gigantic Pisgah National Forest is a twin to the Cherokee.

Scattered across the state are 26 Tennessee State Parks, all of which have camping areas, and most of which offer a wide variety of recreational opportunities. These make for fine stopping points in cross-state travel, and usually there's no trouble finding a site. The system has a total of 1150 of these, with more under construction. Most of the parks are at places with historic or scenic significance, and often they can serve as good base headquarters for exploring adjacent points of interest.

One of the most interesting and extensive camping areas

Backpacking into the mountains is rugged, but fun, even if it does get wet along the way.

Canoes provide lots of adventure on "modern day Huck Finn" river trips.

outside the Smokies Park and the Cherokee Forest is TVA's showplace Land Between the Lakes, a long, 170,000 acre peninsula which has been developed as a national demonstration in recreational and outdoor education. It is accessible from both Tenn. and Kentucky and has succeeded well; LBL offers everything in the way of camping facilities, all the way from modern RV sites to primitive locations, and its position between Kentucky Lake and Barkley Lake make it ideal for water related recreation as well as that found on land. Over 80 percent of this area is forested, and the nature study groups and wildlife observers find this area of prime interest. There is even a herd of American bison. Hunting is permitted on designated portions of the area in season for deer (both whitetail and European fallow), small game and waterfowl. Not the bison, of course.

So you can literally take your pick of places to camp in Tennessee—mountains, lowlands, lakes, streams and rivers included—and with a little advance planning, it could be the trip of a lifetime.

Material and information sources are:
Tennessee Department of Conservation
Division of State Parks
2611 West End Avenue
Nashville, Tennessee 37203

Supervisor
Great Smoky Mountains National Park
Park Headquarters
Gatlinburg, Tennessee 37738

Forest Supervisor
Cherokee National Forest
U.S. Forest Service
Cleveland, Tennessee 37311

Information Office
Land Between the Lakes
Tennessee Valley Authority
Golden Pond, Kentucky 42231

Group Camping by CANOE

by GIRL SCOUT TROOP 567 (MARINERS) of Old Greenwich Connecticut

HOW DO YOU TRAVEL when you want to go group camping in a way that's new and fun? We've learned a good answer: go camping by canoe!

We've tried other ways: island camping by sailboat, to Expo '67 by motorboat; and to the deep woods in mid-winter by snowmobile. A canoe camping trip seemed to offer us an attractive change of pace. We could enjoy a leisurely paddle, get some steady exercise (many camping trips involve sitting half the day, then really heavy labor the other half), and learn some new boating skills.

More than half the Scouts in our troop had never been in a canoe before, so this meant we had to do some careful planning and training. The end result was a three-day trek via this quick mode of travel to an area rich in Revolutionary War history. It was an exciting experience for us all.

Planning Where to Go

For a first trip, we think you would be well advised to pick a small lake and paddle around the perimeter, camping as you go; or travel down a small river or canal, camping on the bank and following the current.

The local library was a valuable aid to us in picking an appropriate waterway. For example, we found the book *Exploring the Little Rivers of New Jersey*, which described the abandoned Delaware and Raritan Canal. This canal

Advance physical training, like push-ups and sit-ups strengthen young muscles so that a reasonable rate of speed on the water doesn't require unreasonable exertion.

is State property and camping is permitted anywhere along the towpath—very convenient. It requires no long portages or "carries", but does have several short ones (150 feet) around the now-inoperative locks—that means lots of interest and variety in levels and views of the countryside. It is within an hour of New York City yet retains a very real wilderness feeling as though the surrounding area hadn't changed much since George Washington made it his headquarters—very picturesque, yet convenient and safe, too.

We felt these points were important; we think you'll agree.

1. The itinerary should start within several hours convenient drive from your home town. This offers family members a chance to station themselves along the route to take pictures, as well as pick up members of the group (even the whole group) in case of *really* bad weather or a health emergency.

2. There should be small towns or logical stopping places along the route where the food committee can replenish supplies, refill water jugs, stop for refreshments, and call home or for medical help. These spots should be surveyed in advance by the trip leaders. A drive to the area and along the waterway will help planners pick good spots for launching and picking up canoes as well as for shopping; this should be done in advance of the trip itself.

3. Camping sites should be conveniently located at intervals so that a days' run can be shortened—even lengthened—if need be. This "elasticity" in the schedule can make up for all sorts of delays in getting underway, for making repairs, or being held up by bad weather. Campsites should be close to the waterside and relatively secluded to discourage unwelcome hecklers or casual visi-

tors. Banks should be low enough to permit hauling the canoes completely out of the water at night, if possible, to prevent damage by wakes from other passing boats.

4. The waterway should be protected and small enough to prevent the wind from building up any kind of rough water. Lots of trees not only provide shade but also break the force of the wind and make paddling easier. For a first-time canoe trip, white water (rapids, riffles, fast current areas) should be avoided, as should attempts to rig make-shift sails which could easily capsize heavily loaded canoes.

Then, as your group gains experience, you may want to venture farther afield.

Making an Actual Plan

Our Troop has a motto: if we worry enough about things that could possibly happen *before* we go on our trip, we will have planned to handle all contingencies without worry *while* we're on our trip. It's a good rule and we recommend it.

When your group knows *where* its members want to go, it is possible to select a team of leaders to direct the planning with the needs of a certain area in mind. This business of picking leaders may sound awfully formal, but it is necessary because decisions have to be made by someone. In addition to a project director picked by popular vote, committee chairmen should be appointed (or elected, or they may even volunteer) for such vital areas as: "Itinerary and Program", "Clothing and Packing", "Tents and Equipment", "Food and Cooking" (includes clean-up crews, too), "Pre-Trip Training", and "First Aid and Safety". By involving as many members as possible in different roles as chairmen, committee workers, and helpers, they all develop a personal stake in seeing that things are well planned, and then carried out according to the plan.

In a series of meetings, it will be possible to agree on the actual route and number of stopovers, even for lunch breaks, as well as approximate times of departure and arrival. These times and places won't be exact, of course, but they'll give your plan a foundation on which to build —after all, you can't schedule a trip until you know who's going where, when, and how long they'll stay.

Clothing and Packing

Boating and camping can be a damp business, unless the weather is near-perfect. A quick rain shower and squall wind can keep paddlers too busy to bail or to protect bedding and clothing from water which puddles in the bottom of a canoe. Reboarding can also bring water aboard—since it is absolutely essential to make sure that the canoe is well afloat before boarding, which means wading it out a little way.

It is therefore a must to pack everything to keep out the dampness.

Clothing and Bedding: All equipment should be packed to keep out wet. A suggested clothing list for a two-night, three-day trip is attached. You will see when you read it that all items can be rolled in a sleeping bag *except* sunglasses, sunhat, suntan lotion, camera, film, and poncho. These last should be packed in a gaudy bag", a bright-colored (easy to spot), water-resistant, zipper-type beach bag with plastic lining, and kept close at hand for use throughout the day. The clothing-filled sleeping bag is packed in a large plastic bag for the day's traveling. Such plastic bags can be bought for about 10¢ at laundromats, where they're sold to bring home clean laundry. Large plastic "garbage" bags from the super-market will also do the job. Extras should be packed for each person. A roll of plastic tape for the entire group should be provided to make a watertight seal.

If the already-made-up bags aren't available, they can be manufactured by the Clothing and Packing Committee from polyethelene sheet film bought by the roll from home-repair and building-suply stores (Sears, Roebuck and Montgomery Ward are good sources). To make seams, tape two raw edges together lengthwise several times and tape again.

Food: Non-perishables should be packed by groups according to the day and meal in which they're to be used: "first day's breakfast" might be marked on the outside of the appropriate carton, for example. We've yet to find a really good substitute for small cardboard cartons for this use; they serve as garbage boxes temporarily when they're emptied, and can be burned easily if need be. They stack well and protect boxes of food (donuts and cookies, for example) from being crushed. However, they do get soggy and should be carefully sealed in plastic. Perishables are

The chosen waterway should be protected enough, as by trees lining the route, that sudden winds won't cause emergencies.

Loafing and drifting are part of the experience, too.

usually bought just before the meal at which they'll be eaten and taken to the campsite in a light-weight, inexpensive styrofoam picnic cooler. A word of caution: the styrofoam coolers are light and keep things cold, but they're extremely fragile and nothing should be stacked on top of them.

Camp Gear: Stoves, axes, lanterns, all metal items which might go to the bottom of the waterway in the event of a capsize, should be lashed firmly into the canoe, or at least tethered. Stove fuel should be brought in small quantities and stored in spill-proof cans in a shady spot. Matches should be dipped in parafin wax before starting on the trip, then sealed into a Mason-type jar. Flashlight batteries can leak in hot weather and shouldn't be packed with clothing or in sleeping rolls.

Loading Canoes: Getting the canoes to the launch site is always a problem. In most cases, there are rental dealers along all popular waterways—write Grumman Boats, Marathon, N.Y. for their directory of over 100 canoe rental locations—and it's best to get the craft from them. Sometimes you can launch from a dealer's location; at other times, the dealer will often be willing to deliver the canoes to the launch spot of your choice. In any case, he's your

best source of information on transporting overland. You may have to pay for any damage to the canoes, so be careful!

For our trip we used Grumman 15-footers. Small and light as they were, we found each would hold three Scouts, all the personal gear for these girls, plus a food box and tent. Our Bassett-hound mascot, Olivia, even traveled in one of the canoes and loved it. Even if not mandatory in your state, there should be a life preserver, buoyant cushion, or life jacket for each passenger, readily accessible in each canoe, plus a light of some sort in case of travel after dark. Each canoeist should know his or her specific seat in a specific canoe, and should be partly responsible for seeing that none of the gear carried in that craft is left behind.

Tents and Equipment

We prefer to take light, two-man tents (in which we sandwich three) than heavier, four-man varieties. You can bring your own tent poles or you can cut them; use dead wood for poles and pegs making sure they're kept together in sets with the tent, and lashed aboard. Dirty tent pegs shouldn't be rolled in the tent because the dirt

Each member of the group has her own duties. While some pitch flys and attend to dinner preparations, others may relax until their turns come at cleaning up later.

Careful planning and a congenial group make for a fine experience for all, happy memories and perhaps a return engagement.

clogs the pores of the cloth and ruins the water-proofing; insect-repellent sprays should *never* be used directly on tent fabric because it dissolves the water-proofing.

When you're cooking for a group you will find it's often difficult to schedule meals cooked over a wood fire, especially in misty or damp weather. Dry wood, even in a rainstorm, can be obtained in the woods by snagging dead branches down from standing trees. Use a weighted line (even a shoe lace) thrown over the branch to pull it to the ground. Quick-igniting charcoal products like "Brix", available at the super-market, is one solution—even this fairly stable fuel should be handled with care.

When the woods are dry and authorities ban open fires, it is necessary to bring your own cookstove. We prefer a single-burner alcohol stove of the marine variety. On it, we've actually done all the necessary cooking for a group of up to 25 persons.

Driving tent stakes requires a hand axe; there's no way to use a heavy rock as effectively. Moreover, if the weather's threatening and tents need to go up fast, it may be

well to have one axe per tent rather than just one for the entire group.

Food and Cooking

Simple food, well prepared in clean pots, and plenty of it—these are the rules for any outdoor expedition. When you're canoeing, you must also consider weight. Canned food can only be part of the menu on a canoe trip, therefore.

We recommend that milk and other dairy products have small place in menus, especially for breakfast. They can leave a fatty residue in mouth and throat, as well as make a hard-working paddler sick to the stomach. Eggs can be cooked in advance, especially for the first morning's breakfast, and eaten hardboiled and cold. Donuts are sugary and offer good, quick energy, as do the sugar coated cereals. Individual cereal packs are best.

Mid-morning, hard candy sour balls in fruit flavors can be allowed to dissolve slowly in your mouth—the sourer they are, the better they quench your thirst.

Lunches may be prepared and packed in individual bags at breakfast time so that each canoeist has one. A plastic jug of water can rapidly be converted to lemonade or fruit punch with instant powders. Sandwiches of the peanut-butter'n'jelly variety stick to the ribs and travel best; never use mayonnaise on sandwiches in hot weather.

Dinner should be of the one-pot variety. For example, just before stopping for the evening meal, an ample supply of ground beef can be purchased at a shore-side town. The amount should be about ⅓ lb. per person, kept in the styrofoam cooler until suppertime. If stores aren't available, bring the meat well wrapped in foil and frozen solid in the cooler; it may still be frozen by suppertime. Brown the meat in the bottom of a large pot with some diced onions. Prepare "Ground Beef Stroganoff" by adding one can of undiluted cream of mushroom soup per two pounds of meat; serve over crisp chow-mein noodles. Or, instead prepare "Campfire Stew" by substituting a similar amount of undiluted vegetable soup for the cream of mushroom type; serve with or without noodles.

Next night for a change of pace, steam an amount of the three-minute instant rice in your large pot. Then add canned chicken chunks or tunafish chunks with canned peas and several cans of undiluted cream of chicken soup. Spaghetti can be made using one of the excellent dry-mix systems which includes pasta, sauce and cheese in one packet. Double the amounts to feed paddle-hungry canoeists, though.

We recommend paper plates and cups along with plastic utensils for the ultimate in cleanliness. Upset stomachs and other problems can be caused by unclean eating equipment. Pots should be scrubbed with soap pads, and/or wet earth, then rinsed and boiled over the stove to sterilize them.

Training

Canoeing isn't something we do often enough. It calls for muscles we don't use very much otherwise, as well as little-used skills. In any community, however, there are bound to be competent outdoorsmen and women who know all about canoeing. These people—often local dealers in canoes and camping equipment—are glad to lend you their skills.

We have used Grumman aluminum canoes and have found them stable, light, and very durable. We've been able to do things we knew would not be possible with wood-and-canvas canoes—loading the craft on land, for example, and carrying them loaded. While these things haven't so much as dented our aluminum craft, we advise you be extremely careful with the traditional canoes. One of the areas where you can use the help of experts is in portaging or carrying the canoes around on dry land. We thought at first that it would be easiest to avoid unloading our canoes by getting together a large number of Scouts and carrying them with all gear aboard. *It doesn't work,* and in two later carries we found the job went quicker and easier by toting the empty canoes in the traditional overhead fashion, then returning for our equipment.

Advance training for the trip should include exercising—push ups and sit-ups to strengthen arm, shoulder, and abdominal muscles—as well as practice loading, launching, and paddling sessions. These will give you great confidence, as you learn that canoes aren't *nearly* as tippy as everyone says they are.

First Aid and Safety

Any activity in the woods or on the water carries danger with it. We preface every trip by having a local first aid authority speak to our Troop to give us pointers. We carry a first aid kit in every second canoe. We have one adult advisor for every 6 to 8 scouts. We use the buddy system whenever we plan to walk, hike, swim or explore away from our group.

Safety in canoeing is largely a matter of good sense, we think: Horseplay doesn't make good sense. Neither does going without life preservers and the appropriate first aid supplies.

Anti-bug lotion is important, along with suntan lotion, and pain-relieving sprays in case of sunburn. Each of our first aid kits included a bar of old-fashioned yellow laundry soap for combatting poison ivy. We also had a snake-bite kit.

Canoe Camping When You Don't Own a Canoe

If you want to camp by canoe, but you don't own one; rent one. Renting is possible almost anywhere you'd want to go. To find a livery in the area of your choice write to Grumman Boats, Marathon, New York 13803 for a free copy of their *Rent-a-Canoe-Directory.* You might also request their guide *Group Camping by Canoe.* That's free, too.

Suggested Clothing and Personal Equipment List

1. One pair of shorts
2. One pair of long pants
3. One sweater or sweatshirt
4. One pair of sneakers
5. Several pairs of absorbent cotton or wool athletic socks
6. Personal toiletries
7. Several cotton shirts
8. Camera and film
9. One bathing suit
10. One towel
11. Pair lightweight waterproof boots
12. Raincoat, slicker, or poncho
13. Ground cloth or air mattress if poncho is not used under sleeping bag
14. Sunhat and sunglasses
15. Suntan and mosquito lotion
16. Flashlight and extra batteries

Suggested Camp Equipment List

1. Several large aluminum pots
2. Styrofoam cooler
3. Spatulas and long-handled spoons
4. Plastic utensils with paper plates and cups
5. Hand axe(s)
6. Hand-held spotlight for emergency use
7. Rolls of toilet paper and toweling
8. Folding shovel (entrenching tool(s))
9. Portable stove and fuel
10. Waterproofed matches
11. Soap pads and cleaners or liquid detergents

Have a Great Trip!

consider the

farm ponds

by NAT FRANKLIN

AS USUAL, last year I spent a good deal of time traveling and camping in many places far away from my home in the humid Midwest. Camping is my business and I enjoy it, too. But one of the most memorable times of all occurred little more than an hour from my own doorstep.

It's difficult to say what awakened me on this soft and clinging morning. It may have been a pair of redwinged blackbirds quarreling just outside the tent. Or it may have been a vagrant breeze spilling dew from the white oak tree above onto taut canvas. But no matter because I didn't even bother to dress; instead I went for a dawn skinny dip in the pond which was only 25 feet or so beyond the tent flaps. Ah, paradise! Try that at daybreak sometime and let me know if anything else has ever been so absolutely refreshing. For me it was reliving happy times of a boyhood past.

That done—and still no one else stirring about in camp—I pulled on pants, picked up a flyrod, a bucket and followed a thin trail to the opposite side of the pond to collect my breakfast. As usual, that proved to be very easy. In no more than 30 minutes I had seven bluegills and one small bass. I needed slightly longer than that to collect a quart of blackberries in the bucket. But by the time I had finished dressing the fish, I could hear noises back in camp. Admitted that it may have been my imagination, I also could smell the coffee brewing that far away. No breakfast anytime anywhere ever tasted better than the berries with cream (bought from a farmer nearby) and panfish filets fresh from thhe water; take my word for that.

If the above account sounds too-good-to-be-true or contrived, it isn't. Or if it reminds you of a commercial . . . well, it *is* . . . but for a brand of camping I will describe, rather than for any product. To be specific, it is for farm pond camping and the morning I related took place on a typical midwest farm pond rather than in a remote Canadian wilderness.

No actual figure exists, but various Federal and state agricultural agencies estimate that there are more than a million farm and ranch ponds suitable for recreation scattered across America. That statistic may be modest because it would include only those which were originally built with government assistance and therefore recorded. Still when considered all together, these small impoundments comprise a vast amount of water and recreational opportunity. Too often they are overlooked by outdoorsmen, but especially by campers.

Of course not all farm ponds—perhaps not even most—are open to camping. All exist on private lands and for a variety of reasons, many of the landowners do not want to be bothered with others using their facilities or wandering over their farms. In fact many would take (at least initially) a very dim view of strangers or anyone else pitching a camp

← If escape from crowds is the main reason to go camping, the nation's numerous farm ponds are made to order. This one is typical and is located in southern Ohio.

near a valuable water supply. But I have found farmers and ranchers to be at least as friendly and considerate as other Americans. Permission to camp (in fact—to trespass) has been granted to me more often than refused when a proper and courteous approach was made.

But how does a camper go about getting such permission?

The first step is to locate a pond or ponds and the best way is to leave the main highways behind and to drive the backroads where the traffic is thin and the road signs have long ago rusted in peace. Do this reconnaissance well before the camping season begins—or at least before you personally plan to camp. Keep an eye opened for small lakes which are far from any farm dwellings or buildings and the farther the better. When you spot something which looks like a good camping possibility, try to locate the owner who will probably be living in the nearest farm home.

What follows should be a matter of honesty and low pressure salesmanship. Tell the farmer that you are a city person, but one who likes to get out into the country—and in fact one who *needs* to get out occasionally to escape. Continue that you and your family especially enjoy camping and would appreciate camping beside his pond some weekend later on. Quite possibly you will be refused before getting even that far, but if not, point out that you are a responsible camper who never litters or leaves gates open. In fact, you could add, you are willing to pay for the privilege.

The main point which cannot be overemphasized is to make contact with a landowner in advance and to have permission to camp before you ever leave home. Never drive into a farm yard, camping rig in tow, and ask to go camping then and there. Unless you know the farmer, or unless he is in the business of renting camp privileges on his ponds (which some landowners are), your chances are nearly nil.

We might as well be perfectly candid about this and mention some tricks which pay off and mistakes which do not. Often women or neat, polite, barbered children may better succeed in first contacting a farmer than a man. So if your wife has an engaging personality, let her do the talking. On the other hand, a car full of unkempt kids, a noisy pet or a radio blaring rock music are likely to turn him off and that should be easy enough to understand.

Once you have permission, a farm pond camping trip can be a most pleasant, even an exciting holiday. Normally there are far more things to do close at hand than near a large public or commercial campsite, but of course that depends on the individual. The farm pond is not ideal natural habitat for *all* campers. If your greatest enjoyment on a trip comes from comparing your rig with others, from conviviality, noise, and simply from "meeting new people," don't even consider a farm pond expedition. It will be too peaceful, too serene, too dull. But if you relish quiet and escape—if you genuinely love the undisturbed outdoors and all it offers—the forgotten farm pond is the place for you.

Much has been written about farm pond fishing, which averages very good because most impoundments are built

An important dividend of farm pond camping is the good fishing which begins just outside the tent flaps.

on land which is more fertile than the average. The fishes usually found are largemouth bass and bluegills, both of which (especially the bluegills) are easy to catch and delicious to eat. No elaborate tackle or great skill is necessary for this angling.

You cannot figure to have plug-ins because they simply do not exist and you may have to depend upon your own ingenuity to get along. But that adds to rather than detracts from the game. Some aspects of camping have become so easy nowadays that a sense of achievement is lost, especially for younger people. What's wrong with boiling pond water before you use it, of doing without electric or electronics for a spell, or even of digging a pit latrine? Nothing at all! The perimeter of a pond is a good place to practice basics, to learn how to build a fire and to cook over it. Here is a good spot to be totally renewed.

The farm pond is certainly an ideal place to discover and observe the wonders of nature all around. I have already described catching and picking my own breakfast, but that is only the beginning. Other fruits and berries ripen in season; you should know all about them. During a fall camping trip, many nuts are certain to be available in the nearest farm woodlot. Look also for mushrooms, which thrive in moist situations, but unless you know them well, carry along a guide to distinguish the edibles from non-edibles. Wild edible greens grow everywhere.

There are wildflowers to enjoy and birds to watch around the fringe of every small impoundment. You may also be able to capture enough bullfrogs for a meal, or by putting out baited bank hooks, to catch the ingredient for a robust turtle soup. Everywhere are wildflowers, insects, even small reptiles which can be an unending source of interest to young campers with an expanding curiosity. And all these things exist untrammeled and unspoiled by countless other campers as is usually the case with everything growing around public campgrounds.

A farm pond camping holiday also offers a chance to see what happens nowadays on the modern American farm. That in itself may be a revelation. Children particularly are fascinated with animals and can learn a good deal about raising and caring for everything from poultry to polled Herefords. It may even become possible to participate in such farm activities as haying, milking, rounding up cattle and horses. It isn't unusual for enduring friendships between camping and farm families to develop. Visitors may even be able to better understand today's high prices for groceries.

Camp menus can be vastly more attractive with farm products purchased from your host. The most delicious eggs for breakfast are always the freshest and newly churned butter (try doing this yourself in camp) is a commodity all but extinct in our cities today. Of course you can buy garden-fresh vegetables and orchard fruits all through the season at a fraction of the supermarket cost.

a light plastic pram, a canoe or inflatable raft makes little difference on a limited body of water, but it will be useful in fishing or collecting frogs. These ponds are excellent places to teach safe and proper handling of any watercraft to young ones.

The technique of camping on a farm pond is little different than camping anywhere else. Unlike in a public campground, it may be necessary to clear a small area of tall grass or brush (with a hand sickle) before pitching a tent. Care also should be taken to select a level spot high enough

Summertime plinking and varmint hunting are other possibilities for farm pond campers, but be sure to ask permission of the landowner.

I am partial to the less sophisticated camping rigs—and in fact to tents or tent trailers because only these really retain the pioneer flavor of living outdoors. But any device up to and including the self-contained motor home is suitable as long as it is agreeable to the landowner. Access to some ponds may not be possible with heavy vehicles or heavy trailers. Or following a heavy rain, it may not be possible to get them out of a campsite by any easy means. Keep that in mind.

One item of equipment which can be most valuable to the farm pond camper is a small cartop boat. Whether it's

to be dry—even in the event of a sudden heavy shower. A summer rain may on rare occasions raise the water level in a pond by a couple of feet.

Given the choice, I would rather load camping gear into my Jeep Wagoneer and aim it westward to settle somewhere in the incomparable Rocky Mountains of the West—which is (in my opinion) any serious outdoorsman's promised land. But when that isn't possible—or when short weekends are the only periods available to get out of town—the farm ponds are my escape valves.

And as time passes, I treasure them more and more.

TEXAS GULF CAMPING

Campers who prefer the wild, natural and open beaches choose the undeveloped areas of Padre Island or Mustang Island, pictured here. There is no fee for the use of these areas.

COAST

by MICHAEL DEAN KELLY

COMBINE MILD WINTERS, breezy summers, endless beaches, fresh and salt water fishing, excellent highways and friendly people and you pretty well have the ingredients for a fine place to vacation any month of the year. A prime candidate is the Texas Tropical Coast in the Corpus Christi region. This area has seemingly bloomed during the past few years as a haven for the vacationer who likes to get next to the outdoors, smell the salt air and cook over an open grill. A mixture of a National Seashore, two state parks, beach-oriented county campgrounds and a multitude of private trailer parks and campgrounds make for a varied opportunity for the recreational vehicle traveler.

The most expensive campground on the Coast will cost $3.50 per night, or you may camp on the beaches of Padre and Mustang Islands for no money at all. Corpus Christi itself has only limited facilities, with a campground on Corpus Christi Beach, good areas on Highway #9, and on Padre Island Drive, en route to Padre Island.

The finest facilities are located in the Rockport area, where huge trees, plenty of water, and a vacation atmosphere prevails. In the winter particularly, Rockport does it big. The lowest temperature in the coldest months hovers in the 60's. Maybe it's too cool for most to swim in the surf, but the pools get a workout. This area, just 30 miles up the beach from Corpus Christi, is on the hug-the-coast-highway towards Houston. The prime reason for locating so many grounds here is obvious. This is where the large live oak trees come down to meet the water. The mode of living is casual. It's scenic, fishing is fine any month of the year, and the fall-winter duck and goose hunting is tops.

Rockport and neighboring Fulton Beach are the favored

cities for artists. There are bird sanctuaries here, and just up the road is the Aransas Wildlife Refuge, home to dozens of species never seen north of the Mason-Dixon Line and winter home of the near-extinct whooping cranes. Color film disappears at an alarming rate in the hands of bird-watcher/ photographers.

Nationally-franchised campgrounds are relatively few in the Texas Coastal Bend in general, but three are located in as one of the area's most attractive locations.

Rest rooms and showers are near each and there is a 1620 foot lighted fishing pier that juts into St. Charles and Copano Bays. Campers can fish at no charge, but there is a $1-per-night charge to enter the park.

If you recall the Padre Island of 10 years ago, chances are you will be in for a surprise as you approach it today. As you drive over JFK Causeway from Corpus Christi's

Padre Island National Seashore does not have every camping facility, but campers of many persuasions from tenters to mobile homers, enjoy the shore, the dunes and delightful summer breezes.

Rockport. There is the Ancient Oaks KOA, Lakewood Safari, and a Ramada Inn campground. These are three of the newest, largest and most complete in the area. In this region many people come down for three months to avoid ice and snow altogether. These three grounds have all-underground utilities, all are a stone's throw from Aransas Bay, and both the KOA and Safari have well-stocked lakes within their bounds.

In addition there are other, smaller campgrounds in the region and nearly all offer access to the water. During the winter season they have special rates.

Not far up the coast from Rockport, and across Copano Bay, is Goose Island State Park, 307 beautiful acres of recreation. Goose Island has open shelters with picnic tables, barbecue pits, electric hookups and water for $2.50 nightly. The other hookups in the wooded area are a dollar cheaper and there are open camping areas, too. Goose Island rates

south side, you will note a bridge in the distance. It towers above the Intracoastal Canal. Reach the top of that bridge and you will note tall condominium apartments, plush hotels on the beach, cabin cruisers docked at the back door of tropical homes. To the right is an 18-hole golf course, luxuriously covered with exotic palms, Australian pines and bountiful flowers.

The outdoor or camping enthusiast need not be discouraged, however. Only a few miles more and you're back into the Padre Island of yesteryear, where you may camp on the beach, fish from a pier, swim, surf or beachcomb. There are a few additional restrictions, progress necessitates that, but Padre is pretty much as you remember it.

Practically any aerial photo of Padre Island that you have seen shows campers, tenters and a GI-surplus parachute or a bedspread stretched between two automobiles for shade. The same photo could apply today. Campers are welcome

In the Corpus Christi area is the town of Rockport boasting one of the larger commercial campgrounds. This is Ancient Oaks KOA—bay and beach are only a few blocks from the grounds.

on most of Padre Island's beaches at no cost. The only limitations are in parts of the Padre Island National Seashore in the Nueces County Park at the northern tip of the Island, and just south of the Padre Isles commercial development. The focal point of the Padre Island County park is Bob Hall Pier—a structure which extends about 600 feet into the Gulf. In discussing distances or locations on Padre Island, everything is measured north or south of this pier. There are organized camping facilities in this rustic park; not fancy, but adequate. Sites offer only water and electricity at $2 per night, with a three-night limit. There are no sewer connections, but a central dump station is included. True bathhouse facilities are open in the summer only, but outside rinse-off showers and rest room facilities are open the year-around.

A camping area in the park with no hook-ups is only $1.50. Reservations at either this park or the county park

at Port Aransas, can be made by writing Nueces County Parks, 10901 S. Padre Island Drive, Corpus Christi, Texas 78418.

For a 14-mile stretch south of Bob Hall Pier, free, unlimited camping is permitted on the beach. Of course, there are no public facilities and no utilities. Shade is non-existent, except for what the camper can improvise. Please note too, that south of Bob Hall Pier, there are no gasoline stations for about 100 miles. Padre Island National Seashore, and Malaquite Beach are favorites of campers. Malaquite can be reached either by driving down the beach or on a fine paved road down the middle of Padre Island. The road ends at Malaquite—the last developed area in the National Seashore. This development is minimal. Parking areas are paved, there is a sewage dump station and chemical toilets and trash receptacles are available. Since the facilities are limited there is no charge for their use. No reservations are accepted; it's first come, best spot.

Just south of the Malaquite campground, about a mile away, is the Mecca of organized, commercial recreational activity of Padre Island. Like an extra-terrestrial beast, a concrete boardwalk stretches for 450 feet beside the Gulf. This is the pavillion at the National Seashore. The structure, with paved parking for hundreds of cars, offers a view of miles and miles of sandy beach, the blue water of the Gulf

100-mile long island.

South of the channel the wilderness camper can really be on his own. Ask a ranger for a check list of birds; it's a long one. You'll likely see rabbits and coyotes here too. Camping here takes you away from civilization and here you can see the gulf coast as it was.

More complete camping facilities may be found in the Flour Bluff area of Corpus Christi along South Padre Island

It takes only a few minutes to erect a fly and tent and after that everyone is free to enjoy the fishing, swimming, or just relaxing in the warm sunshine.

of Mexico and every variety of concession facilities. It provides the comforts of modern living for the camper who wants it both ways. Included in the rentals available are beach chairs, umbrellas, floats, towels and souvenirs. There are 750 lockers, showers, rest rooms, private cabanas and barbecue pits on the beach. The restaurants offer food and drinks 12 months of the year.

South of the Malaquite area, and further down the National Seashore, open beach camping area again prevails. If you are at Little Shell or Big Shell, only four-wheel drive vehicles can navigate. Be forewarned.

Some of the best surf fishing and beachcombing may be found in this region and further south down Padre. Getting a camper of any size through these shell deposits may be a little "sticky" however. Deflating tires often helps. Nothing in the way of civilization remains from Malaquite down to the Port Mansfield channel, at nearly the bottom tip of the

Drive. These are privately-owned campgrounds, generally offering facilities for mobile homes as well as campers and other recreational vehicles. While not on the water, they are near shopping and service areas, and only minutes from Padre Island.

The deep-sea fishing capitol of the Corpus Christi area is Port Aransas, where as the saying goes, "they bite every day". About 1300 inhabitants live in the Mustang Island city, only 30 miles from Corpus Christi. In peak periods, particularly during the summer, the population can swell to 10,000. From June through October sailfish, marlin, kings, mackerel, and some tarpon are found in the waters off "Port A". Fishermen come here from all over North America. The big gamefish move in during the winter but redfish, and trout (weakfish) inhabit the nearby bays, and if you go out to the 200-300 feet depth, you'll be at the snapper banks for red snapper, grouper or warsaw on any day of the year.

An attraction for youngsters at the campgrounds in the Rockport area, are ducks, geese and turkeys that tramp through the grounds like these strollers at the Rockport KOA.

It's not necessary to be a millionaire to go deep sea fishing at Port Aransas, either. Party boats, or head boats as they are sometimes called, go out every day. A 12 to 16-hour trip to the snapper banks runs between $25-$30. You can go for king, ling or mackerel for $7 and bay fishing costs even less than that.

Campgrounds in Port Aransas are plentiful, inexpensive, and most are small. Port Aransas Park, too, has a free, lighted fishing pier for its visitors. There are sites with water, electricity and tables at $3 per night while the water-only pads are $2.50. The time limit on space here is seven days in summer, 14 in winter. Hot showers and restrooms are available the year 'round.

Mustang Island, like Padre, also has nearly unlimited free beach camping but has no shade or utilities. You can pitch a tent on most of the beach area and enjoy an undeveloped sojourn.

About 40 miles from Corpus Christi, its salt water and its beaches, lies Lake Corpus Christi, with 200 miles of shoreline. This fresh water lake is known as Lake Mathis. On the south side of the lake, just out of the town of Mathis, is Lake Corpus Christi State Park. There are 300 campsites in the park, and it boasts of two fishing piers where you may catch catfish, gaspergou and white bass. Black bass are here and you just might be lucky enough to catch one. There is also a swimming beach and boating and water skiing available.

Other camping areas dot the lake shore, too.

For complete information on camping, campgrounds and trailer parks in the Corpus Christi area, drop a note to the Tourist Bureau, Box 1147, Corpus Christi, Texas 78403. They will send you maps, brochures and folders on what to see and do in this delightful vacation region. A phone call, 512-882-5603, will bring even quicker results.

Walk Through

Freeze-dried foods especially for the camper are excellent; but similar foods found in super-markets are often far less expensive and serve the purpose equally well.

by ED PARK

EVERY NOW AND THEN I'll see an article in one of the outdoor magazines about the fabulous dried and freeze-dried foods that have hit the market in recent years. Designed for the backpacker, mountain climber, or anyone else who needs ultra-lightness in all his gear, these foods have won wide usage and wider acclaim.

The main reason the usage has not matched the acclaim, I'd guess, is because of the cost. These special-use items, while great to have and use, are just a bit rough on the pocketbook of the ordinary guy who gets out and wanders about a lot. With inflation tearing the guts out of that same guy's pocketbook, it's a bit hard to justify $5 for a deluxe freeze-dried dinner for two very often.

So I'll pass on a bit of advice I use extensively myself. In my work as an outdoor writer I travel over quite a bit of North America, from Mexico to the Arctic ocean. I go by car, airplane, canoe, boat, skis, snowshoes, snowmobile and foot. If room and weight aren't too important, I take along inexpensive canned goods, picking up fresh food along the way. Easy. But if weight *is* important, I rely heavily on dried foods. I can add the water later easier than I can carry it.

Anyway, my basic advice is to skip the foods in the specialty outdoor stores—except for special expeditions of course—and concentrate on those lightweight foods one can find in any large super market, at super market prices.

In preparing this article, I took my clipboard in hand and went for a walk in the local grocery, making notes and jotting down prices as I went. Then I went to a local outdoor store, a place that specializes in backpacking gear. There I also jotted down prices. Let's take a look at some of my notes and see what we can come up with—advice for the backpacker, the boat camper, the everyday tent camper—anyone who needs to keep down both the weight and the cost.

First I'll comment on prices—taken directly from the items on the shelves, on the same day, and for comparable qualities of food. Such a comparison is a real eye-opener. (Note: Food prices have fluctuated drastically in recent months, therefore the prices given here should be used for comparison only—Ed.) In the backpacking specialty store, soda crackers sell for $1.17 for 14 ounces. You can buy 16 ounces for only 25¢ at the super market. The specialty store has a mixture of nuts and raisins which they advertise as a "high-energy trail snack." It's a darn good snack food, great for eating on the trail—but they want 89¢ for 5 ounces of the mixture. You can buy the same mixed nuts

a Super Market

and raisins at the grocer's and get more than twice as much for the same price. The specialty store puddings cost 57¢ for 5 ounces while the grocery price is just 24¢ for almost 7 ounces. For the same 8½-ounce package of corn bread mix, you'll pay 57¢ at the specialty store but only 12¢ at the super market.

It quickly becomes apparent that if you buy much of this type of dried food, you'll save a bundle on the food bill if you buy all the products you can at the super market.

Dried soup mixes will run about 49¢ for a 1-ounce package at the specialty store, but only 36 to 45¢ for 3 to 5 ounces at the supermarket. Dried fruits are expensive anyplace, but when you see a price of 85¢ for 1 ounce of dried apples or peaches at the backpacking store, then trot down down the street to find just 63¢ for 8 ounces of dried apples, or 97¢ for 12 ounces of dried peaches, you quickly see where to shop. Jerky is a favorite of just about anyone who has tried it. I make my own, so never buy it in the stores anyway, but the supermarket will sell it for about half the cost of other places. If we investigate the powdered drinks, we'll also notice a similar difference in prices. The specialty store cocoa was 50¢ for 4 ounces, while the super market would sell me 16 ounces for 59¢. Ice tea mix ran about three times as much, and powdered orange or lemon drinks ran nearly the same.

I don't intend to imply that the backpacking specialty stores are places to avoid, because they do handle excellent foods that are not available anyplace else, and I certainly use my share of their products. They handle such delicious one-dish meals as beef or chicken stew, beef and rice, chili, Chinese dishes, beef Stroganoff, and so on—all done up in nice, lightweight, freeze-dried packages. But what I'm trying to point out is that some things are available for much less cost in the local super market—items that you can purchase there first, then fill in the gaps with the more expensive foods from the specialty stores.

As we wander down the super market aisle, we see other dried foods that can easily become part of the camper's grub box. Foods like dried milk, dry and hot cereals, toasts, cookies, pancake mixes, candy and many different kinds of bread, roll and bisquit mixes. There are many gravy and sauce mixes which are delicious when poured over a variety of hash brown, mashed and scalloped potatoes, or over any number of rices, macaronis or spaghettis. And of course there are the old favorites such as dried beans or peas, the basic ingredients for many filling meals. The section with

rices contains many, many varieties of meals that will please any appetite.

For many years now I have been using one common product that I feel is one of the better meals-in-a-box on the grocer's shelf. This is beef Rice-A-Roni, a rice and macaroni mixture, with just the right combination of spices and herbs, that makes a very flavorful and filling dish. If my trip also includes any hunting, I'll add to the dish whatever game we've bagged, but even without any additions, it makes a good meal. One box of Rice-A-Roni costs about 40¢ and weighs 7½ ounces. This much is enough to be a full meal for two, along with something to drink.

Something I want to stress—regardless of what you choose for meals, or where you buy them—try them out at home before you take them along on a trip. For one thing, you need to find out if you like the stuff. Most of what I've tasted has been excellent, but every now and then I'll run into a brand of dried or freeze-dried foods that seems, to me, to have a pretty wierd collection of spices. I'd hate to be out on a two-week canoe trip and find I could hardly choke down the food I'd brought along.

Another important consideration is the details of preparation. Every now and then somebody in camp will break out a new package of food only to discover it requires an oven —or a cupful of something we don't have, or requires an electric mixer for 2 minutes, or some such. By preparing each item at home, at least once, you'll avoid these pitfalls.

A final reason for trying everything at home is to determine amounts. I have yet to find a package of food that was as filling as the manufacturer says it is. A package for four will do well to serve two. If it says it will serve two, you can almost bet that one active man will eat it all. They tend to be a bit shy on their estimates of what a person will eat when he's active outdoors. But if this is determined at home, you'll be able to compensate and do alright. One brand of dried foods, available through mail order, has been a part of most of my outings for years. Their food is good, and not too expensive. But I quickly learned that we needed the four-man sizes of everything for two of us.

It's true that the new dried and freeze-dried foods on the market have been a great help to the camper. It's even more true that you don't need to go to high-priced specialty stores to buy most of it. Just take a walk through the aisles of any super market and note what you see. Then try them out at home, and you'll end up with a whole new list of foods for those coming camping trips.

BOOKS TO TAKE CAMPING

by PEGGY PETERS

species on a single page. (Incidently, we have found that the range of some birds is wider than indicated on the map.) In Peterson, the pictures and text are in separate areas.

These two small volumes are available almost anywhere, while guides to very particular areas are available locally. National parks often have selected books for their own area. If the feathered ones are of more than passing interest, do ask for bird check-lists wherever you may be. These are widely available, generally free, and, when used in conjunction with the guide, are very valuable.

Guides to the wildflowers. Indispensible to anyone who is constantly saying, "What's that red one over there?", or "that looks a little like our thistle back home . . . but not quite". Because of the enormous variety of flowers, the guides are generally for one particular area only. *A Field Guide to Rocky Mountain Wildflowers* might be your choice if this is where you will camp; another is in the same *Peterson Field Guide* series, but is specifically for Northeastern and Northcentral North America. And there are others. These are excellent for the plants pictured in color, but I find the line drawings difficult to identify. One almost needs the plant in one hand and the guide in the other. Easier, though less complete, are the guides containing fewer species, but picturing those in full color. Be sure to choose the book showing both blossom and leaves.

Once identified, it is often interesting to read a bit farther and learn whether the plant in hand might have medicinal properties; some were used by the Indians as dyes; still others are edible. A few wildflowers or their roots were widely used by early pioneers (for example, Mormon tea); others are devoured with relish by wild creatures. (Bears eat wild blueberries—stems, leaves and all.) A few are poisonous. For the adventurous it might be interesting to try a few of the edible variety. (Having done this upon occasion myself I feel there should be another catagory: "edible if desperate".)

In places where it is permitted why not take a few

LET'S CHECK OFF the items on our list: food, fish hooks, film; bedding, boots, and books. BOOKS? Absolutely.

Almost every camper in preparing for the trip, whether it be fishing with the boys, touring with the family or a holiday for two, assembles some sort of list. It can and does run in small increments of complexity from a minutely detailed type-written assemblage to a few mental notes hastily appended to "what we always bring". Too infrequently does it include a small, traveling library.

Some pleasure reading is nice to have along: it will rain at times and it just might be a pleasant experience to sit snug in a corner and read something you've been meaning to get at for so long. Then, too, there are times when a good book can fill otherwise lost time—as while you're waiting for the dryer to finish at the laundromat or for the ferry to arrive. But the really valuable pieces for the camper to have at hand are information books, especially comprehensive guides which will add to your knowledge and enjoyment.

We never go anywhere, either within the U.S. or elsewhere, without the very best bird guide we can find for the area because birds are one of our major interests. Of course the binoculars are a necessary adjunct, as a hand lens is to anyone interested in botany. For the birds of the U.S.—and there is an astounding number of species—there are two favorites: Roger Tory Peterson's *Field Guides* which are chosen because of Dr. Peterson's unique system of indicating one field mark which quickly identifies the species, and *Birds of North America* by Robbins, Bruun and Zim. This later book is selected because it includes a range map, a brief description of the bird and a picture of the

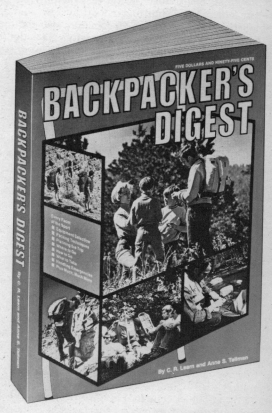

blossoms indigenous to the area and press them. Along with pictures of your camping trip, the flowers and perhaps some leaves or rocks comprise a more complete picture of where you were and what you saw.

I defy the camper to pass three people and not find cameras on at least two of them. Cameras come in such a wide range of complexity, price and size that there is literally one for everyone and everyone seems to have his. Nothing wrong with this. Photographs make probably the single best record of the camper's journey. The problem lies in the way all this equipment is used. How often have you seen a traveler obviously in awe of the mountain scene before him try to capture it from a distance of several miles with a lens of normal length. How often, too, has the visitor placed his family next to a descriptive sign, say, Yellowstone Park, with the sun directly behind the group. Worthless. And needless. Erwin A. Bauer has a book entitled *Outdoor Photography* (Harper & Row, publishers) which enables everyone to take the kind of pictures he wants—just the kind he thinks he's getting when the shutter clicks. Do make this book part of your traveling library.

Consultation with the other members of the camping party might induce you to include books on mushrooms, shells, trees or minerals.

If the Easterner comes West some knowledge of geology is almost manditory. The towering, jutting peaks of the Tetons; the monolithic red sandstones of Utah, the Grand Canyon, the deserts. All new; all fascinating; all crying for explanation. For a general picture read *This Changing Earth* by John A. Shimer; Barnes & Noble Inc. If this seems too lacking in plot when you start it at home, bring it along. The photos and line drawings are fascinating when the solid features are in front of you. Small books and articles on a particular area are usually available on the spot. Grand Teton Park, for instance, sells *Creation of the Teton Landscape* by J. D. Love and John C. Reed, Jr. Here are photos of the great, black dyke on the east face of Mt. Moran, a feature noted by all but understood by few, and a concise explanation of its presence. It explains also the mechanics of mountain-building, volcanic activity, glaciation, erosion and the multitudes of other factors which were ultimately responsible for this magnificent range.

There are two books by Vinson Brown which are available in paperback editions which will be of interest especially to the adolescent and pre-adolescent. One is *Knowing the Outdoors in the Dark* and the other, *Reading the Woods*. These are each $2.95 and published by Collier Books, a division of Macmillan Co. in New York City. These two I recommend as gifts to be given well before the start of the camping trip. They cover a wide variety of subjects on the outdoors and have a plentitude of photographs, drawings, tables and graphs which illustrate the text. Take them along with the rest on the trip; they make excellent reference material.

Another trio of books must be included in the camping library. These are *Fishermen's Digest* (9th edition) and *Hunter's Digest,* both edited by Erwin A. Bauer and *Backpacker's Digest* by Learn and Tallman, all three are published by Digest Books, Northfield, Ill. These are especially recommended as they neatly fill the requirements of two categories: pleasure reading and information reading. There is a third plus: excellent photographs; some the editor's own, and others by contributing authors. These are large, attractive, paperbacked editions worth the camper's careful attention.

For the cook(s) in the family: two volumes. The first shouldn't really be called a volume at all, it is in actuality more of a booklet. The title is *Wild Game Cookbook* and it is a compilation of recipes by the Jackson Hole Art Associ-

ation. It has no index and the contents run from recipes for Braised Bear Paws (with the note: "works with all kinds of bears; blacks, browns or grizzlies") to Spruce Tip Syrup. Interspersed with this sort are some that are more likely to be used by the camper-cook experimenting with new, local products. Chokecherry pie, for one. Or how about cutthroat shisk kebab or sourdough pancakes? For this unique book, write Jackson Hole Art Association, Jackson, Wyo. 83001 and include $2.00.

The second book is Angier's *Feasting Free on Wild Edibles,* a Stackpole Books publication. For the roving gourmet this will be THE book. It illustrates and describes hundreds of available foods from lamb quarters, through beach plums on to nuts and roots. It tells when and how to pick them and just how they are best prepared. Obviously this would be useful not only while camping, but at home, too. The edibles included are from every area in America.

Whether it's the packrat instinct or an inherited tendency from our pioneering forebearers, we all seem to gather up what is available elsewhere and bring it home. At the very end of a vacation trip there may be tons of berries to harvest for jam-making; shells to collect for children's collages or to decorate a mirror frame; pine cones and seed pods for Christmas wreaths and perhaps bayberries to scent home-made candles or soaps. The list is as endless as is the number of books to help and instruct in their use.

Browse through the bookstore; write for what is unavailable there; read before your journey and en route. Everything you learn will enrich and add meaning to the camping experience.

Picture Your Camp Trip

by JIM TALLON

Pictures showing the flavor of your trip will be valuable. Note here the old cook-stove, typically western Dutch oven, "Lumberjack" syrup and the cook wearing cowboy boots.

Here's an example of good composition. Note the horizontal and diagonal lines. Use wide angle lens for this effect.

"HE SLEEPS with his camera, you know."

Oh, no. I didn't know he was that far down the drain. Is there anything that can be done for the poor fellow?"

Well, let us hope that nothing will be done for this poor fellow, for he isn't exhibiting any psychological abnormality, he's just following professional advice on one way to come home from a camping trip with really worthwhile pictures.

I almost always sleep on the ground at Organ Pipe Cactus National Monument in southwestern Arizona. When dawn breaks I sometimes see more feathers than a chicken farmer —Gambels' quail, California curve-bills, cactus wrens. Maybe a hair suit or two with a coyote or ground squirrel tucked inside. As a bedded-down photographer I got some fine early-morning shots I would certainly have missed had I fumbled through a pile of noisy camp gear. I've also got some fine candid shots of fellow campers while on a float trip down the Salmon River in Idaho by this method.

Once, at Many Glacier Hotel in Glacier National Park I awoke at sun-up to see the straight-up mountains mirrored dramatically in Swiftcurrent Lake. My camera was beside me, not out in the car, and I took pictures from the hotel window clad tastefully in my jockey shorts. Had I taken time to dress and rush to the car, the light would have changed; had I run outside in my jockey shorts, *I* might have been the photographic subject rather than the scenery.

Of course, the camera needn't repose within a half-inch of your ribs; good photography doesn't require *that* much dedication—wrapped in a jacket and lovingly laid at the head of your sleeping bag will do. On a Colorado River sandbar within the bowels of the Grand Canyon, or on the windswept beaches of the west coast of Mexico where sleeping out is the rule, I find a camera cared for in this way is well-protected from moisture and blown-sand. I have learned to unzip my sleeping bag and latch on to the camera in one smooth motion. It's even easier to do in our van conversion where the camera resides on a shelf near our bed.

If both were included in a popularity poll, photography might edge out golf. Yet, in spite of this popularity and the fantastic new improvements in camera equipment and films, most of the millions of pictures tripped off each year would be more aptly placed in the trash can than framed and in a prominent place.

Think of the pictures your camping friends have taken and of the slide shows you've sat through. If you have (painfully) witnessed the same percentage of failures I have and if that is near the national average—campers badly need some help. Therefore, the point above, if a bit labored, is not to suggest that campers who want good pictures develop a mania for bedside photography, but to instill in them the importance of keeping a camera near at hand all the time. This in itself will go a long way toward improving their photography. They can then click off a frame or two instead

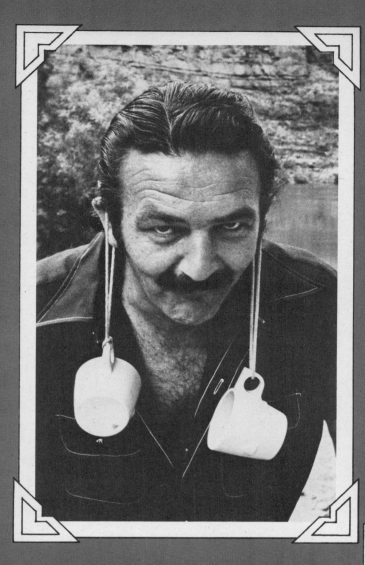

Put a little humor in your pictures and move in for close-ups.

Human interest shots are great. The more candid the shot, the better. Long lenses allow you to take pictures like this without the subject being aware of your presence and becoming stiff.

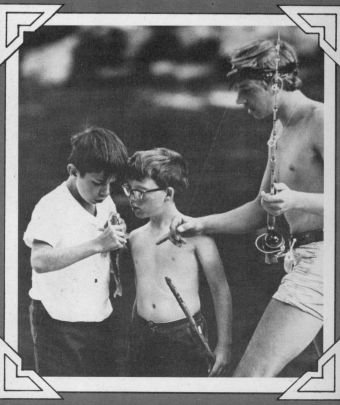

Again, a good example of scenic composition. Vertical lines of the trees, a nice curve on the lake. The small figures give scale to the scene, and add life.

There are good ways and bad ways to show off your camping rig. Where would you classify this shot?

of lamely saying, "Gee, that would make a great picture. Wish I had my camera with me."

After a lifetime of photography, with thousands of pictures in print and several articles on photography published, I am often asked to give talks to various groups on how they can improve their pictures. A number of these sessions were conducted at camper clinics and camper clubs. Here I learned that campers are no different from anyone else when it comes to photography. Most seem to believe that owning an expensive camera will guarantee them good pictures; they fail to realize that a picture, like beauty, begins in the eye of the beholder, and that the camera is just a means to an end.

Of course you can't take pictures without a camera. The better that camera and the more diversified the lenses and accessories, the more control you have over photography. The photographer must be completely familiar with his tools. He should "dry-fire" with his equipment until the use of it is nothing more than a reflex action. Only then is he able to give his full thought to taking photographs. A carpenter doesn't think about his hammer when he's pounding nails; you don't think about every little movement of the steering wheel when you're driving your car.

For our purposes as camping photographers, the 35mm single-lens reflex (SLR) with interchangeable lens capabilities is best. This type of camera is more compact and offers more versatility than any other system. You can buy fisheye lenses, zooms, telephotos and countless other accessories to fit nearly every brand. My own complement of lenses ranges from an 18mm wide angle to a 800mm telephoto. The 18mm covers a figure standing just four feet away with arms spread wide, and unlike the fisheye, gives little distortion. The 800mm draws in wildlife to fill the viewfinder. However, I use these lenses much less frequently than the focal lengths between, and as a camping photographer you can do an admirable job of photography with a lot less.

As a professional, I have owned just about every type of camera made, including practically all of the "quality" brands of 35mm cameras. At the present time I am dragging around a quadruplet of cameras some professionals consider an amateur brand. Until the devaluation of the dollar, this brand, with a bayonet mount and a fast 1.4 lens sold for under $200. Several years ago under the stress of a tight budget, I sold my aging "professional" 35's and bought three new bodies of the less expensive brand with the intention of phasing them out near the end of their "useful life,"

Don't forget to keep a camera with a telephoto on it near your sleeping bag. You may be rewarded with a shot like this one morning.

or about every-other-year under professional wear and tear. My cameras got a lot of abuse. On horseback at a gallop, I have had cameras come together backed by enough G's to pull the wings off a jet airplane. I have fallen into rock-piles wearing them and the cameras took it better than I did. I even had one totally submerged in water for a few seconds. In this case, I took out the film and left the back open; then removed the lens and raised the mirror so air could circulate through the camera. I shook it half a dozen times, then set it in the sun for a couple of hours, making sure the camera didn't get so hot something would melt. After that it worked fine; no trip to the repair shop needed. And the printed results from these cameras inspired one editor to tell me they reproduced superior to some of his 4″ x 5″ color, a format four times as big. What I'm saying here is that you don't have to spend $600 to get a quality camera with quality optics.

Unless the camper has professional aspirations, he should not saddle himself with a ton of photographic equipment. We don't want to turn the camping experience into a total photographic study. As I said earlier, a camping photographer can do an admirable job with just a little equipment. Here is a list of camera gear that will put him in charge of most photographic situations he will encounter on a camp trip:

1. Camera body and normal lens
2. 28mm wide angle
3. 135mm telephoto
4. 400mm telephoto (optional, for wildlife fans)
5. tripod
6. bellows

Now let us back up a bit. Let me re-emphasize the importance of "dry-firing" your camera. This doesn't mean you have to trip the shutter, but look in that viewfinder and interpret what you see; change your lenses until you become familiar with them. I have friends who are good photographers, but after years of taking pictures they still live under the illusion that wide-angle lenses are used solely to cover larger areas, and that telephotos are just for magnifying subjects. They do other things as well. Wide angles, for example, emphasize the foreground. Say you want to show a camp scene with the most important part of it being the cook working over an open cookfire. You move in close, still retaining your tent or RV in the background where it becomes of secondary interest. The shot says "camping" overall, but you direct your viewer to the camp-cook.

Telephotos, too, can be used for such "special effects." The longer the telephoto, the shallower the depth of field—the area of sharp focus. You can back up and use a telephoto to emphasize the cook through "selective focus." That is, you focus sharply on the cook and allow the tent or RV to be in the out-of-focus area. Too, telephoto lenses compress distances. You can pull a fence, a row of trees, a farm house, and distant mountains together to create an eye-catching photograph. Taken with a normal lens, the picture would be only so-so.

As for the tripod, it will permit you to take sharp pictures below hand-holdable shutter speeds (This is 1/30th of a second with a normal lens, proportionately higher with telephotos.) This would be necessary when the light level is very low. The tripod will also support the camera for "self-timed" shots. You can get in some of the shots yourself. Cock the self-timer, trip it, and you have approximately 10 seconds to get in front of the camera.

The bellows extends the camper's photographic possibilities to cover nature subjects closer than the range of normal lenses will allow. That is, lenses without bellows. The lens is removed and the bellows attached to the front of the camera, and then the lens attached to the front of the bellows. This gadget works with any lens, but best on normal lenses and telephotos. With a 400mm-bellows combination, you can focus close enough to fill the frame with small mammals like ground squirrels, insects and flower blossoms. Yet, stay far enough away that you don't frighten off the live subjects.

The price of the equipment mentioned above is remarkably low. In the advertisements in the back of the photography magazines, I have seen all three focal length lenses for under $40 each. Tripods and bellows cost about $20 each. At this kind of price the lenses cannot be expected to last forever mechanically, but the optics are of a quality to satisfy the non-professional. Some of the pictures I have taken with "cheap" lenses have appeared on the covers of magazines.

Every photographer has his favorite film(s) and specific reasons for using it (them). I recommend that you stay with Kodachrome II whenever you can. This is the sharpest film made, allows grainless blow-ups and slides, and usually costs less. High Speed Ektachrome makes a good back-up film when the light level is too low for Kodachrome II, but it is rather grainy and doesn't have the snappy colors of the slow speed film. Still, just after dawn or in the dim light of the forest, it can mean the difference between pictures and no pictures.

Thus far I have neglected to mention black and white, and color negative films. It seems that no one but camera club types, advanced amateurs, and the professional photographer uses black and white films today. The turn to color by the average camera fan has been so complete that I feel black and white film isn't worth covering in this article, especially since campers are usually in situations best pictured with color film. And through color negative films, like Kodacolor is extremely popular with the instamatic class, I can't recommend it for our use, at least not on a regular basis. Kodacolor film results in prints which too often, to me, have an artificial look. In contrast, the transparencies come alive with color when seen with a viewer or projected on a screen. If you like, you can have prints made from the slides. There is a plus with Kodacolor, however: if you make an exposure error with Kodacolor, the lab can correct it when they make your prints. With Kodachrome II and High Speed Ektachrome (and all transparency films), you must be correct with your exposure or live with the mistake.

Exact exposure. This means the exact amount of light coming through lens and shutter opening and registering on the film. Today, for many photographic situations, "exact exposure" is literally built into most 35mm SLR cameras—an internal exposure meter that is coupled to lens and shutter. You line up two needles, either by adjusting the f-stops—which controls the amount of light coming through the lens; or with the shutter speed—which either cuts the light in half or doubles it with each subsequently higher or lower speed. My technique is to set the shutter speed first; usually 1/60 or 1/125 using the normal or wide-angle lenses for non-moving subjects; and going to higher speeds for moving subjects and telephotos which are harder to hold steady. For example, a 250mm telephoto would require 250th of a second; a 500mm tele, 1/500th of a second. For your lenses use the shutter speed closest to your focal length. Next I rotate the f-stop ring on the lens until the needles line up. It's that simple. Under average situations this works fine; under others you must do a little thinking for the meter. For example, if light is coming directly into the lens it will give you an inflated reading. You will badly under-expose your pictures if you do not adjust for it. To learn how to compensate for this, thoroughly read and re-read the section of your camera manual pertaining to the built-in meter.

At this point we have covered the basics of producing, mechanically and optically, good camping pictures, or pic-

In a photo like this both your RV and the scene are complimented.

tures that camping makes available to us. Now we get to the most difficult part of photography: What is a good photograph? Essentially, and perhaps over-simply, it is one that pleases the viewer. Taking good photographs is a technique developed through trial and error. And involved are variables such as figure placement, color content, directional lines of interest, and balance.

Rather than pin yourself in with a bunch of rules that perhaps no one understands, turn your attention to published pictures—in newspapers, magazines and books. See what you like and determine why you like it. You can get some excellent composition ideas by watching movies and television. Not every picture you see in print is good. Sometimes an editor may be desperate to illustrate an article and use pictures he normally wouldn't if he had a better selection. See if you can spot these. Too, you might subscribe to photography magazines. I get several and read them thoroughly, but I find them catering to offbeat photography, rather than the straight-forward picture. Still, you can learn from them.

Once you get the hang of composition and have accumulated some nice slides, you'll want to show them off. Rather than use a hand viewer, you'll get more satisfying results by assembling them into a slide show. You'll need a projector and a lenticular screen; beaded screens don't show off the color and sharpness as well and are literally out-of-date. Just as you do for your camera equipment, shop wisely for a projector. You may well find several prices for the same model and brand of projector. The simple projectors are usually the most trouble-free.

Another piece of advice—before leaving on your camp trips make a few notes, a script, so to speak. Shoot a few frames of packing your gear and of points of interest along the way. Once at camp, get shots around the area showing people and their activities: hunting and fishing; and don't forget those wildlife and flower close-ups. Your show should run about 80 to 100 slides, and you may have to make several trips to get the shots you want. Be sure to cull out poorly composed and wrongly exposed shots.

Photography is wholly compatible with camping. With decent camera equipment, a bit of thought, and some practice, you can relive your camping experiences again and again.

The Carefree World of Camping

Camping just may be the most flexible pastime of all. It is for whole families who escape to a pre-Cambrian island of a lonely lake in northern Ontario.

Or speaking of carefree holidays, how about this one in a Coleman Minuteman camper—the modern Conestoga—where father and son chose lures to go fishing just a good cast away.

Paradise Found (for anglers, that is) is a lonely canvas camp, pitched in air-conditioned evergreens, far from any other fishermen, in northern Manitoba.

Ladies of many families — young and old — often long for seashores and here mother and daughter entertain a flock of gulls on South Padre Island, Texas.

Not all camping is pure joy—not by any means. But how better for a serious big game hunter to get back into the boondocks where game is most abundant? This nimrod alone bagged a fine bull elk in Montana's Pioneer Mts.

Camping is also for groups—lodge, professional, family reunion, neighborhood, fraternal—just name it. These have joined together on a covered wagon trek with outfitter L.D. Frome of Afton, Wyoming.

For a pair who can handle heavy backpacks and who *really* want to get away, why not head for the high Rockies?

These old buddies have been camping together every year since they came back from World War II. No other kind of vacation quite matches it for rehashing old times, both good and bad.

Camping can have more than a nominal sense of adventure. Here the editor is prepared for anything, including a late spring snowfall, when on a fishing trip to alpine lakes of Montana's Rockies.

For some campers, and it helps if they are very young, a physical challenge is the most important of any trip. From here they can look down and see their campsite in the shadows several thousand feet below them.

But let's say it's a rainy, blustery day outside. Fishing wouldn't be much fun and hiking in a soggy woods appeals to no one here. So spend the day soaking up the luxury of the trailer instead—and hit the trail tomorrow.

This is solitude surely enough for a young man and his beagle. But it is also more than that. Somewhere down that waterway ahead is adventure. The current will carry the canoe through a dark forest—and to another memorable campsite.

Tow a jeepster behind your motorhome and there's no limit to the places you can see—the sights you can enjoy. Here the trail from road's edge leads into the strange formations of South Dakota's Black Hills.

Eagle Lake in the High Sierra during California's early springtime is the site of this idyllic camp. And that camper is also a co-editor, enjoying the morning sunshine among tall ponderosa pines.

Many campers instinctively look for natural beauty in a campsite—and this family certainly found it in a wayside of British Columbia, not far from the Skeena River.

Speaking of simple pleasures, cooking a camp breakfast on an outdoor stone fireplace must be among the simplest—and best. Anybody's appetite is apt to be double what is normal anywhere else.

Quayside at Rockport, Texas (right). Even in January it is warm and bright. The carefree camper here has come far from the deep snows in Wyoming. Why not pause here for a while and thaw out slowly, ever so slowly . . . Meanwhile—back in Wyoming (below), but six months later—it's no time to sit around and contemplate. Unload the bikes from the camper, leave the campground behind and pedal out into some of the most magnificent scenes in America.

July. Summertime. A fishing trip for father and sons. Take your choice of the Montana Rockies where a snowbank still lingers beside a trout lake. Or try a float trip on Utah's Green River where it isn't even necessary to pitch a tent.

No matter whether it's grilling up pork chops on a griddle, concocting something fancy in a spic and span camper, broasting chicken over hickory or leaving a Dutch oven to simmer over coals while you explore elsewhere, the cook is the captain of any camping trip.

Meet three real artists—camp cooking artists, that is. Number one relies on his Coleman beside the Missouri River at Gates of the Mountains. Take a two-pound trout, (lower left) filet and broil it slowly over aspen coals. Number three (lower right) is deep frying ruffed grouse for a hunting buddy at Ghost Lake, Wis.

We feel sorry for the camper who hasn't yet discovered fishing—even though we know he eventually will. That big pike, top left, lost a duel to a camper in Manitoba. The others are just the kinds of perfect campsites an angler often finds when he wanders from the beaten tracks. Even the youngest in the family can catch fish—but if she is wise, not bigger ones than her father—if she wants to go again.

Campers can treat themselves to the best in natural beauty and scenes of national heritage. Kids of all ages —8 to 80—like both and never miss a chance to climb on the cannon that won the Battle of Lake Erie.

Carefree campers can learn a lot, too. Setting up a tent is a skill that develops into other skills later on.

What better way than camping to pursue a favorite hobby? And painting is just one possibility, no matter where a camper pitches his tent.

Add also one vote for doing nothing. Get that camper trailer set up, shoo the kids toward the swimming hole, then relax.

A great thing about camping is the way it leads to other wholesome activities such as horses and riding trails. Some use a campsite as only a starting place, the beginning of a survival hike, the base for working on Boy Scout awards and merit badges.

In all of the National Parks and Forests, hiking trails fan out in all directions from every campground and these are the routes to the most carefree days of all. They're free, they belong to you, so why not use them?

Somewhere down that waterway is a comfortable campsite we can reach by canoe and by gently paddling with the current. Maybe we can go swimming or cating along the way. Now just where is that launching site?

That's the Snake River and according to many campers who have wandered widely around the states, one of the most exquisite scenes in America. Campers somehow seem to enjoy all the best things in life.

This mule is about to carry somebody's gear on a pack trip in the Canadian Rockies. Not every mule stands this still when loaded down with 100 pounds of duffel. It's safe to say the campers will have a lot more fun on this than the animals. Some may not consider houseboating (right) as camping and we won't argue that here. But it is as carefree as any pastime and that is qualification enough to be included here. Look at it as camping afloat.

For many carefree campers, a camp simply must be pitched near water and the closer the better. But that isn't any wonder and fishing is just one of the reasons. At least we see more and more campers carrying along small boats nowadays—you can count us among them.

Natural Areas Administered by the National Park Service and Related Properties

Acadia National Park, Maine: Rugged coastal area on Mount Desert Island, highest elevation on eastern seaboard; picturesque Schoodic Peninsula on mainland; half of Isle au Haut, exhibiting spectacular cliffs. *Address:* Route 1, Box 1, Bar Harbor, ME 04609.

Agate Fossil Beds National Monument, Nebr.: World-renowned quarries containing numerous, concentrated, well-preserved Miocene mammal fossils representing an important chapter in the evolution of mammals. *Address:* c/o Scotts Bluff National Monument, P.O. Box 427, Gering, NB 69341.

Arches National Park, Utah: Extraordinary products of erosion in the form of giant arches, windows, pinnacles, and pedestals. *Address:* c/o Canyonlands National Park, Moab, UT 84532.

Badlands National Monument, S. Dak.: Ruggedly eroded layered sedimentary deposits containing great numbers of prehistoric animal fossils. *Address:* P.O. Box 72, Interior, SD 57750.

Big Bend National Park, Texas: Spectacular mountain and desert scenery; variety of unusual geological structures; in the great bend of the Rio Grande. *Address:* Big Bend National Park, TX 79834.

Biscayne National Monument, Fla.: Significant example of a living coral reef in the Upper Florida Keys: includes portions of Biscayne Bay. *Address:* P.O. Box 1369, Homestead, FL 33030.

Black Canyon of the Gunnison National Monument, Colo.: Sheer-walled canyon with shadowed depths accentuating the darkness of ancient rocks of obscure origin. *Address:* c/o Curecanti National Recreation Area, 334 South 10th St., Montrose, CO 81401.

Bryce Canyon National Park, Utah: Contains perhaps the most colorful and unusual erosional forms in the world. In horseshoe-shaped amphitheaters along the edge of the Paunsaugunt Plateau of southern Utah stand innumerable highly colored and grotesque pinnacles, walls, and spires. *Address:* Bryce Canyon, UT 84717.

Buck Island Reef National Monument, V.I.: One of the finest marine gardens in the Caribbean, including coral, grottoes, sea fans, gorgonias, and tropical fishes. Underwater trail. Rookery of frigate birds and pelicans; habitat of green turtle. *Address:* c/o Virgin Islands National Park, P.O. Box 806, St. Thomas, VI 00801.

Canyonlands National Park, Utah: Geological wonderland of rocks, spires, and mesas rising more than 7,800 feet. Extensive petroglyphs made by Indians about 1,000 years ago. *Address:* Moab, UT 84532.

Capitol Reef National Park, Utah: Sixty-mile uplift of sandstone cliffs with highly colored sedimentary formations dissected by narrow high-walled gorges. Dome-shaped whitecap rock along the Fremont River accounts for the name. *Address:* Torrey, UT 84775.

Capulin Mountain National Monument, N. Mex.: Symmetrical cinder cone, an interesting example of a geologically recent extinct volcano. *Address:* Capulin, NM 88414.

Carlsbad Caverns National Park, N. Mex.: Largest underground chambers yet discovered; a series of connected caverns with countless magnificent and curious formations. *Address:* P.O. Box 1598, Carlsbad, NM 88220.

Cedar Breaks, National Monument, Utah: Huge natural amphitheater eroded into the variegated Pink Cliffs (Wasatch Formation), which are 2,000 feet thick at this point. *Address:* c/o Southern Utah Group, NPS, P.O. Box 749, Cedar City, UT 84720.

Channel Islands National Monument, Calif.: Large rookery of sea lions, nesting sea birds; unique plants and animals. Monument includes Santa Barbara and Anacapa Islands. Land area, 1,119.98 acres. *Address:* P.O. Box 1388, Oxnard, CA 93030.

Chiricahua National Monument, Ariz.: Varied rock formations created millions of years ago by volcanic activity. *Address:* Dos Cabezas Star Route, Willcox, AZ 85643.

Colorado National Monument, Colo.: Sheer-walled canyons, towering monoliths, and weird formations hewed by erosion in sandstone. *Address:* c/o Curecanti National Recreation Area, 334 South 10th St., Montrose, CO 81401.

Crater Lake National Park, Oreg.: Lake of unique blue in heart of once-active volcano; encircled by multicolored lava walls 500 to 2,000 feet high. *Address:* c/o Klamath Falls Group, NPS, P.O. Box 128, Klamath Falls, OR 97601.

Craters of the Moon National Monument, Idaho: Fissure eruptions, volcanic cones, craters, lava flows, caves, and other volcanic phenomena; 43,243 acres designated as wilderness, Oct. 23, 1970. *Address:* P.O. Box 29, Arco, ID 83213.

Death Valley National Monument, Calif.-Nev.: Large desert almost surrounded by high mountains; contains lowest point in Western Hemisphere; famous in history of the West. Federal acreage: 1,776,594.97 in Calif.; 115,240.00 in Nev. *Address:* Death Valley, CA 92328.

Devils Postpile National Monument, Calif.: Symmetrical blue-gray columns rising as high as 60 feet, fitting closely together; a remnant of a basaltic lava flow. On Pacific Crest National Scenic Trail between Yosemite and Kings Canyon National Parks. *Address:* c/o Sequoia and Kings Canyon National Parks, Three Rivers, CA 93271.

Devils Tower National Monument, Wyo.: An 865-foot tower of columnar rock, the remains of a volcanic intrusion. First national monument. *Address:* Devils Tower, WY 82714.

Dinosaur National Monument, Colo.-Utah: Spectacular canyons cut by Green and Yampa Rivers through upfolded mountains. Quarry containing fossil remains of dinosaurs and other ancient animals. Federal acreage: 149,443.79 in Colo.; 49,637.03 in Utah. *Address:* P.O. Box 101, Dinosaur, CO 81610.

Everglades National Park, Fla.: Largest remaining subtropical wilderness in coterminous United States; extensive fresh- and salt-water areas, open Everglades prairies, mangrove forests abundant wildlife including rare and colorful birds. Third largest national park. *Address:* P.O. Box 279, Homestead, FL 33030.

Florissant Fossil Beds National Monument, Colo.: Wealth of fossil insects, seeds, and leaves of Oligocene Period preserved in perfect detail; also remarkable display of standing petrified sequoia stumps. *Address:* P.O. Box 164, Florissant, CO 80816.

Glacier Bay National Monument, Alaska: Great tidewater glaciers and examples of early stages of postglacial forests; rare species of wildlife. Largest area in National Park System. *Address:* c/o Alaska Group, NPS, P.O. Box 2252, Anchorage, AK 99501.

Glacier National Park, Mont.: Superb Rocky Mountain scenery, with numerous glaciers and lakes among the highest peaks, forms part of the Waterton-Glacier International Peace Park established May 2, 1932. *Address:* West Glacier, MT 59936.

Grand Canyon National Monument, Ariz.: Part of the Grand Canyon of the Colorado River containing Toroweap Point with its unusual view of the Inner Gorge and lava dam of recent era. *Address:* c/o Grand Canyon National Park, P.O. Box 129, Grand Canyon, AZ 86023.

Grand Canyon National Park, Ariz.: Most spectacular part of the Colorado River's greatest canyon, 217 miles long and 4 to 18 miles wide; exposure of rocks representing vast geologic time. A Living History area. *Address:* P.O. Box 129, Grand Canyon, AZ 86023.

Grand Teton National Park, Wyo.: Series of peaks comprising the most impressive part of the Teton Range; once a noted landmark of Indians and "Mountain Men." Includes part of Jackson Hole, winter feeding ground of largest American elk herd. A Living History area. *Address:* P.O. Box 67, Moose, WY 83012.

Great Sand Dunes National Monument, Colo.: Among largest and highest dunes in United States. Deposited over thousands of years by southwesterly winds blowing through the passes of the lofty Sangre de Cristo Mountains. *Address:* P.O. Box 60, Alamosa, CO 81101.

Great Smoky Mountains National Park, N.C.-Tenn.: Loftiest range east of the Black Hills and one of the oldest uplands on earth. Diversified and luxuriant plantlife, often of extraordinary size. A Living History area. Federal acreage: 274,803.77 in N.C.; 239,864.84 in Tenn. *Address:* Gatlinburg, TN 37738.

Guadalupe Mountains National Park, Tex.: Mountain mass rising from desert contains portions of the world's most extensive and significant Permian limestone fossil reef. Also features a tremendous earth fault, lofty peaks, unusual flora and fauna, and a colorful record of the past. *Address:* c/o Carlsbad Caverns National Park, P.O. Box 1598, Carlsbad, NM 88220.

Haleakala National Park, Hawaii: World-famous 10,023-foot Haleakala volcano (dormant), with large and colorful crater in which grows a species of the rare silversword; Kipahulu Valley; Seven Pools; native and migratory birdlife. *Address:* c/o Hawaii Group, NPS, Pacific International Bldg., 677 Ala Moana Blvd., Suite 512, Honolulu, HI 96813.

Hawaii Volcanoes National Park, Hawaii: Scene of impressive active volcanism on the island of Hawaii; luxuriant vegetation at lower elevations; rare plants and animals. *Address:* c/o Hawaii Group, NPS, Pacific International Bldg., 677 Ala Moana Blvd., Suite 512, Honolulu, HI 96813.

Hot Springs National Park, Ark.: Forty-seven hot mineral-water springs used in the treatment of certain ailments. *Address:* P.O. Box 1219, Hot Springs, AR 71901.

Ice Age National Scientific Reserve, Wis.: Contains nationally significant features of continental glaciation. First national scientific reserve. *Address:* c/o Regional Office, NPS, 143 South 3rd St., Philadelphia, PA 19106.

Isle Royale National Park, Mich.: Forested island, largest in Lake Superior, distinguished for its wilderness character; timber wolves and moose herd; pre-Columbian copper mines. Land area, 133,844 acres. *Address:* 87 North Ripley St., Houghton, MI 49931.

Jewel Cave National Monument, S. Dak.: Caverns in limestone formation, consisting of a series of chambers connected by narrow passages; many side galleries; fine calcite crystal encrustations. *Address:* c/o Wind Cave National Park, Hot Springs, SD 57747.

Joshua Tree National Monument, Calif.: Representative stand of Joshua-trees; great variety of desert plants and animals, including the desert bighorn. *Address:* P.O. Box 875, Twentynine Palms, CA 92277.

Katmai National Monument, Alaska: Dying volcanic region includes the Valley of Ten Thousand Smokes; scene of a violent eruption in 1912; home of the world's largest land carnivore, the brown bear. Second largest area in the National Park System. *Address:* c/o Alaska Group, NPS, P.O. Box 2252, Anchorage, AK 99501.

Kings Canyon National Park, Calif.: Mountain wilderness dominated by two enormous canyons of the Kings River and by the summit peaks of the High Sierra. General Grant Grove (formerly General Grant National Park), with its giant sequoias, is a detached section of the park. *Address:* Three Rivers, CA 93271.

Lassen Volcanic National Park, Calif.: Lassen Peak, only recently active volcano in coterminous United States, erupted between 1914 and 1921; impressive volcanic phenomena. A Living History area. *Address:* Mineral, CA 96063.

Lava Beds National Monument, Calif.: Unusual exhibits of volcanic activity; principal theater of Modoc Indian War, 1872-73. *Address:* c/o Klamath Falls, OR 97601.

Lehman Caves National Monument, Nev.: Caverns of light-gray and white limestone, honey-combed by tunnels and galleries decorated with stalactites and stalagmites. *Address:* Baker, NV 89311.

Mammoth Cave National Park, Ky.: Series of underground passages; beautiful limestone gypsum, and cave onyx formations; deep pits and high domes; river 360 feet below surface. A Living History area. *Address:* Mammoth Cave, KY 42259.

Marble Canyon National Monument Ariz.: Spectacular canyon, containing 3,000-foot walls of red sandstone and white limestone, extends 50 miles along the Colorado River between Glen Canyon National Recreation Area and Grand Canyon National Park. *Address:* c/o Grand Canyon National Park, P.O. Box 129, Grand Canyon, AZ 86023.

Mount McKinley National Park, Alaska: Mount McKinley, 20,320 feet, highest mountain in North America; large glaciers of the Alaska Range; caribou, Dall sheep, moose, grizzly bears, timber wolves, and other wildlife. Second largest national park. A Living History area. *Address:* c/o Alaska Group, NPS, P.O. Box 2252, Anchorage, AK 99501.

Mount Rainier National Park, Wash.: Greatest single-peak glacial system in the United States radiating from the summit and slopes of an ancient volcano; dense forests; subalpine flowered meadows. *Address:* Longmire, WA 98397.

Muir Woods National Monument, Calif.: Virgin stand of coast redwood. Named for John Muir, writer and conservationist. *Address:* c/o San Francisco Bay Area Group, NPS, Point Reyes, CA 94956.

Natural Bridges National Monument, Utah: Three natural bridges carved out of sandstone; highest is 220 feet above the streambed, with span of 268 feet. *Address:* c/o Canyonlands National Park, Moab, UT 84532.

North Cascades National Park, Wash: Wild alpine region of jagged peaks, mountain lakes, glaciers, plant and animal communities. *Address:* Sedro Woolley, WA 98284.

Olympic National Park, Wash.: Mountain wilderness containing finest remains of Pacific Northwest rain forest; active glaciers; rare Roosevelt elk; Pacific shore. *Address:* 600 East Park Ave., Port Angeles, WA 98362.

Oregon Caves National Monument, Oreg.: Cave passages in limestone with intricate flowstone formations. *Address:* c/o Klamath Falls Group, NPS, P.O. Box 128, Klamath Falls, OR 97601.

Organ Pipe Cactus National Monument, Ariz.: Sonoran Desert plants and animals found nowhere else in United States; traces of historic trail, Camino del Diablo. *Address:* P.O. Box 38, Ajo, AZ 85321.

Petrified Forest National Park, Ariz.: Extensive natural exhibit of petrified wood; Indian ruins and petroglyphs; portion of colorful Painted Desert; 50,260 acres designated as wilderness. *Address:* Petrified Forest National Park, AZ 86025.

Pinnacles National Monument, Calif.: Spirelike rock formations 500 to 1,200 feet high, with caves and a variety of volcanic features. *Address:* Paicines, CA 95043.

Platt National Park, Okla.: Numerous cold mineral-and fresh-water springs including bromide waters. *Address:* P.O. Box 201, Sulphur, OK 73086.

Rainbow Bridge National Monument, Utah: Greatest of world's known natural bridges, a symmetrical arch of salmon-on-pink sandstone, rising 309 feet above gorge. *Address:* c/o Glen Canyon National Recreation Area, P.O. Box 1507, Page, AZ 86040.

Redwood National Park, Calif.: Coast redwood forests containing virgin groves of ancient trees, including the world's tallest. Park includes 40 miles of scenic Pacific coastline. *Address:* Drawer N, Crescent City, CA 95531.

Rocky Mountain National Park, Colo.: Rich in scenery; Trail Ridge Road sightseeing on the Continental Divide; 107 named peaks over 11,000 feet; wildlife; wildflowers; 410 square miles of the Rockies Front Range. *Address:* Estes Park, CO 80517.

Saguaro National Monument, Ariz.: Cactus forest containing giant saguaro unique to Sonoran Desert of southern Arizona and northwestern Mexico. *Address:* P.O. Box 17210, Tucson, AZ 85710.

Sequoia National Park, Calif.: Great groves of giant sequoias, world's largest and among the oldest living things; magnificent High Sierra scenery, including Mount Whitney (14,494 feet), highest mountain in coterminous United States. *Address:* Three Rivers, CA 93271.

Shenandoah National Park, Va.: Outstanding portion of Blue Ridge Mountains with Skyline Drive on crest; vistas of historic Shenandoah Valley and the Piedmont; hardwood forests; wealth of wildflowers. *Address:* Luray, VA 22835.

Sunset Crater National Monument, Ariz.: Volcanic cinder cone with summit crater formed just before A.D. 1100. Upper part colored as if by sunset glow. *Address:* c/o Grand Canyon National Park, P.O. Box 129, Grand Canyon, AZ 86023.

Theodore Roosevelt Island, D.C.: Wooded park in Potomac River, a living tribute to the conservationist 26th President. Blending memorial by Eric Tugler contains Paul Manship's 17-foot statue of Theodore Roosevelt and four 21-foot tablets inscribed with Roosevelt's tenets on nature, manhood, youth, and the state. *Address:* c/o George Washington Memorial Parkway, 1400 Wilson Blvd., Suite 102, Arlington, VA 22209.

Timpanogos Cave National Monument, Utah: Limestone cavern on side of Mount Timpanogos; noted for coloring and helictite formations. *Address:* R.R. 1, Box 200, American Fork, UT 84003.

Virgin Islands National Park, V.I.: Park of lush green hills, quiet coves, and white sandy beaches covering three-fourths of St. John Island, Early Carib Indian relics; remains of Danish colonial sugar plantations. Underwater trail. *Address:* P.O. Box 806, St. Thomas, VI 00801.

Voyageurs National Park, Minn.: Beautiful northern lakes, forests; interesting geology and history. Land area, 139,-128.00 acres. *Address:* P.O. Drawer 50, International Falls, MN 56649.

White Sands National Monument, N. Mex.: Glistening white gypsum sands, with dunes 10 to 45 feet high; small, light-colored animals adapted to environment. *Address:* P.O. Box 458, Alamogordo, NM 88310.

Wind Cave National Park, S. Dak.: Limestone caverns in scenic Black Hills, decorated by beautiful boxwork and calcite crystal formations; elk, deer, pronghorn, prairie dog towns, bison herd, and rare black-footed ferret. *Address:* Hot Springs, S. Dak. 57747.

Yellowstone National Park, Wyo.-Mont.-Idaho: World's greatest geyser area, with about 3,000 geysers and hot springs; spectacular falls; Grand Canyon of the Yellowstone. Rich in wildlife. First and largest national park. Federal acreage: 2,039,216.98 in Wyo.; 149,031.90 in Mont.; 31,488.00 in Idaho. *Address:* Yellowstone National Park, WY 82190.

Yosemite National Park, Calif: Mountainous region of unusual beauty seen from Tioga Road; Yosemite Valley and other inspiring gorges; Nation's highest waterfall; Three groves of giant sequoias A living History area. *Address:* P.O. Box 577, Yosemite National Park, CA 95389.

Zion National Park, Utah: Colorful canyon and mesa scenery, erosion and rockfault patterns that create phenomenal shapes and landscapes; former volcanic activity. *Address:* Springdale, UT 84767.

Recreational Areas Administered by the National Park Service and Related Properties

Amistad National Recreation Area, Tex.: Contains United States part of the Amistad Reservoir on the Rio Grande. *Address:* P.O. Box 1463, Del Rio, TX 78840.

Apostle Islands National Lakeshore, Wis.: Twenty picturesque islands and an 11-mile strip of adjacent Bayfield Peninsula along south shore of Lake Superior. *Address:* 206 6th Ave. West, Ashland, WI 54806.

Appalachian National Scenic Trail, Maine-N.H.-Vt.-Mass.-Conn.-N.Y.-N.J.-Pa.-Md.-W.Va.-Va.-Tenn.-N.C.-Ga.: A scenic trail of approximately 2,000 miles follows the Appalachian Mountains from Mount Katahdin, Maine, to Springer Mountain, Ga. One of two initial units of the National Trail System. Federal acreage by state unavailable. *Address:* (Northern unit)—c/o Regional Office, NPS, 143 South 3rd St., Philadelphia, PA 19106. (Southern Unit) —c/o Regional Office, NPS, 3401 Whipple Ave., Atlanta, GA. 30344.

Arbuckle National Recreational Area, Okla.: Manmade Lake of the Arbuckles provides water recreation for extensive Midwest area. *Address:* P.O. Box 201, Sulphur, OK 73086.

Assateague Island National Seashore, Md-Va.: A 37-mile barrier island with sandy beach, migratory waterfowl, and wild ponies. Federal acreage: 14,507-15 in Md.; 5.32 in Va. *Address:* Route 2, Box 294, Berlin, MD 21811.

Baltimore-Washington Parkway, Md.: A 29-mile approach to the Nation's Capital containing 19 miles administered by the National Park Service; 10 miles by Maryland. Includes Greenbelt Park, a natural woodland of 1,100 acres. *Address:* c/o Catoctin Mountain Park, Thurmont, MD 21788

Bighorn Canyon National Recreation Area, Mont.-Wyo.: A 71-mile long reservoir created by Yellowtail Dam on the Bighorn River; extends 47 miles through spectacular Bighorn Canyon. The Crow Indian Reservation borders a large part of the area. Federal acreage: 33,548.00 in Mont.; 28,438.00 in Wyo. *Address:* P.O. Box 458 YRS, Hardin, MT 59035.

Blue Ridge Parkway. N.C.-Va.-Ga.: Scenic parkway which averages 3,000 feet above sea level, following Blue Ridge Mountains, embracing several large recreational areas, and preserving mountain-folk culture. A Living History area. 469 miles completed or under construction; estimated length when completed, 659 miles. First national parkway. Federal acreage: 45,428.66 in N.C.; 28,630.99 in Va.; 8,413.00 in Ga. *Address:* P.O. Box 7606, Asheville, NC 28807.

Cape Cod National Seashore, Mass.: Ocean beaches dunes, woodlands, fresh-water ponds, and marshes on outer Cape Cod, for centuries a landmark and haven for mariners. *Address:* South Wellfleet, MA 02663.

Cape Hatteras National Seashore, N.C.: Notable for its beaches, migratory waterfowl, fishing, and points of historical interest, including the Cape Hatteras Lighthouse overlooking the "graveyard of the Atlantic." First National Seashore. *Address:* P.O. Box 457, Manteo, NC 27954.

Cape Lookout National Seashore, N.C.: Series of barrier islands of the lower Outer Banks, embracing beaches, dunes, salt marshes, and Cape Lookout Lighthouse. *Address:* P.O. Box 690, Beaufort, NC 28516.

Catoctin Mountain Park, Md.: Part of the forested ridge that forms the easern rampart of the Appalachian Mountains in Maryland, with sparkling streams and panoramic vistas of the Monocacy Valley. A living History Area. *Address:* Thurmont, MD 21788.

Coulee Dam National Recreation Area, Wash.: Franklin D. Roosevelt Lake, formed by Grand Coulee Dam (part of the Columbia River Basin Project). *Address:* P.O. Box 37, Coulee Dam, WA 99116.

Curecanti National Recreation Area, Colo.: Includes Blue Mesa Lake, Morrow Point Lake, and Crystal Reservoir, components of the Curecanti Unit of the Colorado River Storage Project. *Address:* 334 South 10th St., Montrose, CO 81401.

Delaware Water Gap National Recreation Area, N.J.-Pa.: Outstanding scenic area along Delaware River to encompass 37-mile-long Tocks Island Reservoir when U.S. Army

Corps of Engineers completes dam. Federal acreage: 14,237.01 in N.J.; 6,787.96 in Pa. *Address:* Int. 80, Columbia, NJ 07832.

Fire Island National Seashore, N.Y.: Part of a barrier island off the south shore of Long Island, with outstanding qualities of natural history and opportunities for beach-oriented recreation. *Address:* c/o New York City Group, NPS, 26 Wall St., New York, NY 10005.

George Washington Memorial Parkway, Va.-Md.: Embraces many landmarks associated with the life of George Washington. When completed will extend between Mount Vernon and Great Falls on the Virginia side of the Potomac, and from Great Falls to Chain Bridge on the Maryland side. A Living History area at Great Falls Park, Va. Federal acreage: 3,549.29 in Va; 2,580.80 in Md. *Address:* 1400 Wilson Blvd., Suite 102, Arlington, VA 22209.

Glen Canyon National Recreation Area, Utah-Ariz.: Lake Powell formed by the Colorado River behind one of the highest dams in the world. Federal acreage: 1,094,425.80 in Utah; 92,018.00 in Ariz. *Address:* P.O. Box 1507, Page, AZ 86040.

Gulf Islands National Seashore, Fla.-Miss.: Historic forts, sparkling white sand beaches near Pensacola, Fla; Fort Massachusetts and primitive offshore islands in Mississippi. Federal acreage: 6,254.00 in Fla.; 3,978.00 in Miss. Land area, 20,430.00 acres. *Address:* c/o Florida Group, NPS P.O. Box 2764, Tallahassee, FL 32304.

Indiana Dunes National Lakeshore, Ind.: Contains 200-foot-high sand dunes on Lake Michigan's southern shore; separate natural units of beaches, dunes, and hinterlands. *Address:* R.R. 2, Box 139-A Chesterton, IN 46304.

Lake Chelan National Recreation Area, Wash.: Beautiful Stehekin Valley and portion of fjordlike Lake Chelan adjoining southern unit of North Cascades National Park. *Address:* c/o North Cascades National Park, Sedro Woolley, WA 98284.

Lake Mead National Recreation Area, Ariz-Nev.: Includes Lake Mead, formed by Hoover Dam, and Lake Mohave, by Davis Dam, on the Colorado River. Federal acreage: 1,221,077.25 in Ariz; 691,614.8 in Nev. First national recreation area established by act of Congress. *Address:* 601 Nevada Hwy., Boulder City, NV 89005.

Natchez-Trace Parkway Miss.-Tenn.-Ala.: Historic route following general location of the old Indian trail between Nashville, Tenn., and Natchez, Miss., known as the "Natchez Trace," important in early travel. 317 miles completed; estimated length when completed, 450 miles. Federal acreage: 28,252.73 in Miss.; 6,547.68 in Tenn.; 3,845.89 in Ala. *Address:* R.R. 5, NT-143, Tupelo, MS 38801.

Ozark National Scenic Riverways, Mo.: Nearly 150 miles of the free-flowing Current and Jacks Fork Rivers, with significant caves and springs. The first national riverway. *Address:* P.O. Box 448, Van Buren, MO 63965.

Padre Island National Seashore, Tex.: A 67.5 mile stretch of a barrier island along the gulf coast noted for its wide sand beaches, excellent fishing, and abundant bird and marine life. *Address:* P.O. Box 8560, Corpus Christi, TX 78412.

Pictured Rocks National Lakeshore, Mich.: Superlative scenic area on Lake Superior with multi-colored sandstone cliffs, broad beaches, bars, dunes, waterfalls, inland lakes, ponds, marshes, hardwood and coniferous forests, and numerous birds and animals. First national lakeshore. Land area, 65,568 acres. *Address:* c/o Isle Royale National Park, 87 North Ripley St., Houghton, MI 49931.

Point Reyes National Seashore, Calif.: A peninsula near San Francisco noted for its long beaches backed by tall cliffs; lagoons and esteros; forested ridges; offshore bird and sea lion colonies. Part of area remains in private pastoral zone. A Living Farm area. *Address:* c/o San Francisco Bay Area Group, NPS, Point Reyes, CA 94956.

Prince William Forest Park, Va.: The forested watershed of Quantico Creek, where pines and hardwoods have replaced worn-out farmland. *Address:* P.O. Box 208, Triangle, VA 22172.

Ross Lake National Recreation Area, Wash.: Mountain-ringed reservoir in Skagit River Canyon, separating north and south units of North Cascades National Park. *Address:* c/o North Cascades National Park, Sedro Woolley, WA 98284.

St. Croix National Scenic Riverway, Wis.-Minn.: About 200 miles of the beautiful St. Croix River and its Namekagon tributary. An initial component of the National Wild and Scenic Rivers System, Federal Acreage: 1,600.70 in Wis.; 95.22 in Minn. *Address:* P.O. Box 579, St. Croix Falls, WI 54024.

Sanford National Recreation Area, Tex.: Manmade Lake Meredith on the Canadian River, a popular water activity center in the Southwest. *Address:* P.O. Box 325, Sanford, TX 79078.

Shadow Mountain National Recreation Area, Colo.: Shadow Mountain Lake and Lake Granby, two units of the Colorado-Big Thompson Project, adjacent to the west entrance of Rocky Mountain National Park. *Address:* c/o Rocky Mountain Group, NPS, Estes Park, CO 80517.

Sleeping Bear Dunes National Lakeshore, Mich.: Notable for its beaches, massive sand dunes, forests, and lakes, two offshore islands and Lake Michigan shore. *Address:* 400 Main st., Frankfort, MI 49635.

Suitland Parkway, Md.-D.C.: A 9-mile landscaped parkway between Washington, D.C., and Suitland, Md., and between Bolling Air Force Base and Andrews Field. Federal acreage: 607.46 in Md.; 123.12 in D.C. *Address:* c/o National Capital Parks-East, 5210 Indian Head Hwy., Oxon Hill, MD 20021.

Whiskeytown-Shasta-Trinity National Recreation Area, Calif.: A scenic mountain region excellent for fishing, boating, and sightseeing at Whiskeytown Lake, formed by a dam across Clear Creek. Forest Service, U.S. Department of Agriculture, administers 172,588-acre Shasta and Trinity-Lewistown Units. *Address:* Whiskeytown Unit, P.O. Box 188, Whiskeytown, CA 96095.

Wolf National Scenic Riverway, Wis.: 24 miles of fast water, ideal for canoeing, fishing and scenic enjoyment. An initial component of the Wild and Scenic Rivers System. *Address:* c/o Chicago Field Office, NPS, 2510 Dempster St., Room 214, Des Plaines, IL 60016.